PROPERTY OF
SOLOMON SCHECHTER DAY SCHOOL OF ESSEX & UNION

YOU, NEW JERSEY AND THE WORLD *is the core of a widely-used New Jersey social studies program created for the state's elementary schools by John T. Cunningham in association with Frank W. Ritzer. A grant from the New Jersey Historical Society helped to make the original program possible.*

EDUCATIONAL ADVISORY BOARD

Marie Chesnutt, Teacher
  Alpine School, Sparta
Joseph H. Davenport, Principal
  P.W. Carleton School, Penns Grove
Robert Hoagland, Teacher
  Millstone Twp. Elem. School, Clarksburg
Marilyn Hook, Teacher
  Rockaway Meadow School, Parsippany
Diane Jannuzzelli, Teacher
  Harrison School, Roselle
Elizabeth A. Mason, Teacher
  Herbertsville School, Brick

Ethel L. Moss, Supervisor
  Camden School Dist., Camden
Carol Petuskey, Teacher
  Deerfield School, Linden
Betty Schwarz, Teacher
  Long Beach Island School, Ship Bottom
Lois Stieve, Teacher
  Viola Sickles School, Fair Haven
Frieda B. Wentz, Teacher
  Deerfield School, Short Hills
Ann W. Yeich, Teacher
  P.W. Carleton School, Penns Grove

Library of Congress Catalog Card Number: 81-67139
Manufactured in the State of New Jersey
100-1185-4289

YOU, NEW JERSEY AND THE WORLD

by John T. Cunningham

Illustrated by: Bill Canfield
Educational Associate: Arlene Sarappo
Design & Production: Marjorie Keating
Cover Photo: Walter J. Choroszewski
Song: New Jersey's The Place For Me
Music by: Marie Chesnutt
Words by: Marie Chesnutt and
Peter S. Massardo

Afton PUBLISHING CO.

BOX 1399, ANDOVER, NJ 07821
201–579–2442
ISBN: 0-89359-000-2

Copyright © 1990 by Afton Publishing Co., Inc.
All Rights Reserved

MAGIC CARPET JOURNEYS

YOUR SONG: "New Jersey's The Place For Me" 9
PICTURE ESSAY: New Jersey is Beautiful! 10

1. MAPS ....
We find that symbols lead the way. We visit a planet. We take off along the "Streets of the World." Maps guide us — to school, to New Jersey, to the world. **15**

2. GEOGRAPHY ....
New Jersey has many "faces." We take a close-up look at six of them. We see the mountains, the highlands, the Jersey shore. We visit the Pine Barrens, cities and farmlands. **33**

3. GEOLOGY ......
This is the excitement of how great violence shaped our state. Here is the story of the millions of years before humans lived here. You'll learn of volcanoes, earthquakes and dinosaurs! **53**

4. INDIANS ......
Let's move backward, thousands of years, to visit the Lenape Indians, New Jersey's first settlers. We see what they ate and wore, where they lived and what they believed. **65**

5. COLONISTS .....
First the explorers came in tiny ships to find the land. We follow colonists to America, watch them get settled, learn about their lives, day by day. **77**

6. REVOLUTION . . . . . *New Jersey was the center of the American Revolution. Five great battles were fought here. George Washington lived here for three winters. Here freedom was won.* **97**

7. IMMIGRANTS . . . . *We see the hardships that made Europeans leave their homes. We cross the Atlantic Ocean and enter America through Ellis Island. We learn that new people still come here.* **115**

8. TRANSPORTATION . *Follow our ancestors as they walked, rode horseback or used stagecoaches, railroads, canals and automobiles. We take off in airplanes. We see ports.* **131**

9. INDUSTRY . . . . . . *People work in New Jersey! There are more than 3½ million jobs here. We see changes, from windmills to modern computers. The world changes. New Jersey keeps pace.* **153**

10. AGRICULTURE . . . . *New Jersey is where farms and cities meet. We visit the egg farms, dairy pastures, vegetable fields as big as football fields, and horse farms. We learn farmers have big problems.* **171**

11. CITIES . . . . *New Jersey has people! Millions live in old cities, started in colonial days. We visit the "Big Six" — then find that new cities are springing up throughout the state.* **189**

12. ENVIRONMENT . . . *New Jersey still is beautiful! We set out to find the open spaces. We find the parks, the trees, the flowers. We must ask: who will keep it clean? You'll find the answer!* **207**

13. GOVERNMENT . . . *Government is not something beyond ourselves. We learn New Jersey has many kinds of governments. We learn that WE are government. WE make the difference.* **223**

GLOSSARY	238
NEW JERSEY "FIRSTS"	240
NEW JERSEY DATES	242
FAMOUS NEW JERSEYANS	246
COUNTIES OF NEW JERSEY	250
INDEX	252

THE IMPORTANCE OF *YOU*

This book is meant for *you*.

It will lead you into New Jersey. It will take you outward to all the world. It might even start you into space.

Each of you will travel through this book on your own special "Magic Carpet." You *do* have one! It is your wonderful imagination!

Imagination *frees* your mind to travel. You can go far back in time—to when dinosaurs were here! You can meet Indians, colonists, and inventors. You can go far out, in imagination, to the moon.

From each of our magic carpets, the view is different. Your view is as good as mine!

Do you want the magic carpet of your mind to take off fast? You need power! You get that from knowledge. The more you know, the better your imagination soars!

So look for anything and everything that will increase your "Carpet Power." Look in other books, in maps, filmstrips and newspapers. Look in encyclopedias.

You have parents or grown friends who work. They know fascinating facts about machines and computers and other products made in New Jersey. You can write to boys and girls in other New Jersey towns.

And don't forget your *own* power! In some things, *you* are the expert. You know how *you* feel. You know what *you* see. Exchange your power. Tell others of your experiences!

Perhaps you have lived in another state or country. Perhaps you were born in another nation. You probably have read something about New Jersey that you think is great news!

Share! *You* have knowledge that is not in any book!

Your Magic Carpet journeys are about to begin!

Happy soaring!

SOME WORDS FROM YOUR CAPTAIN

Hi! Let me introduce myself. I am John T. Cunningham, your captain on these Magic Carpet flights. I will work to make every journey worth taking—but I need *your* brainpower!

My fourth grade teacher was my first Magic Carpet pilot. She helped me to learn about geography, history and people. She taught me to know trees, flowers, animals and birds.

Later, after I graduated from Drew University (in New Jersey, of course!), I began writing for a big city newspaper. Soon, publishers began asking me to write books about New Jersey and its many wonders.

Hundreds of thousands of boys and girls have used (or are using) my school textbooks. I often meet a grownup person who has saved one of my books from the fourth grade. That is a real treat for me!

Your captain—and your friend,

John T. Cunningham

P.S. I will bring along my dog "Duffy" as our "co-pilot." She is my symbol. She loves New Jersey, too! Look for her.

ON WINGS OF SONG

All aboard! Let's try a short Magic Carpet journey, just to get the feel of it.

We'll take off on the wings of a song, **New Jersey's the Place for Me**. It was written by a fourth grade teacher, Mrs. Marie Chesnutt. She wrote the song so that boys and girls in Alpine School, Sparta, could enjoy their "Magic Carpet" journeys around New Jersey.

Each Magic Carpet in this book will begin with a new verse. Your teacher will help you to learn the song. Perhaps your music teacher will help as you learn to sing each new verse.

You'll be surprised. If you sing this song around home, your mother, father, sister or brother will ask, "What is that song?" Teach them. Soon everyone will sing along.

Wouldn't it be great if all children had their own New Jersey song? It would be the symbol of learning about our state!

Enough of reading about the song. Let's sing it! The music, the first verse, and the chorus are on page 9.

Ready? Away we soar into New Jersey—singing!

New Jersey's The Place For Me

High Point (left), New Jersey's loftiest spot, is 1803 feet above sea level. Cape May Point (above), where "diamonds" are found, is at sea level. Between is the Pine Barrens (below), filled with streams, forests and mysterious "ghost towns." Cape May diamonds are not valuable, but New Jersey's beauty is ever precious.

New Jersey is one of the nation's great research centers, with hundreds of modern laboratories. It ranks near the top in raising horses. It is a state on the move. Near Newark and Elizabeth (right), one of the world's great seaports is only a few hundred feet from mighty Newark International Airport. Variety: That's New Jersey!

New Jersey people love sports. They see winter as the time to ski on the slopes of Sussex, Warren and Morris counties. Cold winds lower temperatures and freeze the lakes. That brings out those who fish through the ice. At the Meadowlands Stadium, our football Giants give us a chance to cheer for the home team.

Winter's cold gives way to the warmth of spring and summer. Then, beaches from Sandy Hook to Cape May come to life. Everyone knows the marvelous Jersey Shore! In the Highlands, lakes appeal to sailboaters. Atlantic City's boardwalk, although busy all year, is most crowded in July and August.

13

New Jersey's wonders are as tall as the Statue of Liberty, as unusual as Margate's elephant called Lucy, as golden as our capitol dome and as old as Salem's oak. Each has a story to tell—of freedom, of seaside fun, of state government, of olden times when a tree was young.

MAPS

MAGIC CARPET NO. 1

*Our globe consists of seven continents,
Four oceans then complete the sphere.
New Jersey's just a part of our big earth,
But we're so glad that we live here.*
    Repeat Chorus (see page 9)

Where in the world is THAT place? You find yourself asking this question many times as you read books or watch TV and learn about some unfamiliar areas.

The question is easy to answer: become an expert in map reading!

Before we undertake any Magic Carpet journeys, we must know how to use maps. Let's begin, right at your front door, and move outward around the world.

When we are finished, you will know EXACTLY where in the world you live. It's quite an address!

BIG EARTH, TINY STATE

We promised you a chance to walk on a planet.

It's easy! Open the front door. Step out on a marvelous planet called Earth. It speeds through space, just like a giant spaceship or a "space colony."

Earth is *our* planet. New Jersey is our tiny spot on Earth.

Here we start our explorations. Always remember—what we find here can be useful anywhere that we go.

All explorers must be prepared. They know how to read maps. They understand how rivers flow. They can tell, from a map, where people *might* be living, usually near a stream. They know about weather.

Explorers must know the skills of traveling—on lakes, across deserts, over mountains, across rivers, through snowfields.

That is why exploration begins with your own state. Here, first hand, you will learn about some of what the world offers.

You can only read about other planets or other nations. On Earth, you can look out a window and see a planet and hear its people. You can be part of a nation, the United States.

Near your school you can *see* different features of the world—bays, mountains, rivers, peninsulas, cliffs, capes, islands and many other kinds of areas.

Could an explorer really KNOW what a brook or river was without having seen one? (Actually it would be even better to *swim* in the streams!)

New Jersey is tiny. Alaska, largest of the 50 states, is 75 times as big! Texas is 34 times as big! Why is little New Jersey worth the knowing? The answer is VARIETY! As we will discover, New Jersey has a varied history, varied kinds of people and varied places where we work and play.

Could explorers ever really KNOW what an ocean was unless they saw the waves thunder over the sand? (It would be better to dive into a wave!)

In our little New Jersey you actually can see mountains, rivers, and the Atlantic Ocean. You can see cities and farms. You can see and talk with many kinds of people, from many nations.

You can find out about **climate.** In summer New Jersey has very hot days and nights. In winter, we can get as much as two feet of snow in a single day! Sometimes the winter temperature is 20 degrees below zero.

So start learning about your planet. Open the door!

Big Earth! Tiny state! New Jersey has so many kinds of wonders to explore. New Jersey can help us understand many kinds of people and many kinds of regions. New Jersey can start us to knowing the world.

Let's begin.

Let's get on with our state.

Let's get on with our planet!

LIBERTY IS OURS!

Maps can help solve arguments, answer trivia questions or even help in court trials.

One big question is: WHERE are the Statue of Liberty and Ellis Island? People have been arguing that for more than a hundred years. The question often has been contested in law cases.

Look at the map below. It shows New Jersey to the left and New York State to the right. Between is the official boundary line that divides the state. The scale of miles is on the bottom.

There is no question that both the Statue and the Island are within New Jersey bounds!

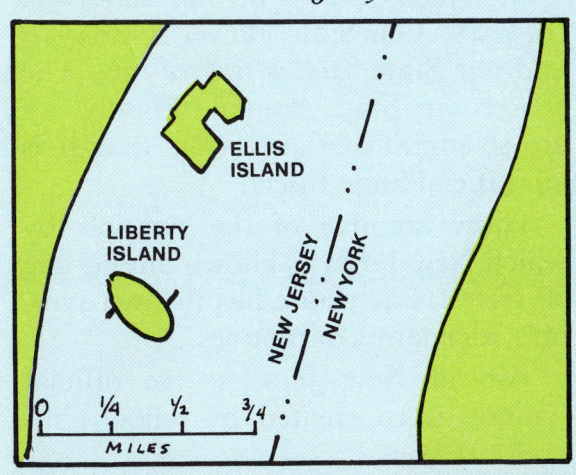

17

SYMBOLS SHOW THE WAY

Whenever New Jersey people travel by car to other states, our license plates tell people that we are from "The Garden State." That is a **symbol** of how we New Jerseyans think of our state. The words are also our state nickname.

Symbols or nicknames are not necessarily "official." However, New Jersey's state animal, bird, flower, tree and insect *are* set by state law.

New Jersey's State Bird is the *Eastern Goldfinch*. Our State Flower is the *violet* and our State Tree is the *red oak*. The *horse* is our State Animal. Finally, we are so proud of the *honeybee* that it is our official State Insect.

Those are five of the symbols by which New Jersey is known among the 50 states. Each state has its own symbols, nicknames or mottoes.

Two of New Jersey's five official symbols were created by school children like you.

Sunnybrae School in Hamilton worked to make the honeybee our State Insect. Sunnybrae's boys and girls wrote letters and contacted legislators. Their hopes were rewarded in 1974 when the honeybee became the official State Insect.

Students in Our Lady of Victories School, Harrington Park, were responsible for our State Animal. They chose the horse and campaigned to make it official. It became the State Animal in 1977.

State garden clubs backed the violet. The New Jersey Audubon Society pushed the Eastern Goldfinch. Many groups supported the red oak.

Every New Jersey region has its own symbols, although they are not "official." Lighthouses symbolize the Jersey Shore. High Point Monument is a symbol of the state's mountains. Pine trees symbolize the great Pine

Barrens of southern New Jersey.

Each state's most important symbol is the State Seal. The State Seal can only be used with permission of the state government. It is put on all laws and important state papers.

New Jersey has an official State Flag. Probably your school flies one along with the American Flag. The State Flag is buff and "Jersey" blue, our official state colors. Ask whether your school has a State Flag.

Symbols are everywhere—in team names (*Giants, Jets, Nets, Jersey Devils, Phillies, Flyers*, to name a few), in team colors and in official seals.

See if your school has any symbols— a nickname, school colors or even a school seal. If your school does not have such symbols, why not think of some possibilities? You could hold an election and let all the students and teachers vote.

Ask your local government about its seal. Look at it carefully. Does it really symbolize what your town or city is all about?

New Jersey's official seal is called the "Great Seal." The blue ribbon at the bottom contains the state's motto, "Liberty and Prosperity," and the date 1776. That was the year that New Jersey became a state.

One of the most important uses of symbols is on maps. A map is supposed to give as much information as possible. That's why mapmakers use small symbols—a tree for a park, a circle for a town, a line for a road, and so on. Once you recognize symbols, maps are easier to use.

"JUST-LOOK-AT-ME!"

Think of a cheerful little bird (about 5 inches long) that changes color in winter, eats seeds and sings "just-look-at-me!" as it darts through New Jersey backyards and downtown parks.

That's the Eastern Goldfinch, our official State Bird.

The Goldfinch eats seeds (as do all finches). It scratches up lettuce seed or grass seed, along with seeds from dandelions, burdock and chicory. It might also eat insects or bugs.

We know the Goldfinch best in the "golden stage," when males are golden yellow all over except for the black caps, wings and tail. In winter, however, the gold turns to olive green, the color of female Goldfinches the year-around.

Spring comes, the gold returns and our state bird sings as it seeks food. The sweet trilling sounds like a canary's song and for that reason (and because they look like canaries), Goldfinches often are called "wild canaries."

The Goldfinch flies in a "roller coaster" fashion, moving swiftly up and down. It sings "per-chick-o-ree, per-chick-o-ree" (or, if you wish, "just-look-at-me, just-look-at-me").

19

LET'S TAKE A LOT OF MAPS

Every time that we begin a trip we have two big choices. We can follow a map—or we can risk getting lost.

When school is open, you leave home and go to school. You don't need something printed to find your way but you carry a "map." It is in your brain.

You know which way to turn when you go out your front door. You know that several streets lead to school. You pass certain buildings that you know are on the right route. Traffic lights are familiar. You recognize big trees along the way.

If you ride a bus, your "brain map" takes you to your bus stop. After school, you know where your bus is parked. You become familiar with the streets and roads that your driver follows.

The first travelers had to remember their trails, just as you do. Then, to help others, they marked the trails by cutting notches on trees. These helped travelers to make the proper turns.

Then travelers going on long trips began to draw their trails on bark or on furs so others could find the same route. Maps had been "born!"

20

Imagine yourself as one of those early travelers. Make your own map. Put on paper the route from your home to your school. Add points that would help others—such as symbols for traffic lights, stores or big trees.

You are now a mapmaker. You have begun to know how to use maps for *your* advantage.

Any journey is better if you take a variety of maps.

Some maps will show just the streets of your town. Some will show all the world. Some will be flat. Some will be rolled up. Some will be in the shape of a round globe.

Some special maps will show the travels or adventures of others. An example would be a map showing where the Revolutionary War was fought in New Jersey. Another kind of map might tell how much rain or snow falls in different parts of our state.

Other maps would show rivers or counties.

If you happened to be *extremely* lucky you might find a pirate treasure map. Pirates needed such a map to find where they buried their gold and silver.

You will note that the **scale** of miles is not the same on every map. One inch on your "way to school" map might equal 100 feet. One inch on a New Jersey state map usually equals about five or six miles. One inch on a world map likely would be equal to 2,000 or more miles.

That sounds tricky, but when you compare maps you will see why the scale of miles must be different.

To prove it, suppose your world map had a scale of one inch equal to one mile. The world map would be about as big as 10 football fields! That area would be so big that you might get lost on the map itself!

The fine road map that you get from your gasoline dealer might have been produced in Convent, New Jersey, home of General Drafting Company.

The skilled **cartographer** *in this illustration is working on one of the many kinds of maps that her company produces. General Drafting turns out maps for most states and for many nations of the world.*

Making one road map can require nearly two years of work. Every detail must be carefully checked and rechecked before drawing a map even begins. It then can take as long as one year just to draw the map!

21

THEY ADD UP TO TWENTY-ONE!

Let's try our first trip on our Magic Carpets. This time we won't take any maps, to test whether or not we need them.

We move upward, speeding through space. Soon we are far away—300 miles away.

Suddenly we must make an emergency landing! Our Carpet floats down into a big field. People approach. They ask:

"Where do you live?"

You answer:

"269 My Street, My Town, New Jersey."

They have never heard of the place. You tell your zip code. That helps. The people at least get your Magic Carpet pointed in the right direction. Somehow you get home.

You must wonder, do you *really* know where on Earth you live? Let's find out before any more Magic Carpet flights!

To start, you live in a house on a street in a town. You also live in a **county**—one of 21 counties in New Jersey. It is very important to know your county and the county "seat," the central town where county business is carried out.

It helps to know about all the counties. The 21 counties add up to the state called New Jersey.

Each New Jersey county is very different from all the others. You can understand that. Counties along the Atlantic Ocean certainly would be different from counties in the mountains.

It is fun to find out about other counties. Each has a *County Clerk* who

New Jersey's 21 courthouses come in many sizes and many designs. Here are three of them—Passaic County on the left, Somerset County on the right and Burlington County in the center. Some courthouses are small wooden buildings, others (such as Union and Camden) are very tall structures. Visit your own county courthouse!

might help. He or she has an office in the **county seat**.

Wouldn't it be great to have "Pen Pals" in other counties? Your teacher or principal can help you find some.

You could stop to *visit* in neighboring counties rather than just passing through on the way to somewhere else.

Visit your own county courthouse, where trials are held and where people born in foreign countries become citizens of the United States.

Knowing about the 21 counties makes where you live a bit clearer. You live in a certain house, on a street, in a town, in a county.

It's time to be airborne again. Next, let's find out about lines that are really the "streets" of the world.

NAMING THE 21

Each county name tells much about the people who first settled the region.

Ten counties were named for places in England—Burlington, Camden, Cumberland, Essex, Gloucester, Middlesex, Monmouth, Salem, Somerset and Sussex.

Two county names came from the Dutch—Bergen and Cape May. Two, Morris and Hunterdon, were named for New Jersey governors—Lewis Morris and Robert Hunter. Two counties remember Revolutionary War generals—Hugh Mercer and Joseph Warren.

Indians gave a name to one county: Passaic. One county (Hudson) was named for an early explorer, Henry Hudson. Atlantic and Ocean were named for the ocean they touch. Union was given that name in 1857 in the hope that America could continue as the United States!

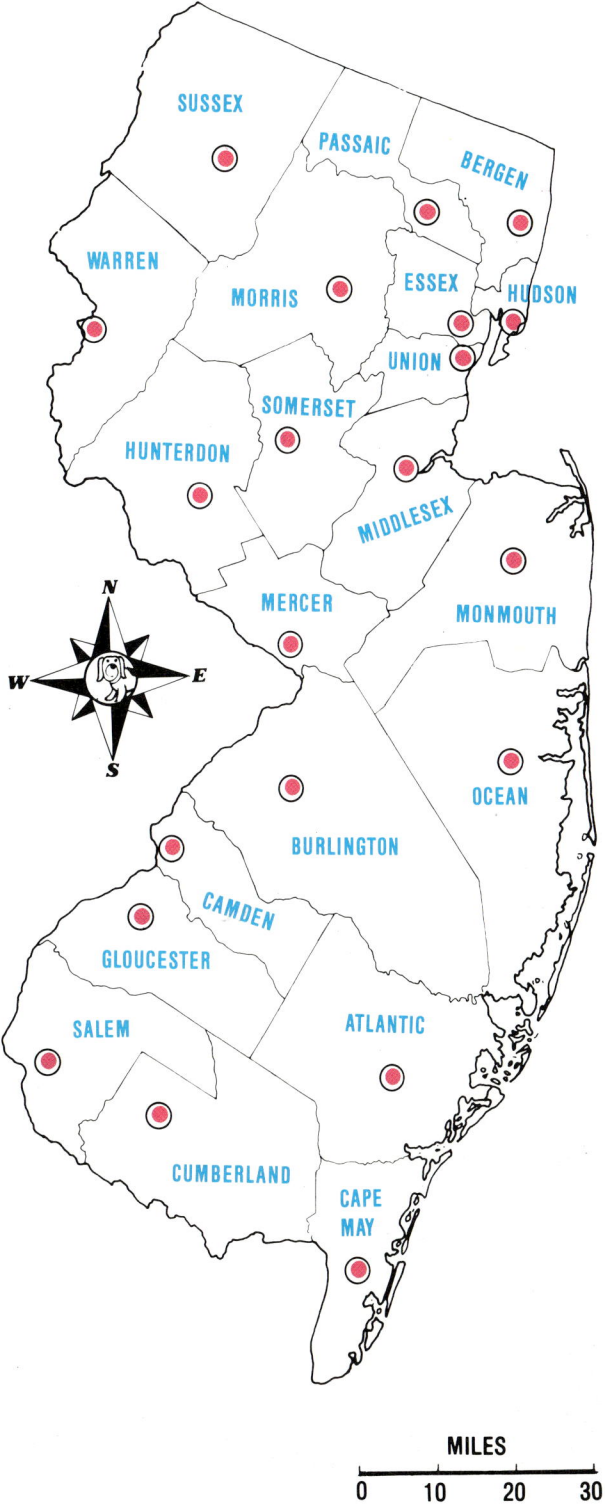

This is New Jersey: twenty-one counties and each very different from the others. County seat locations are shown by red dots in circles. You'll find county seat names on the chart on pages 250–251.

STREETS OF THE WORLD

Imagine that you live at 249 Lisa Street. It intersects with Christopher Avenue, the main street in your town. You easily can direct me to your house:

"Go east on Christopher Avenue to the big stone library. Lisa Street starts at that corner. Turn left on Lisa Street. Our house, number 249, is about two blocks north of the corner."

Pilots who fly jetliners around the world find their routes in exactly the same way. They follow "world streets." Ship captains can follow those same "streets" to tiny, far-off islands.

The "streets of the world" for pilots and ship captains are imaginary lines drawn around the world. The lines are called **latitude** and **longitude**. You will follow them for all of your life.

Take a look at a New Jersey map. Nearly all have lines that run north and south, or east and west.

These New Jersey lines are parts of the world's latitude and longitude lines. Latitude lines run east and west (side to side). Longitude lines, of course, run north and south.

At the ends of the lines on a map, whether of New Jersey or of the world, you will find numbers. These are the exact latitude or longitude numbers.

Note that each number has a tiny circle (°). This is a symbol for **degree**. A degree is part of a circle or globe. One degree equals 1/360th of the circle.

It is not easy to understand, but you'll need the knowledge!

New Jersey's main latitude lines are 39°, 40°, and 41°. Our two main longitude lines are 74° and 75°. Find them on a globe and trace them all the way around the world, north and south or east and west.

Our state's "main street" might be Latitude 40° because it is nearly in the middle of New Jersey. Follow "Street 40°" around the world.

Let's confine our Magic Carpet exploring to New Jersey right now, just to get a feel for latitude and longitude lines.

Let's fly off for four visits, using the map on page 25. Find Jim's town, near

Latitude 39°. Find Jessica's town, very close to Latitude 41° and Longitude 74°.

The third and fourth visits are tricky. Brian lives exactly on Longitude 75°. Jennifer's house is exactly on Latitude 40°.

Oh yes, find *your* approximate "corner" on the latitude and longitude streets of the world. It's a good idea to know where you *are*, before you think of world travels.

We are ready, finally, to soar out of New Jersey and around the world.

Captains of large ocean liners constantly study maps to follow the latitude and longitude lines.

Count on latitude and longitude to help get Jim, Jessica, Brian and Jennifer back home.

Suppose we did not have these imaginary streets of the world.

You would need many words and possibly many maps to make the locations clear. Even then most strangers would have difficulty in finding Jessica's town.

By saying, "She lives very close to latitude 41° and longitude 74°," it is no puzzle at all!

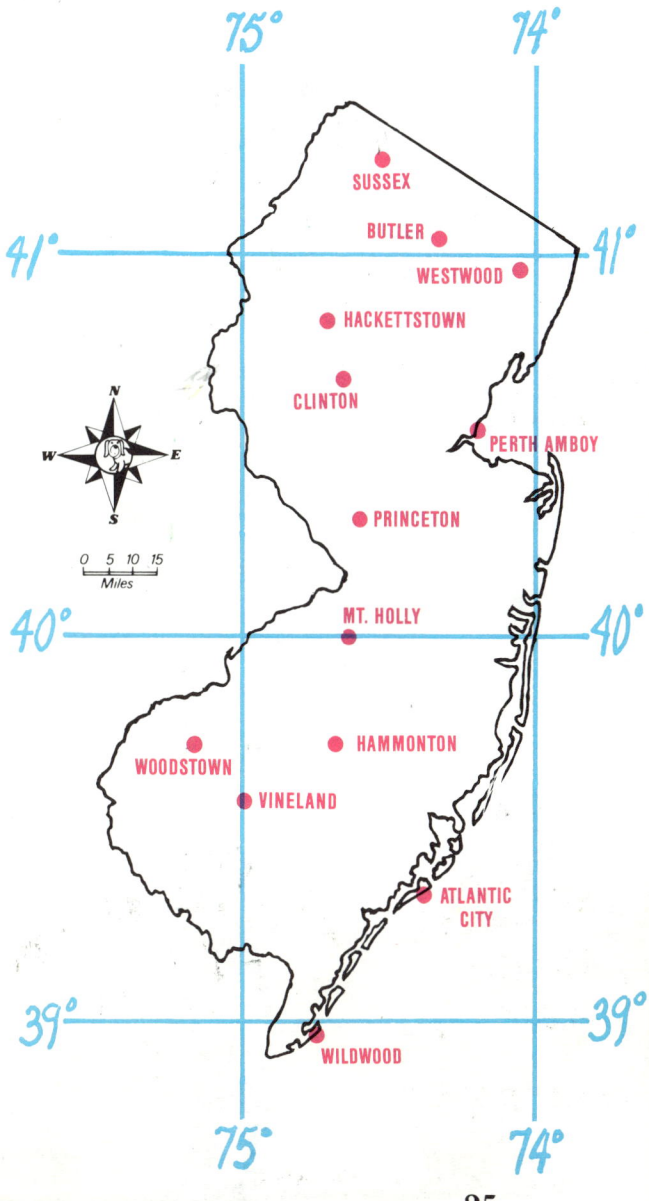

25

AROUND THE WORLD

Let's speed outward. We'll follow the "streets of the world," those imaginary lines called latitude and longitude.

Before you soar, look at a globe. Imagine that you are looking down as a space traveler might view the planet Earth from hundreds of miles high.

You see several things. The Earth is round, of course. Also, the globe has a "blue look." That is because three quarters of the world is salty **ocean** water.

Green areas are what mapmakers call "land masses." The seven biggest land masses are called **continents**.

To see all the world at once, imagine that you could peel the "skin" off the globe and put it on flat paper. It is difficult to make something round into something flat, but a flat map gives us a very good image of the continents and oceans.

The flat map below contains the seven continents and the oceans. New

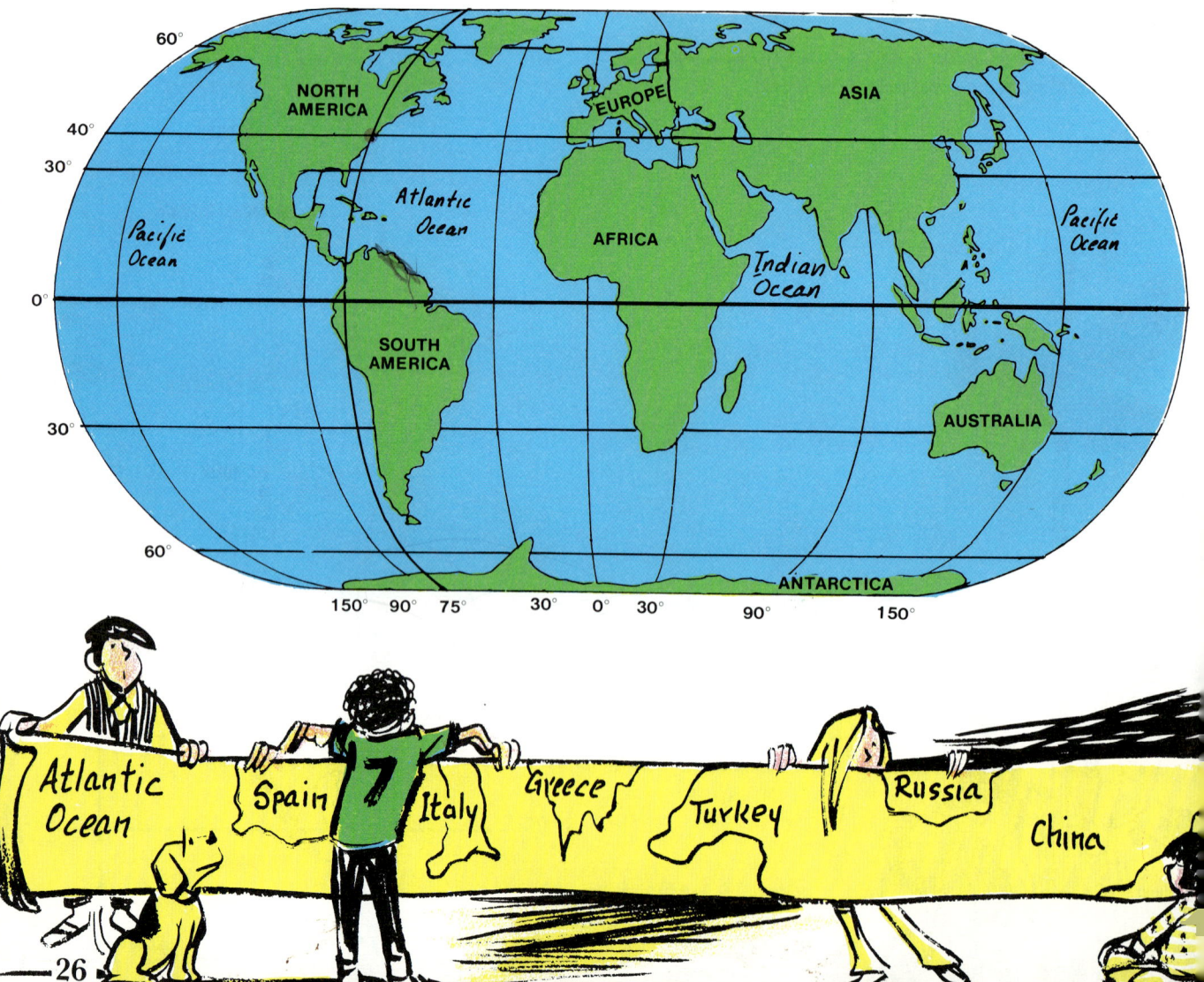

Jersey is just a small red dot on the continent called North America.

Our nearest continental neighbor is South America. There are two great continents called "America," surrounded by the vast oceans called Atlantic and Pacific (the A. & P.!).

Eastward across the Atlantic Ocean are the continents named Europe, Asia and Africa. Still farther east is Australia. Remember, on a globe, Australia can also be *west*, across the Pacific Ocean!

The seventh continent is at the bottom of the world. It is Antarctica, a place so cold that no humans live there permanently. Only a few scientists or explorers visit to study for awhile among the penguins that do live in Antarctica.

If we journeyed north from Antarctica, the climate would get warmer and warmer as we neared the middle of the map. Then, at *Latitude Zero* degrees—the middle of the map—we would reach the **Equator**.

The Equator is one of two lines that we *must* know about if our "streets of the world" are to make real sense.

The Equator goes around the "fattest" part of the globe, yet it is called *Latitude Zero*. It divides the world in half, "top and bottom," north and south. Latitude lines circle the world northward or southward from the Equator.

Ah, then, New Jersey's Latitude 40° is not exact enough! We really must say Latitude 40° *North* to locate for sure New Jersey's "main street!"

If there is a *Latitude Zero*, would it figure that there is also a *Longitude Zero*?

Right! Look at the map. Longitude zero runs north and south through a bit of Europe and some of Africa. As you can guess, longitude lines also go around the globe, east and west from *Longitude Zero*. New Jersey's longitudes are 74° and 75° *West*.

Now we know almost exactly where on earth New Jersey is:

Longitude 75° West

Latitude 40° North

Our Magic Carpet never again will lead us astray on the planet Earth!

OUR "HEMI" OF THE SPHERE

You are about to get another part of your world address: *Western Hemisphere*.

A "sphere" is a round object. It can be anything from a tennis ball to the huge earth.

"Hemi" means half. Quick now, what does **hemisphere** mean?

You can cut a tennis ball in half and have a hemisphere. You could look at the earth from a space ship and see only half a sphere.

Or you could look at a globe of the world. The part that you can see will always be a hemisphere. No matter how you try, you can't see both halves of something round!

The world can be divided into the "Eastern" and "Western" Hemispheres. In "our half," the Western Hemisphere, we find North America and South America. Part of Antarctica is also in this half of the globe.

The rest of the globe is the Eastern Hemisphere. It contains all of the continents of Africa, Europe, Asia, Australia and part of Antarctica.

Our "hemi" of the "sphere" has the same amount of space, of course. However, the Western Hemisphere has much more water—and less land—than the Eastern. Since water is blue on maps, the Western Hemisphere has a "blue look."

"Our" hemisphere extends from the North Pole to the South Pole. The same is true for the Eastern Hemisphere. Naturally the Equator goes through both hemispheres.

WESTERN HEMISPHERE

EASTERN HEMISPHERE

An orange is a sphere. You can use one to prove many things you want to know about spheres or hemispheres.

Peel the orange. The sections are clearly seen. The dividing lines are real on an orange, but think of them as imaginary *latitude or longitude lines. Hold the complete orange one way and the lines are "latitude." Hold it another way and the lines become "longitude."*

Now grasp the orange in the middle. Pull it apart. In each hand you will have half an orange, or a hemisphere.

Certainly it takes some imagining to think of an orange as the Planet Earth, but imaginations are meant to be used—especially by Magic Carpet pilots!

We aren't finished with hemispheres. Now look at the globe directly down from the top. You see the Northern Hemisphere. Is there a Southern Hemisphere? Of course!

The Equator is the dividing line. It divides the Northern Hemisphere from the Southern. We live in the Northern.

The seasons are exactly opposite in the Northern and Southern Hemispheres. This is because of the way that the earth rotates around the sun. As the sun gets farther north or south of the Equator, the seasons change—spring, summer, autumn and winter.

Look again at our longitude lines through New Jersey—74° and 75°. Now, on a Western Hemisphere map, follow Longitude 75° toward the South. In South America, it goes through Columbia, Peru and Chile.

A large Western Hemisphere map, a South American map or a world map in an atlas will show you that Latitude 40° **South** goes through Argentina and Chile.

Because the seasons are opposite, boys and girls in Argentina or Chile are at this minute enjoying a season exactly six months different from that of New Jersey. If you have winter here, it is summer in Argentina and Chile!

But when you get the warmth of summer, boys and girls in Argentina and Chile are in the middle of winter!

EARTH'S MIDDLE

You know about the Equator, an imaginary line at Latitude Zero that divides the planet Earth into Northern and Southern hemispheres.

The Equator might be called "the waistline of the planet," since it is the middle line at the fattest part of Earth. Here, the distance around the world is about 25,000 miles. On an old sailing ship it would have taken about three years to sail around the Equator.

The Equator is also the hottest part of the world. It crosses the northern part of South America, the central part of Africa and goes through several islands in Asia.

Crossing the Equator is special. Usually there is a ceremony, where those crossing for the first time get a special certificate.

FORTY-EIGHT AND TWO AFAR

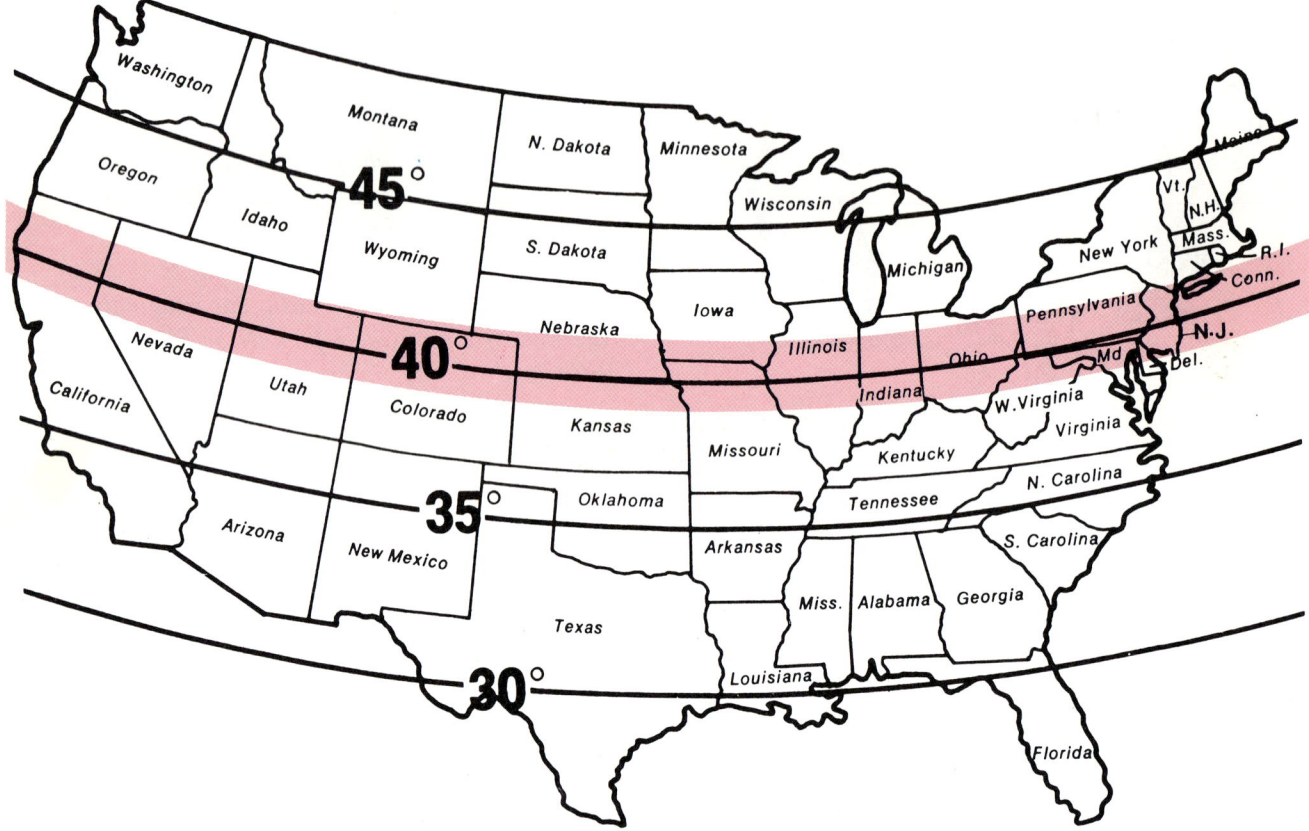

The best part of our address is saved for last: The United States of America!

Or, just write U.S.A. Those initials are known everywhere in the world. U.S.A. means 50 states together, 50 states united.

To help get an idea of what the United States is, imagine New Jersey as a small piece of a giant jigsaw puzzle. See it as a piece that we can move.

Let's push that New Jersey piece westward. We must keep it on a "track" between New Jersey's latitudes—39° to 41°.

Westward we go, first across the Delaware River. As we move, Cape May slides over Washington D.C., our nation's capital. Our piece moves over much of Pennsylvania and Maryland.

Our piece moves over the slow-moving Ohio River and close to the track where the famed Indianapolis "500" automobile race is held every May. We move past Springfield, Illinois, where President Abraham Lincoln won his first fame.

We cross the wide, muddy Mississippi River and the broad Missouri River. On we move—through the giant grain fields of Nebraska and Kansas, over the snowcapped Rocky Mountains, across the hot Salt Lake desert, and above the high mountains of California. Finally, we reach the Pacific Ocean.

If that sounds a bit like the song, "America The Beautiful," it should! This is what America is all about!

As we've moved our New Jersey token westward, we have crossed or touched 12 states. And, exciting though the journey between Latitudes 39° and 41° might be, this strip along our "latitude streets" is only a small part of the United States of America!

Forty-eight of our 50 states touch one another. Two states, Alaska and Hawaii, are so far away that they do not fit within the scale of our map on page 30.

Far off to the northwest is Alaska. A small part of Alaska is about 600 miles from the State of Washington, the closest state. Most of Alaska is more than 1,000 miles away from Washington.

The biggest of all states, Alaska, became our 49th state in January, 1959.

Way out in the Pacific Ocean, 2,400 miles west of California, is Hawaii, made up of several small islands. It became the 50th state in August, 1959.

You could spend the rest of your life learning about the United States. Some of you undoubtedly will!

The more you learn, the prouder you will be to know that your EXACT address is:

Your street. Your town. Your state. Your zip code. U.S.A. Continent of North America.

Plus: *Latitude 40° North. Northern Hemisphere. Longitude 75° West. Western Hemisphere. The Planet Earth.*

THAT address will get you back home from anywhere—even outer space!

John T. Cunningham
Box 1399
Andover, N.J. 07821

YOUR STREET
YOUR TOWN
YOUR STATE
YOUR ZIP
U.S.A.
LATITUDE 40° NORTH
NORTHERN HEMISPHERE
LONGITUDE 75° WEST
WESTERN HEMISPHERE
THE PLANET EARTH

Your postman is never likely to see an address like this, unless each of you in your class chose someone's name and sent the person a letter with this kind of address. It could be fun—and you can be sure that there is no possibility that the letter would be lost!

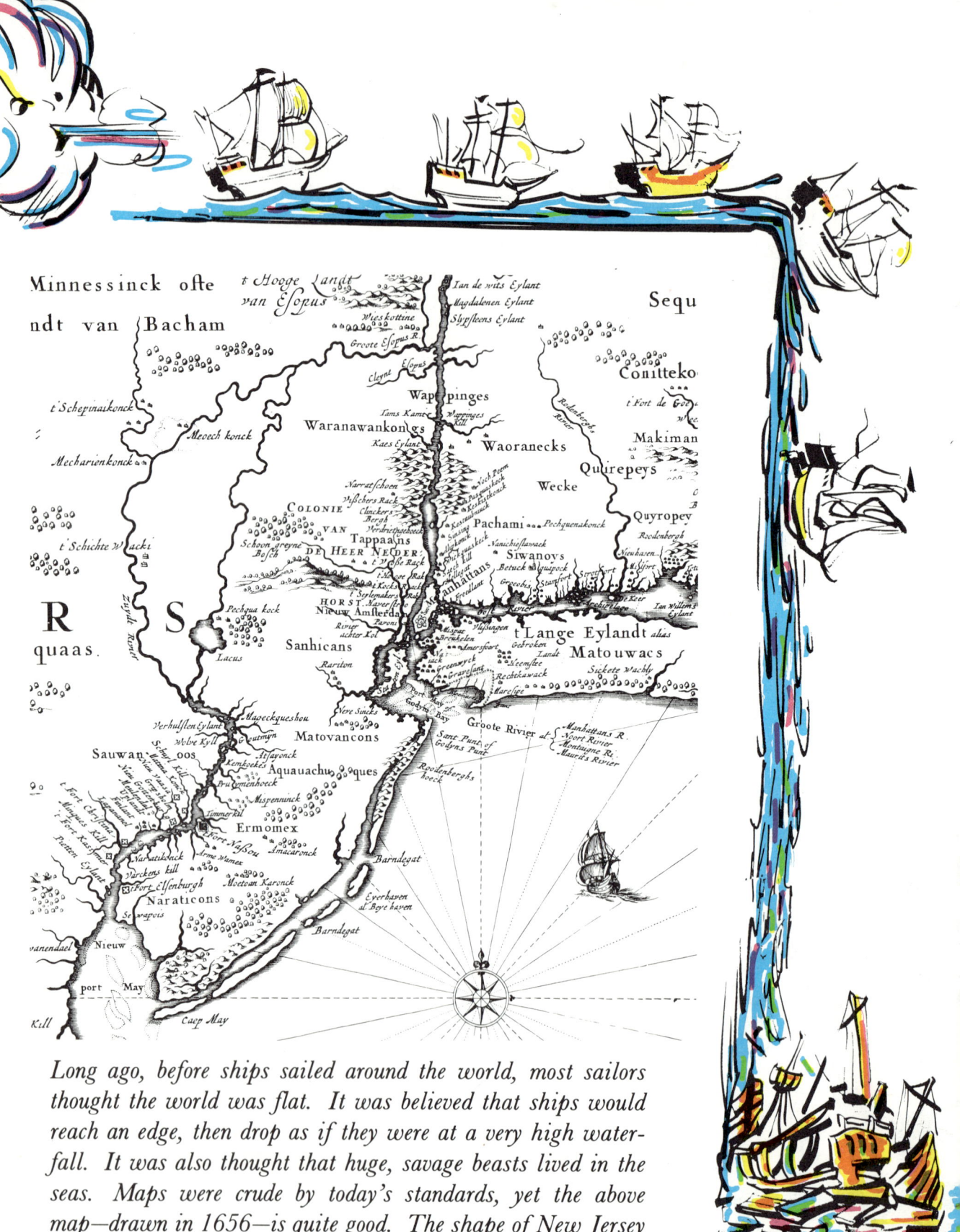

Long ago, before ships sailed around the world, most sailors thought the world was flat. It was believed that ships would reach an edge, then drop as if they were at a very high waterfall. It was also thought that huge, savage beasts lived in the seas. Maps were crude by today's standards, yet the above map—drawn in 1656—is quite good. The shape of New Jersey easily can be seen.

GEOGRAPHY

MAGIC CARPET NO. 2

*New Jersey's land is varied, tip to toe,
Its many faces give it style.
Mountains, lakes 'n' forests, seashore too,
Lure travelers o'er every mile.*
    Repeat Chorus (see page 9)

Let's look New Jersey squarely in the face! It is not easy. Our state has many different "faces."

We will examine all six faces, dividing up New Jersey. These actually are geographical divisions, but it seems so much friendlier to call them faces!

So, we're off, first to the mountain "face." Then we will look at the Highlands and go on to "The Great Pathway," where cities, people and traffic are found. Finally, we will look at the mysterious Pine Barrens, the great farm lands and the sparkling Jersey Shore.

33

NEW JERSEY HAS MANY FACES

Now that we have been around the world—and then some—it is time to do some Magic Carpet flying in our own State of New Jersey!

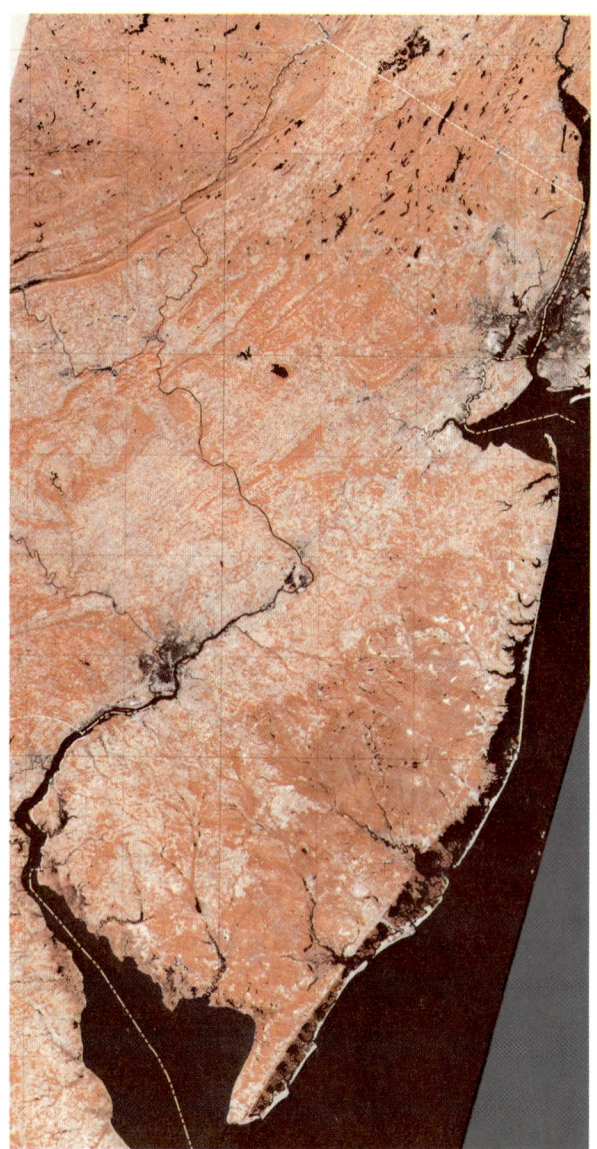

This is how New Jersey looks from a spaceship. There is no boundary line. A mapmaker added that. The shape is easy to see.

First, look at New Jersey's shape. It is easy to find on a United States map. If you were an astronaut, looking down from 200 miles in space, New Jersey could be instantly recognized.

Remember that from a spaceship or an airplane, there are no state lines. However, your eyes quickly would pick up our state's two big sweeping curves to the west. Then your eyes would see the long coastline where our state meets the Atlantic Ocean.

New Jersey has water on three sides. Nine-tenths of the boundary lines are water, either parts of rivers or the ocean. Our state is really a long **peninsula.**

The Delaware River provides the two big curves to the west. Near the "bottom" of the state, the river becomes very broad and is called Delaware Bay.

We share the Delaware River boundary with Pennsylvania and the state of Delaware. We also share Delaware Bay with Delaware.

We call our coastline along the Atlantic Ocean "The Jersey Shore." It is 127 miles long from Sandy Hook to Cape May Point. It is famous for its great sandy beaches.

In the northeastern part of New Jersey, our boundary is the Hudson River. It separates us from New York State.

New Jersey has one more boundary—the straight line across the top. It is shared by the states of New York and New Jersey. It is our state's only straight-line boundary.

New Jersey is tiny, as you well know after getting a look at the world! But in our small area we have varied kinds of land.

Some people call the different areas of New Jersey the "faces" of our state. A state *does* present its "face"—or "faces"—to those who wish to see and to understand.

New Jersey can be divided into six sections, or "faces." They are very different. The map on this page shows the six sections. They vary from high mountains in the northwest to sea level beaches in the east and south.

There are no exact lines for the sections, of course. Nature does not work that way. The areas tend to lap over into one another. The map shows generally where each type of "face" can be found.

Off we speed, starting with the mountains at High Point. We will look closeup at each of six "faces." When we stop, at Cape May Point, we'll know that New Jersey is a land worth seeing!

There are no actual *lines on the ground between states. Boundary "lines" are drawn by surveyors for use on maps. Fortunately, neighboring states are friendly—as New Jersey is with New York State.*

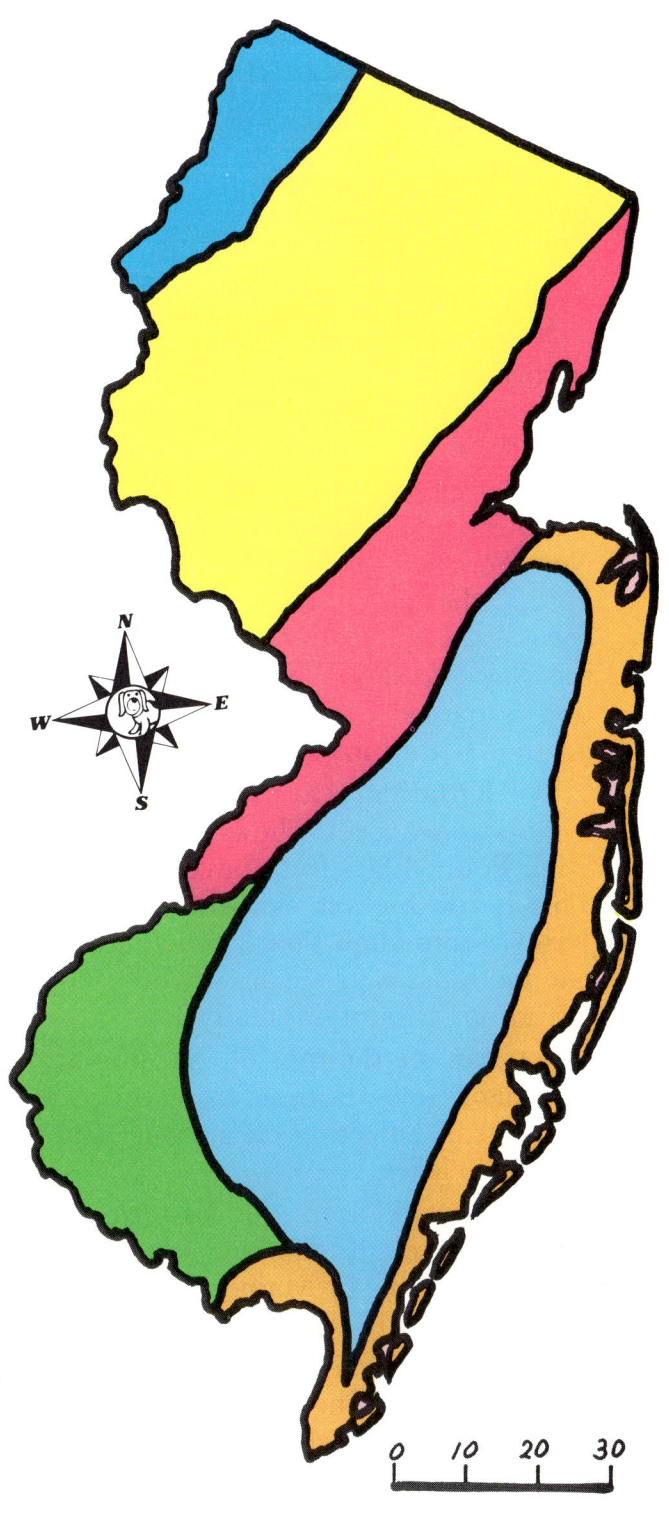

These are the New Jersey "faces" that we will examine closely. Note that the sections vary in size and shape. Each face is colored differently. This is the key to all of the "face" maps to be found on the next 12 pages.

35

THE MOUNTAIN LAND

New Jersey's highest area is in the northwestern part. It begins where our state meets New York near High Point and runs for about 35 miles to the Delaware Water Gap.

"Our" mountains continue into both New York and Pennsylvania. In New York, the mountains are called *Shawungunk*. In Pennsylvania, they are the *Blue Mountains*. New Jersey's portion is named the *Kittatinny Mountains* (or the "Kittatinnies").

The Kittatinnies average about 1600 feet above sea level. The highest spot is High Point, 1,803 feet above sea level. This is the highest elevation in New Jersey. From High Point, you can look out for miles and see how wild these Kittatinny Mountains really are!

You can see the tops of oak, poplar, and maple trees. In that forest, you can see the sun reflecting off several small mountain lakes.

Hikers walk atop the Kittatinnies along the rough Appalachian Trail. The trail begins in Maine and follows mountaintops all the way to Georgia!

Beside the trail, hikers often see rattlesnakes sunning themselves on the warm mountain rocks. At night, hikers camping beside the trail might hear the growl of a bear, the hoot of an owl, or the cry of a wild cat.

You can drive close to part of the Appalachian Trail. If you go to Sunrise Mountain in Stokes State Forest, you can park your car within less than 200 feet of the trail. With very little effort you can hike a bit of the trail.

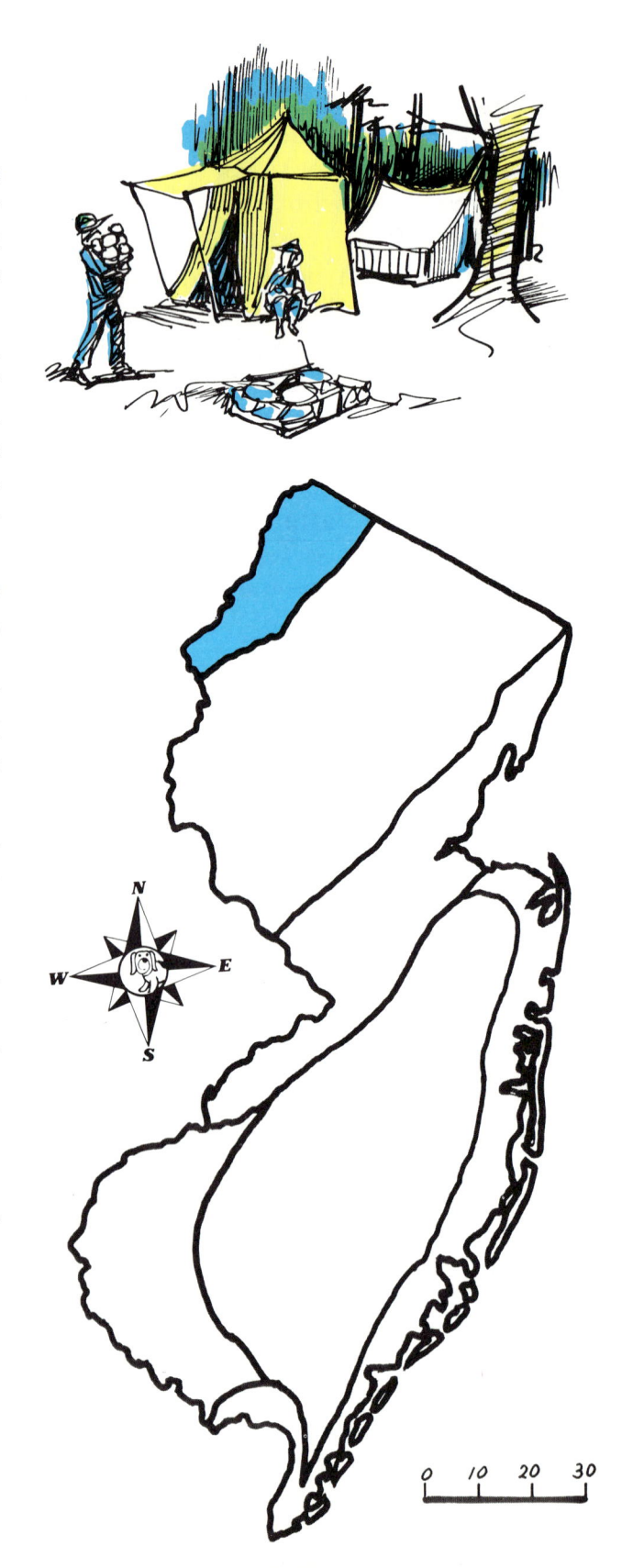

The Mountain Land is for anyone who loves being in the open air—to picnic, to camp, to watch birds or to hike along the rugged Appalachian Trail.

Experienced walkers in top-flight condition can walk the Appalachian Trail from Maine to Georgia.

New Jersey has three sights along the trail certain to make hikers pause—High Point, Sunrise Mountain and Sunfish Pond. Here, young visitors clamber over boulders at High Point.

It was not easy for people to settle here. The rugged rocks made it very difficult to build roads, or even to ride horseback. The rocky soil was not good for growing vegetables. It was easier to let milk cows graze on the steep slopes. Some of the area became a large dairy land.

Most of the "Mountain Land" is now saved for us in parks or forests. These include High Point State Park, Stokes State Forest, Worthington State Forest and the huge Delaware Water Gap National Recreation Area.

The mountain land is a great New Jersey asset. Its trees bring a coolness to the land. Trees also keep rain from running off the hills too rapidly. More than anything, the mountains add beauty and open space to our state.

Occasionally a big black bear, weighing as much as 300 pounds, wanders out of the Kittatinny Mountains and into nearby towns! It makes headlines, for most people do not realize this part of New Jersey is still so wild.

THE HIGH COUNTRY

Just east of the Kittatinnies is the "face" we call the Highlands. These high hills extend south nearly to Trenton and north to the New York border. Much of this beautiful land is still forestland.

The Highlands mountains have unusual names—*Wawayanda, Pochuck, Bowling Green, Bearfort, Kanouse, Ramapo, Watchung, Schooley's, Musconetcong* and the *Sourlands*. One "mountain" is called *Pimple Hills*!

Long ago, in colonial times, the middle part of the Highlands had many small forges that made iron from ore mined in nearly 100 mines. Forests supplied wood for the forge fires.

Today, all the forges are closed. The mines are shut. It is cheaper to **import** iron ore from far away—even from other countries. Millions of tons of iron ore still are underground in the New Jersey Highlands. Someday, perhaps, iron will be mined again.

The Highlands have many other kinds of minerals. "Rock Hounds" know the town of Franklin, where zinc ore once was mined. In the old mine dumps, rock collectors find many rare minerals!

The region has many lakes. The state's largest, *Lake Hopatcong*, is nearly seven miles long. It has about 40 miles of shoreline. New Jersey's other big lake, *Greenwood*, is shared with New York State.

We all have favorite lakes, such as *Mohawk, Swartswood, Culvers, Owassa, Musconetcong* and *Wawayanda*, to mention only a few. *Green Pond* is as big as most of those lakes, but it is called a "pond." Names do not always tell the real story!

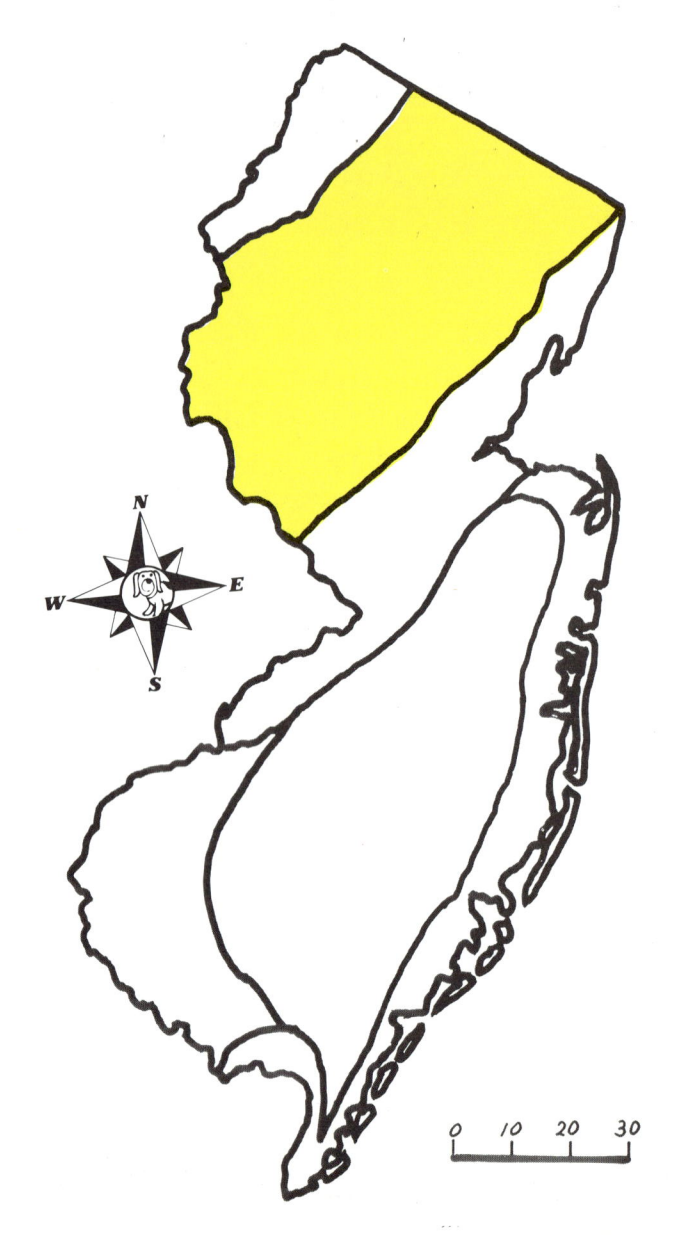

The Highlands also have many **reservoirs**, where water is stored for towns and cities. The most important are Wanaque, Boonton, Spruce Run, and Round Valley Reservoirs. Most reservoirs are not open for swimming or fishing. However, Spruce Run and Round Valley, both state-owned, are wonderful recreation areas.

Hundreds of thousands of people who work in Newark, New York or other cities live in the Highlands. They commute to work daily by trains, cars or buses.

Great changes are taking place in the Highlands. Big companies are constructing huge new buildings on what used to be farmland or forests. More people are working and living here. That means heavy automobile traffic and increased air and water pollution.

The first settlers came for iron. Now business, industry, and home builders seek out the Highlands. Many people believe that we would also be wise to preserve more public park land for recreation, natural beauty, fresh air and water.

The Highlands still offer New Jerseyans the finest in lakeland sports. Yet, as in the photograph above, housing and industrial development are crowding into the wooded hills.

Once, the lakes were only summer resorts. Demands for housing have caused owners to "winterize" their lakeside houses, making it possible to live there in all seasons of the year.

The picture above clearly demonstrates the need to be careful lest the woodlands, farms and waterways disappear.

THE GREAT PATHWAY

New Jersey's best known area is the busy stretch of land between New York and Philadelphia. Neither city is in our state, but both always have been important to New Jersey.

This level region could be called "The Great Pathway." Even in colonial times it was easy to travel on the flat land between New York and Philadelphia. Now, millions of people live in the "Pathway."

Our state's ten most populated places are in this region: *Newark, Jersey City, Paterson, Elizabeth, Trenton, Woodbridge, Camden, Hamilton, East Orange and Edison.*

These days many industries and offices are moving out of the pathway to nearby counties. That is because new highways have made it easier for automobile drivers and truck drivers to move across the state.

People also are moving outward because of the new highways. Townships such as Dover and Brick, are growing rapidly. Towns eastward from Camden are getting more people.

The Great Pathway is still New Jersey's most important "face." Any area filled with cities is certain to be worth attention.

We sometimes forget the importance of cities, where people live and work. Universities usually are in or close to cities. Research laboratories are never far away, for they depend on city factories to make their supplies. Cities contain most of the great libraries and museums. We all depend on our Great Pathway.

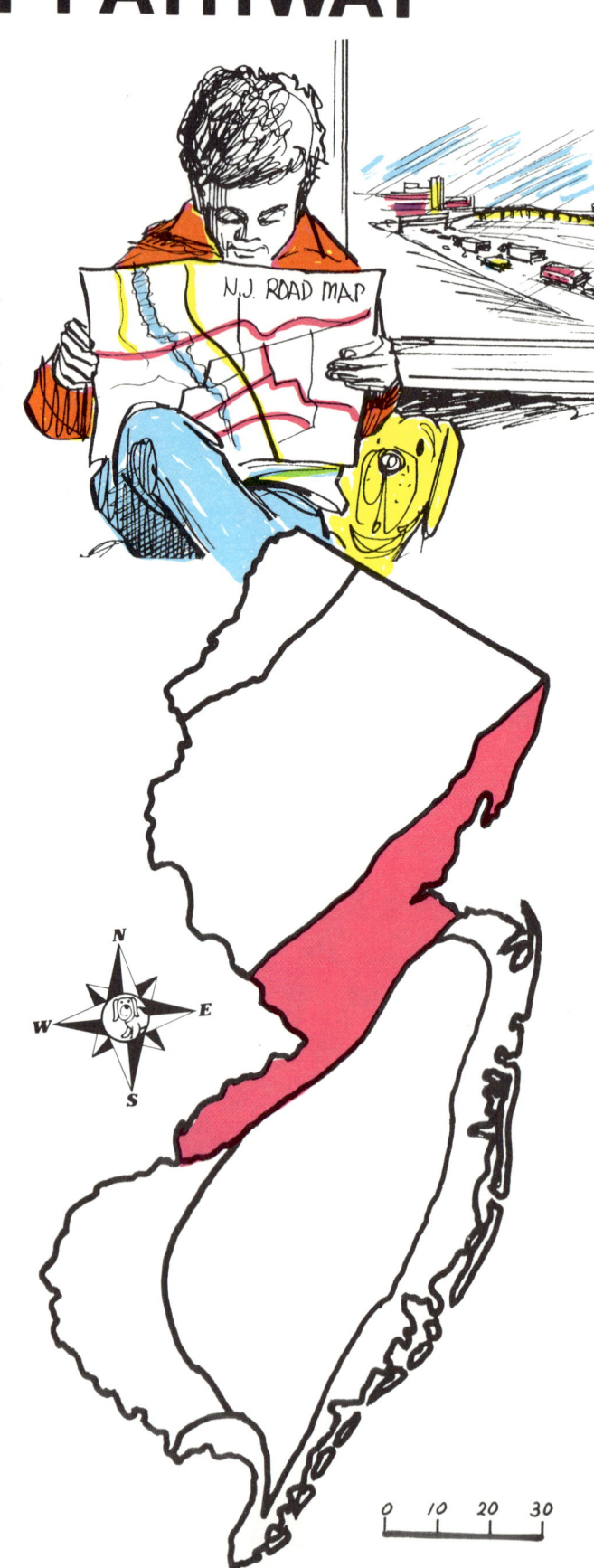

One city familiar to most New Jersey boys and girls is Trenton. Many of you will visit the Capital City. You will see the fine State Museum, the State Library and learn of Trenton's great role in the American Revolution.

Many of you also will visit Newark, to see the Newark Museum, one of the best of all small museums. Nearby is Newark Library, used by thousands of people every day. Many boys and girls attend concerts or other programs in Newark's Symphony Hall. Some of you will visit world-famed Newark Airport and the big, exciting seaports of Newark and Elizabeth.

In Paterson, you can see the mighty Passaic Falls. You will be close to the Statue of Liberty at Liberty Park in Jersey City. Camden is where one of America's great poets, Walt Whitman, chose to live.

The "Great Pathway" is where people gather. It is always important!

Pathways are for traveling, and crowded roads (above) show that New Jersey people make full use of "The Great Pathway" across our state.

Highways carry people into such cities as Newark (left), Elizabeth, Paterson, Trenton and Camden. There people work, attend concerts, use libraries and shop.

The roads also take people outward—to homes in nearby counties, to the Meadowlands Stadium and, in summer, to such fun places as the Jersey Shore.

THE PINE BARRENS

New Jersey's most mysterious and most wonderful section is called the Pine Barrens. This huge area covers about one fifth of the state.

The pine woodland includes about one million acres. It holds all of Fort Dix Army base as well as the Naval Station at Lakehurst. Several very large state-owned forests and parks are here. A big Army jetport is located close to Fort Dix.

Most of this great woodland is flat. The highest point, Apple Pie Hill, is only 205 feet above sea level. A tower atop the hill, used as a lookout for forest fires, gives visitors a marvelous view of the pine forest.

The name, "Pine Barrens," was given by early settlers. They thought the sandy soil would not grow vegetables or fruit. To them, such soil was not fertile and therefore "barren."

Actually, this is one of the richest sections in the state for wild flowers and shrubs. Botanists (people who study plants) come here from all over the world.

People familiar with the Pine Barrens can find many kinds of beautiful wild orchids. They also find such strange growing plants as sundews and pitcher plants. These trap insects and eat the victims!

Most of the "Barrens" trees are pines, but many scrub oaks also are found. The oaks spring up after wild fires burn off pine trees. White cedars grow close to slow-moving, coffee-colored streams.

The Pine Barrens is a place of mystery and history! The woods hold many ruins of "ghost towns," the remains of once-busy villages!

Many school children visit a Pine Barrens "ghost town" called Batsto. Long ago, iron and glass factories were busy here. Batsto's owners lived in the big mansion on a low hill.

Batsto workers lived in small wooden houses near the company store. They had to buy everything in the store and never could save any money. Many people lived, worked and died at Batsto or similar villages. They never knew of the world outside the forest.

If you climb to the tower atop the Batsto mansion, you are high above the evergreen forest. It looks like a great green sea, rolling in from all directions!

Early settlers gave simple names to Pine Barrens land, such as *Penny Pot, Red Lion, Ong's Hat* and *Sooey Place*! You can find *Fellowship* and *Friendship* if you look! It is fun to collect unusual Pine Barrens place names. Try it!

High above the Pine Barrens, from an airplane or a tall fire tower, the great woodland stretches away in all directions. Only an occasional road cuts through the region, one of New Jersey's most amazing natural wonders. Nearly a million acres of land are included in the barrens.

Deep within the woodlands are the remains of "ghost towns," places where the forest rang with the sounds of ironmakers and glassblowers at work. Batsto, a state-owned historic site (left) was such a town. It has been restored for visitors.

43

THE GARDEN SPOT

Our automobile license plates say that New Jersey is The Garden State.

Visitors often wonder about that. They think our nickname really should be "Industrial State" or "City State." They ask, where are the "gardens?" It's a fair question.

The reason for the nickname is found mainly along the lower Delaware River. Many farmers still prosper there because of the deep rich soil.

Land in the "garden spot" is generally flat. The soil is easily plowed. The growing season is long. Sometimes two or three crops of quick-growing vegetables such as lettuce or onions are harvested in one year.

This is not the only New Jersey farm (or "garden") area. Herds of dairy cows are still seen on pastures in Warren and Sussex counties. Horse farms are found in nearly all counties. Chickens are grown in some counties.

However, New Jersey's best farm area is in Salem and Cumberland counties, plus parts of Cape May, Gloucester and Burlington counties.

Some of the vegetable fields of southern New Jersey are almost beyond imagination. Sometimes they stretch away from a roadway as far as the eye can see.

Two or more giant tractors often work at the same time in one field. Unusual machines plant the seeds. Vegetables are harvested with other huge machines especially designed for such crops as beans, corn or soybeans.

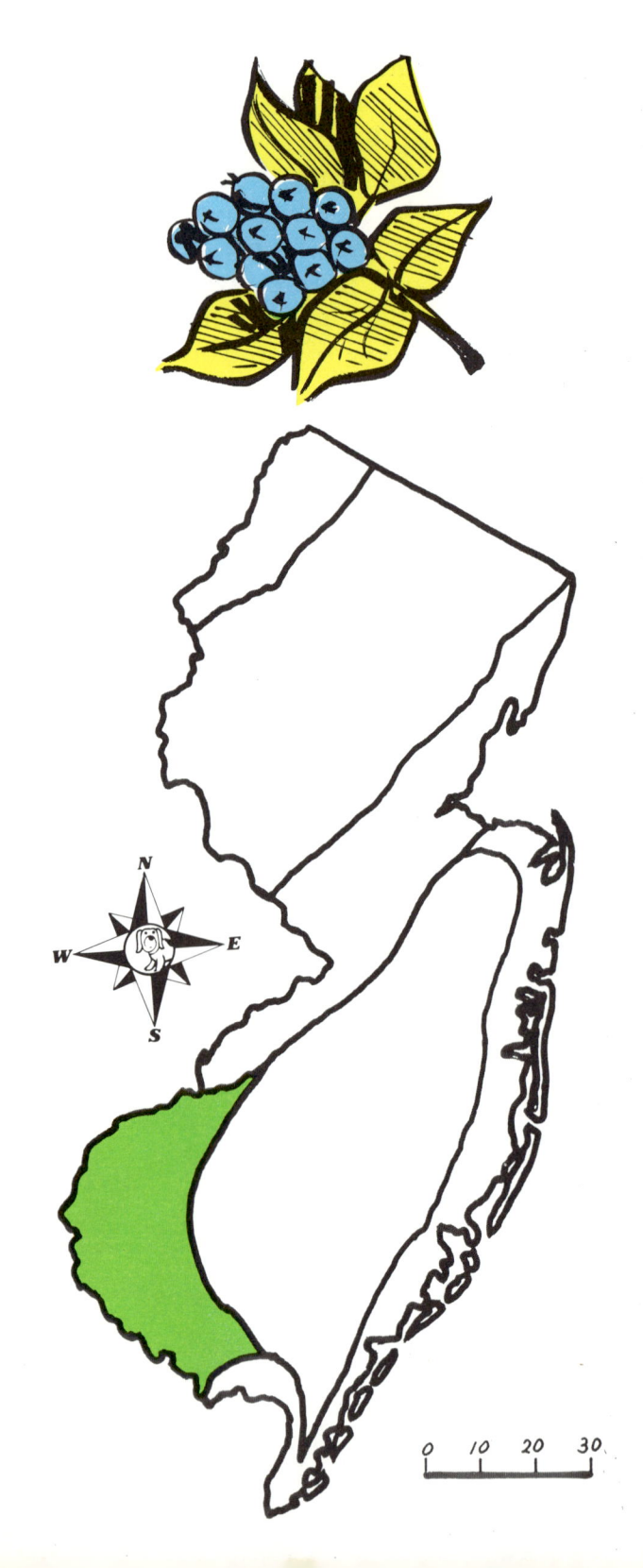

44

Farmers who reap vegetable harvests from the soils of southwestern New Jersey must rely on modern machines—from powerful tractors that pull plows to giant harvesters that can pick anything from tender asparagus to ripe red tomatoes. Such machines make it possible for farmers to plant two or three times every year in the same fields.

The region's farmers also grow fine fruit, especially apples, peaches, blueberries, strawberries and cranberries.

One famous southern New Jersey farm product is the tomato. Some farmers grow tomatoes for canning factories. However, most tomatoes are grown for sale in stores or at fruit and vegetable markets where your parents might shop.

There have been farms and farmers in this southern New Jersey area for more than 300 years. Truly, as the earliest settlers wrote, this land has been blessed by nature. It *is* "The Garden Spot."

JOHNSON'S BIG BITE

Robert Gibbons Johnson stood on the steps of the Salem County courthouse in the summer of 1820 and told astonished neighbors that he would eat a tomato. The audience shuddered. Tomatoes, they thought, were deadly poisonous!

Johnson calmly took a bite. Many people turned their heads away, not wanting to see him die a horrible death. He lived of course; tomatoes were not poisonous. Johnson knew it, because he had eaten the fruit before. After that, everyone grew (and ate) tomatoes.

THE JERSEY SHORE

New Jersey faces the Atlantic Ocean along 127 miles of sandy coastline. We call this "The Jersey Shore."

Colonists thought that the Jersey Shore was worthless, because they could not grow crops in the white sand. Most avoided the beaches as if they were deserts.

Whale hunters settled more than 300 years ago at Cape May and at Harvey Cedars on Long Beach Island. A few fishermen and clam diggers later worked along the shore. Since there were not many places where good ports could be located, the Jersey Shore had few settlers.

Then a great business began—very slowly—when a few fishermen's wives offered rooms for people who liked the sea and the beaches. The first such "summer guests" came about 200 years ago.

Entertaining summer visitors became very profitable. Today, millions of people visit the Jersey Shore every summer. Those "worthless" sands yield very big "harvests" of tourist dollars.

Once it was believed that the Jersey Shore "season" ended when boys and girls went back to school in September. It is true that not many families visit the beaches except in summer. However, the casinos at Atlantic City are busy every month of the year, even in the coldest days of winter.

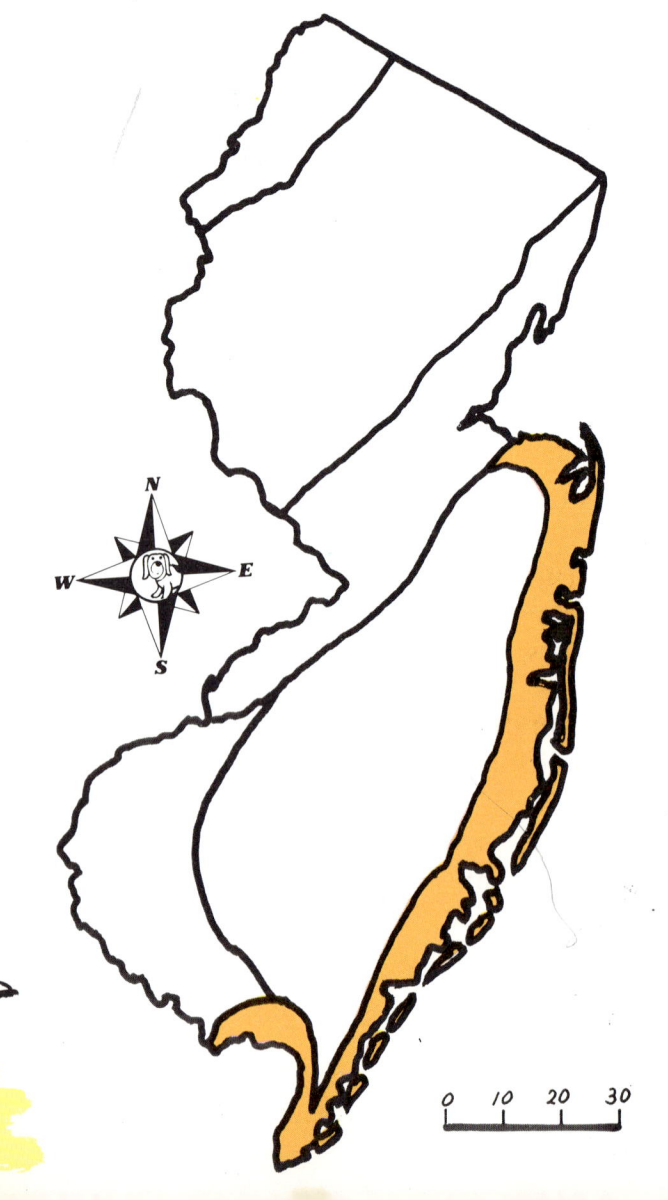

There are really two sections of the Jersey Shore. The northern region, from Sandy Hook to Bay Head, is attached to the mainland. From Bay Head south to Cape May, the resort towns are all "at sea," on sandy peninsulas or on islands.

Most of the mainland coast in the north is low and quite level where it meets the ocean. Near Sandy Hook, however, hills almost 200 feet high overlook the sea. They are called the Atlantic Highlands. From the ocean, these hills are an impressive landmark!

Long ago, lookouts with spyglasses watched from the Atlantic Highlands to see far-off vessels. Large twin lighthouses were built there in 1862 to warn ship captains of the dangerous coastline. The Twin Lights are still in place.

Many familiar shore towns are on islands. Atlantic City is on an island. So are Ship Bottom, Beach Haven, Ocean City, Wildwood and many other towns. Everything—lumber, bricks, glass, food—must be brought in from the mainland.

In early days, all visitors and all supplies were taken to the islands in boats. Imagine how much fun it must have been to sail out to the islands when few people lived there!

The widest and best New Jersey beaches are on the southern islands. One of the broadest beaches along the Atlantic coast is in Wildwood. At low tide, you can wade out more than one-quarter of a mile!

Between the shore islands and the mainland are wide **bays**. Some bays in Cape May County are called "**sounds**." The bays and sounds are fine places for fishing, clamming, sailing, waterskiing and swimming.

The lighthouse on the tip of Sandy Hook peninsula is the oldest continuously-lit beacon in the Western Hemisphere. The light first went on in 1764. The white tower rises 85 feet above the Hook's sand.

Called "Twin Lights," the towers on the Navesink Highlands are not identical. The south tower is square but the north tower has eight sides. Each tower is 73 feet tall. Built in 1862, the "twins" are no longer lit.

Summer visitors learn to call Barnegat Light by the name "Old Barney." The 162-foot-tall tower, red on top and white on the bottom, was finished in 1857. It no longer is lit. Visitors can climb 217 steps to the top.

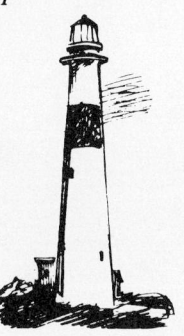

One of Atlantic City's symbols is Absecon Light. Finished in 1857, the white tower has a broad blue stripe near the top. The old lighthouse is 167 feet tall, highest of the Jersey Shore beacons. It was last lit in 1933.

Far to the south is Cape May Light, close to the point where Delaware Bay meets the Atlantic Ocean. The all-white tower, 165 feet tall, was completed in 1859. The beacon's light is turned on every afternoon at 4.

Five lighthouses along the Jersey Shore are reminders of days when the beacons warned ships of dangerous areas. Only two of the lights are still used. Radar does a better job of warning ships.

47

WIDE AND DEEP

Rivers are vital. They supply water. Ships and people can travel on them. They can be boundaries between towns, states and nations.

New Jersey has about 6,400 miles of streams. If that were all one river in a straight line, you could travel to California and back on 6,400 miles of waterways. Not all New Jersey streams are rivers. Most are just tiny brooks, which is where rivers start.

Our state's two most important rivers are the *Delaware* and the *Hudson*. We share them with other states. Neither the Delaware nor the Hudson rises in our state. Both start in New York State.

Big ships can travel up the Delaware as far as Trenton, where the river flows so rapidly over large rocks that even canoe paddlers have difficulty. Most ocean-going ships dock along the Delaware in either Philadelphia or Camden.

The Hudson River is very busy on both sides. On the New Jersey side, Hudson County always has been important to shippers. Now new piers and docks are being built in Jersey City and Bayonne.

Most ships in the New York-New Jersey area dock at the deep water ports at Newark and Elizabeth. Huge cargo ships come in from New York Bay. They follow the Kill Van Kull at

Bayonne to Newark Bay, where the Newark and Elizabeth ports are located.

"Kill" is an old Dutch word meaning creek or channel. Thus Kill Van Kull really means "the channel of Van Kull." Van Kull was a Dutch family name.

New Jersey's best known inland rivers are the *Passaic* and the *Raritan*. Both rivers were named by the Indians. The Passaic and Raritan both begin near Mendham. They find very different pathways to the sea. The Passaic enters Newark Bay at Newark. The Raritan flows into Raritan Bay at Perth Amboy.

Find the paths of the Passaic and Raritan. You will be surprised at how far rivers must travel before they reach sea level.

In the state's northern area are such rivers as the *Pequest, Musconetcong, Wallkill, Ramapo, Pequannock* and *Millstone*.

Along Delaware Bay are the *Salem, Cohansey* and *Maurice* rivers. *Maurice*, by the way, is pronounced "Morris." All three rivers are important for shipping some South Jersey products. Some South Jersey rivers are called creeks, such as the *Rancocas* or *Raccoon* creeks that flow into the Delaware River.

Along the Atlantic Ocean coast are such good-sized rivers as the *Manasquan, Egg Harbor, Mullica* and *Toms* rivers.

You will find that many New Jersey streams have Indian names. Our first people, the Indians, knew how valuable rivers were for travel, drinking and to water their gardens.

Colonists also used the rivers and creeks to travel inland from the ocean. Rivers were called thoroughfares, the main "roads" from place to place.

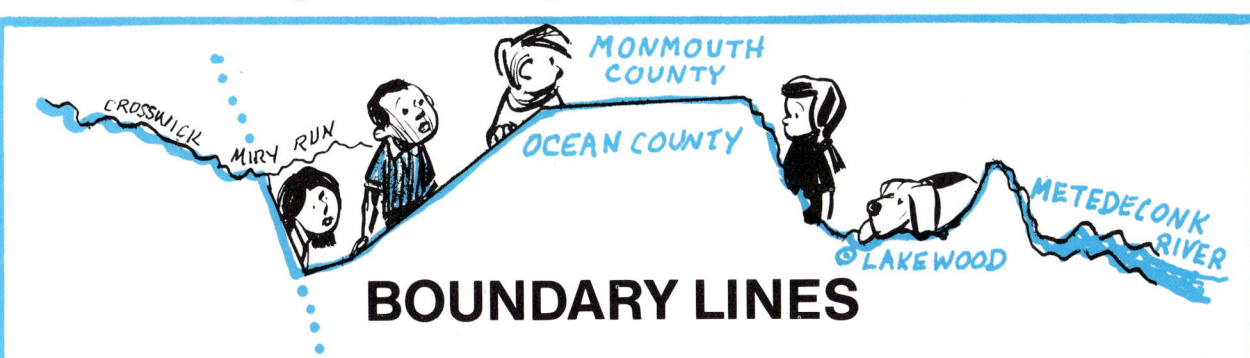

BOUNDARY LINES

Rivers often set boundaries between nations, states, counties or towns. We humans have added our own straight-line boundaries.

Look at your own county boundaries on a map. Which were set by nature? Which have been established by people?

Nineteen of New Jersey's counties share boundaries with other states or are along the Atlantic Ocean. Look for the two "inland" counties.

Do any counties in New Jersey have all-natural boundaries? Which of the counties share the straight-line boundary with New York State?

Your town or city boundaries can be fascinating to study. Town boundaries often have been changed. Sometimes areas break away from a larger city. Sometimes, in reverse, small towns become part of a larger town.

Perhaps someone in your town government, probably the town engineer, can tell you of your town's boundaries.

Someone in your local historical society could tell you how boundary lines once were set. Large boulders, tall trees or barns were used then to define boundaries.

Boulders, trees or buildings can disappear. When boundaries are "natural," such as a river, they are likely to last.

49

SKIING AND ONIONS

New Jersey actually gets a great deal of precipitation (rain or snow) each year. Only 13 states get more than our state's average of about 45 inches per year. Some states get very little. Arizona averages about 7 inches per year, lowest among states. Bad storms have dropped more than 8 inches of rain on New Jersey in one day!

New Jersey is only 166 miles long from High Point to Cape May. Yet it has a great variety of weather. Depending on where you are, the climate can be like either New England or the South.

Southern New Jersey farmers near Delaware Bay often plant such crops as onions early in March. At that time, northern New Jersey mountains usually have enough snow left for skiing!

The ocean at Cape May or Wildwood can be warm enough for swimming in late October. The ocean does not grow cold just because summer holidays end! At the same time, ice may form on northern New Jersey mountain ponds.

Climate affects farmers very much. Southern New Jersey farmers can have as many as 50 to 60 more growing days each year than northern New Jersey farmers. (*See map*).

New Jersey usually has enough rainfall to grow most fruits and vegetables, but there can be long periods when the rainfall is slight. Reservoirs get dangerously low and the hot sun dries out the fields and forests. Southern New Jersey farmers depend on pumps to **irrigate** rows of growing vegetables. They make their own "rain!"

Harsh weather can strike the state. A winter snowstorm might drop two feet of snow on northern New Jersey. That slows automobile traffic almost to a halt.

Savage Jersey Shore hurricanes can flatten boardwalks, wreck homes and ruin beaches.

GROWING SEASONS

DAYS
- 140 to 160
- 160 to 180
- 180 to 190
- 190 to 200

Ice storms are even worse. Cold rain freezes on trees and electric or telephone wires. Heavy ice snaps off limbs that break wires. Thousands of homes are without lights or telephones, sometimes for days.

The worst New Jersey storms are late summer hurricanes. These start far to the south. When they hit the Jersey Shore, wild winds roar at 80 to 100 miles or more an hour!

Hurricane winds can twist huge trees completely out of the ground. Rain pours down, six inches or more in one day. Ocean tides rise high. Homes and beaches near the ocean are in danger.

When the hurricane sweeps inland, rivers overflow their banks. High winds break limbs off large trees.

Extremely bad weather, fortunately, is not normal in New Jersey. The weather usually is quite pleasant—or at least millions of people who live here year after year think so!

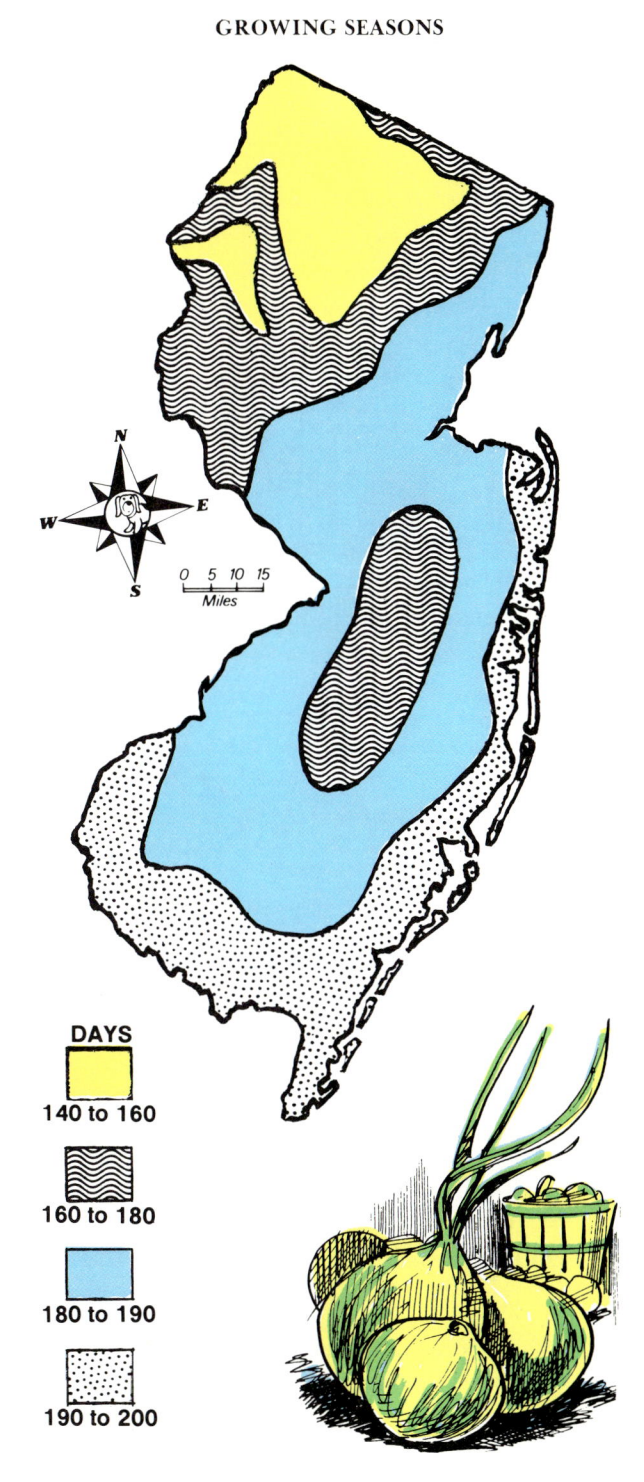

That dotted band along the Jersey Shore and Delaware Bay, on this map, means good weather for both farmers and seaside vacationers. New Jersey's summer temperatures often rise into the high 90's. Winter can bring lows of 20 degrees below zero (the record is 34 below). Temperatures along the Jersey Shore are much milder, in both summer and winter.

51

THE "FACES" OF 1844

New Jersey's "faces" (as seen in its towns) were shown in a book printed in 1844. Two artists, John W. Barber and Henry Howe, drew about 100 pictures for the book. Here are some of them.

The heart of old Bloomfield

Morris Canal flowing past Rockaway

Covered bridge at Phillipsburg

Busy Bridgeton on Cohansey Creek

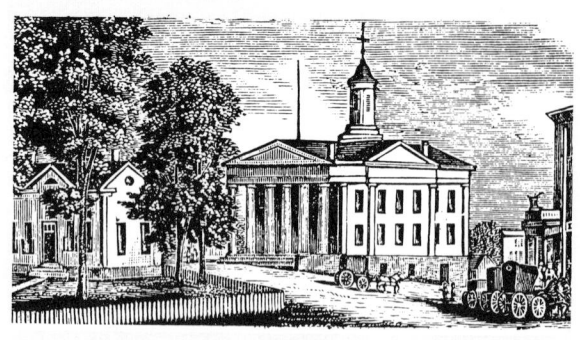

Sussex County's courthouse at Newton

A busy afternoon at Toms River

The center of thriving May's Landing

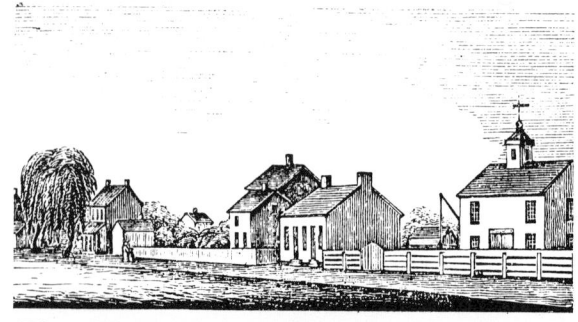

The village of Cape May Courthouse

These are "woodcuts," meaning the pictures had to be cut on wooden blocks for printing. If you like this sampling, perhaps your teacher could borrow "Barber & Howe" from the library.

52

GEOLOGY

MAGIC CARPET NO. 3

♪ *Geology unlocks earth's ancient past,
Prehistory is always near.
We'll look around, discover age-old times,
And all the relics we find here.*
    Repeat Chorus (see page 9) ♪

Earthquakes! Volcanoes! Dinosaurs! Mastodons! New Jersey had them all, many millions of years ago.

How do we know?

Scientists, called geologists, have studied the ancient past. They have found evidence of all the violence that shaped our planet and our state.

Come along. Let's find those distant prehistoric times. Who knows? As our eyes get accustomed to seeing the long ago past, we might even find a dinosaur footprint. Other New Jersey boys and girls have done just that!

WE CALL IT GEOLOGY

If you live in the northern third of New Jersey, your area probably was once under a thick layer of ice!

If you live in the southern half, the place where your school yard is now was once hundreds of feet beneath an ancient sea.

All about us we can find evidence of what is called **prehistoric time**—the time before humans lived on earth. There were no people here to write what they saw, felt and thought.

Most of what we know about prehistoric time is learned through a science called **geology**. Experts in geology, called **geologists**, are men and women who examine the earth, above and below the surface. They find what our planet was like millions of years ago.

Traces of prehistoric time are found in different kinds of rocks and soils, in animal bones preserved for millions of years or in **fossils**.

Geologists tell us that the earth is *millions* and *millions* of years old—even *billions* of years old!

It is difficult even to imagine the number of years needed to form our planet. There were years of violence:

Tremendous natural forces pounded one another!

Steam poured forth from cracks in the earth!

Earthquakes shook the land!

Out of all this violence came the land that is now called New Jersey.

It is easy to find geological evidence. Huge boulders can be seen on top of the ground in many parts of northern New Jersey. These tell of the great ice

54

New Jersey's most important geological monument likely is this "rock in the glen," from which Glen Rock got its name. Weighing 270 tons (more than 500,000 pounds!), the boulder was carried by glacial ice in northern Canada to New Jersey. When the glacier went north about 20,000 years ago, the rock remained.

block (or **glacier**) that brought those rocks here from far away.

The most dramatic boulder is found in the Bergen County town of Glen Rock. It is about the size of a small house. It is so unusual that the town was named for this "visitor" brought by ice.

South Jersey newspapers often describe the finding of bones of ancient sea animals or sea shell fossils. These prove that South Jersey once was an ocean bottom. Sewell, in Gloucester County, is one place where many prehistoric bones or shells have been found in soft sand.

Our land was not called New Jersey then. No human beings were around to give names to places. The Delaware River, Hudson River and Atlantic Ocean were there, but not *by those names*, or by any names.

Let *us* be geologists in the next few pages. Geologists really are detectives who find clues to the distant past.

Sometimes a geologist's study of prehistoric time will seem very difficult because of scientific words. Consider those words as "clues" or as a "code." Have some fun using them as you become skilled "geology detectives!"

55

THE VIOLENT YEARS

Great violence was needed to transform this planet called Earth into a place where humans could live.

Remember, humans have lived on our old Earth only a very short time—perhaps as "little" as a million years. A million years is only the blink of an eye in geological time.

Wild forces once tore at our planet. Mighty mountains were pushed up, then crumbled away. Volcanoes poured red hot lava across the land. Rushing streams wore away hard rock surfaces. Wild winds blew. Rains poured down for hundreds of years.

The best place in New Jersey to see the effects of those ancient powerful forces is the *Delaware Water Gap*.

Look up at the Gap from the highway that runs through it. We see layers of different colors, telling of different periods of time when the Earth's surface was being formed. Then, we look more closely, and note that the layers are in a crooked pattern. This shows the terrible power that twisted this rock mountain!

Delaware Water Gap was carved through the mountain by a stream that is now called the Delaware River. The

Delaware Water Gap is lasting proof of the power of water. After earthquakes and rock upheavals had twisted the mountain, the river began to wear away the hard rock. It took millions of years, but the river used sand, small rocks, boulders and other substances to cut the gap down 1,200 feet to where the river now flows.

water itself did not do the cutting, but it pounded sand and pebbles at the hard rock surface and wore it away.

In those days, many many millions of years ago, the river was about 1,500 feet wide. As it wore down, the river bed became more narrow and much deeper. The Delaware River at the Gap is now only about 300 feet wide.

As you stand and look up at the Gap, realize that this river sliced downward more than 1,200 feet from the top.

Our best known prehistoric volcano was located near the present town of Boonton. It erupted, or overflowed, at least three different times over long periods of years. Great flows of red hot lava poured out. The molten rock flowed across the flat land like water. The lava formed the three ridges of what we call the Watchung Mountains. These mountains stretch from near Paterson to Far Hills.

"QUAKE" TIME

Earthquakes still give New Jersey strong warnings that powerful forces can make the earth shudder. Humans cannot control nature.

New Jersey has had about 65 known earthquakes in the past 200 years. The worst have caused loud rumbling noises deep within the earth. These noises usually are followed by sounds that have been described as being "like explosions."

Most of our "quakes" have been recorded in an area from Monmouth to Bergen counties. People who have experienced our earthquakes say that the rumblings have rattled china closets or shaken small objects off shelves or tables.

No lives ever have been lost and no buildings ever have been destroyed in a New Jersey earthquake. Don't worry—but never forget that nature's awesome power must be respected.

Water is powerful. If rain floods across your baseball field, it can cut deep gullies between the bases. What you see are "little canyons" or "water gaps" on a small scale.

Today, thousands of families live peacefully on the cooled-off lava of the Watchung Mountains. Your parents or older friends drive over this volcanic region each day, probably without even *knowing* that their highways and homes are built on lava!

The most remarkable evidence of volcanic flows can be found in the Palisades along the Hudson River. This rocky cliff, created by lava streams, rises as much as 500 feet above the river.

THE TERRIBLE LIZARDS

After millions of years of violence, life came to the Earth.

Almost 200 million years ago, tremendous beasts walked across what is now New Jersey. Our area was then a hot tropical swamp, just right for the animals that we call dinosaurs. The word means "terrible lizards."

Some of New Jersey's dinosaurs were as much as 30 feet tall. But not all dinosaurs were giants. In fact, some were smaller than a pet cat. The footprints of one dinosaur found in New Jersey shows that it was only a foot tall.

The first complete dinosaur skeleton found in the United States was discovered near Haddonfield in 1858. It was about 28 feet tall. This dinosaur was called *Hadrosaurus*.

Hadrosaurus was dug up by a farmer, who did not know the value of his find. He gave many of the bones to friends. When a Philadelphia museum

When the dinosaur Hadrosaurus roamed what is now New Jersey, this area was a steamy, hot swampland. Hadrosaurus was a "duckbill," whose bones often have been found.

wanted to preserve the dinosaur, the bones had to be gathered from many places. Leg bones were being used to hold doors open in nearby homes!

The original skeleton of Hadrosaurus is in the Academy of Sciences Museum in Philadelphia. A model is in our New Jersey State Museum at Trenton.

Although it was a giant, Hadrosaurus was not ferocious. It ate shrubs and leaves from tall trees. Its chief enemy was *Laelaps*, which stood about 20 feet tall. Laelaps was a fierce meat eater. Laelaps and Hadrosaurus often fought to the death!

Laelaps had long curved claws and knife-shaped teeth. It leaped like a kangaroo. Think of a 20-foot-tall kangaroo! A fine skeleton of a Laelaps was found in a sand pit at Barnsboro, near Sewell.

Many other skeletons of the dinosaur period have been found in

Two boys who found a dinosaur print like this at Roseland were alert enough to call for expert help. Such a print must be very carefully handled to make sure that the stone does not break. Scientists prefer to leave a dinosaur or fossil print in the place where it was found.

New Jersey. These include giant crocodiles, huge lizards, great turtles, and other sea animals up to 40 feet long.

There are differing opinions about why dinosaurs disappeared after inhabiting the earth for millions of years.

Many geologists believe that dinosaurs became extinct when their environment changed. As the seas rose and fell, living areas could disappear. If the climate changed, vegetation might not grow and the giants would not have proper food.

Some scientists believe that dinosaurs did not die out gradually. They say all might have perished at once because of violent changes in the earth's atmosphere, possibly clouds of volcanic dust that shut out the sun.

ANOTHER GIANT

Dinosaurs had been gone for many millions of years when another giant beast came to what is now New Jersey. It was the **mastodon**—*a huge, hairy creature about the size of an elephant.*

The first mastodon skeleton discovered in our state was found in 1869 on a Mannington Township farm in Salem County.

Mannington Township's mastodon caused great excitement. A Rutgers University professor took the skeleton to the Rutgers Geological Museum. It is still there.

Several other mastodon skeletons or mastodons bones have been found in New Jersey. The most famous probably was one uncovered near Vernon in Sussex County in 1954. That skeleton is in the State Museum, where it is often called "Matilda."

When mastodons disappeared is not known. They might have been here as "recently" as 3,000 years ago—not a long time when measured in geological terms!

THE ICY TIME

Thick ice covered northern New Jersey about 40,000 years ago, part of a glacier that slid over the surface of all North America!

A glacier is simply a great, moving layer of ice, sometimes miles deep and thousands of miles wide.

There are still glaciers in the world. One, for example, is in the Rocky Mountains in the state of Montana. This area is called Glacier National Park. Other glaciers are found in Alaska.

It is difficult even to imagine what it was like in glacial days. Cold winds blew constantly! Every day was winter—for thousands of years! If any human *had* been here, it would have been like living in a giant refrigerator with the door closed!

When "our" glacier finally began to melt, it released water that flowed over the earth. The melting waters filled in the valleys between the hills and formed several very large lakes in northern New Jersey.

The greatest of our prehistoric lakes were *Lake Hackensack* and *Lake Passaic*. There were no towns then, but we can use modern towns names to locate them.

Lake Hackensack extended from Woodbridge to beyond our border with New York State. It was three or four miles wide and about 50 miles long. The lake remained for thousands of years before it drained away.

Lake Hackensack left behind marshlands between Bogota and Perth Amboy. These marshlands are the

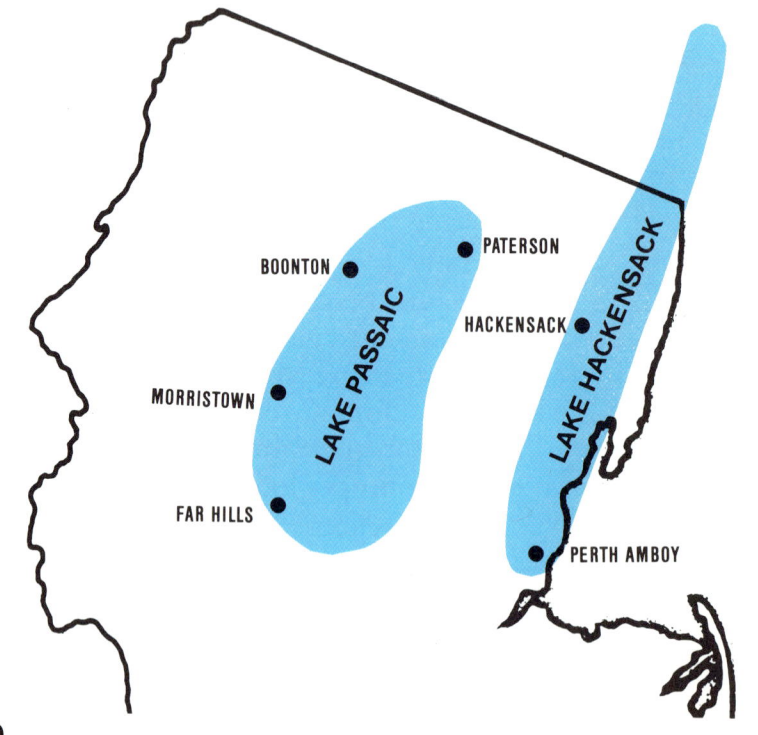

It is not likely that any human eyes ever saw either Lake Hackensack or Lake Passaic. That really is too bad, for both were huge. Try to imagine either or both of those prehistoric bodies of water. Lake Passaic was about four times as big as modern Lake Hopatcong. Lake Hackensack was about seven times the area of Hopatcong, now our largest lake.

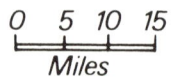

Exploring the Great Swamp National Wildlife Refuge requires a guide. For one thing, the area covers 6,000 acres, much of it wet bogs or briar patches. It is also patrolled by U.S. Government workers to protect the birds and other wildlife. Anyone who is able to get a guide, in a canoe or walking, is very fortunate.

well-known "Jersey Meadows." People crossing New Jersey from New York to Newark travel across the meadows, filled with railroad tracks, truck yards and factories.

The "Jersey Meadows" now are known widely because of the Meadowlands Sports Complex near Rutherford. Sports fans know of the racetrack and the professional teams that play in the stadium or arena.

The other great prehistoric lake, Lake Passaic, was formed in a valley west of the Watchung Mountains. This lake extended from Far Hills to Paterson. Measure its length and width on the map on page 60.

Eventually Lake Passaic's waters drained away near Paterson. They fell 70 feet over a rocky cliff to form the falls at Paterson. As the lake vanished, it left behind the Passaic River.

Lake Passaic's bottom remains as marshy ground in Morris County. About 6,000 acres of the lake bottom are preserved in The Great Swamp National Wildlife Refuge. It is protected by the United States government.

Many students of all ages go to the Great Swamp to study flowers, trees and birds—and to realize that this fertile ground was once the bottom of ancient Lake Passaic!

WHERE TO FIND PREHISTORY

Evidences of prehistoric times are everywhere!

If you live in southern New Jersey, where the land is flat, it was leveled by millions of years of seas that rose and fell.

If you live in the hills of northern New Jersey, your slopes were formed in prehistoric times.

Geological change is not just a matter of the distant past. Each day the ocean washes against the Jersey Shore, shifting the sands and changing the coastline.

Measured day to day, or even year to year, the ocean's changes are scarcely visible. But, within less than 300 years, the ocean front at Long Branch has been cut back 1,000 feet from where it was when the first settlers came.

Cape May Point is 1,000 feet north of where it was 300 years ago.

The long peninsula called Sandy Hook has grown about two miles beyond where it was when the first explorers came more than 300 years ago.

Fossil remains are found often in New Jersey.

Sometimes fossil discoveries are very unusual. Several young schoolboys found hundreds of dinosaur footprints in an old rock quarry in Roseland.

The boys worked to preserve the quarry so that other boys and girls might see the footprints. Thanks to those boys, Essex County now has a noted dinosaur area.

Similar finds of fossils by schoolboys and schoolgirls are reported from time to time in the newspapers. Perhaps *you* might be lucky enough to find some such evidence of geological prehistory!

Dinosaur and **mastodon** bones also are dug up by people who are building reservoirs, highways, shopping centers, or new housing developments. A very large mastodon was found at Vernon when a man was bulldozing land to make a new lake. Many prehistoric skeletons are found in the soft, sandy southern New Jersey soils.

Another unusual discovery of dinosaur footprints was made near Lincoln Park not long ago. Efforts were made to preserve all the tracks as a "living museum," but that could not be done. Fortunately, several footprints were saved in the Lincoln Park Library.

Keep your eyes open! There might be the remains of a dinosaur or one of its descendants almost underfoot!

These boys and girls from Fair Haven in Monmouth County are seeking fossils in a stream not far from their school. Evidences of the geological past are nearly everywhere—but the greatest fun can come in locating dinosaur footprints, as boys and girls have done in several parts of New Jersey. Perhaps you can find one!

PREHISTORY ON THE BEACH

Don't think that everything that lived during the time of the dinosaurs has disappeared. You can see a "prehistoric" creature on the Jersey Shore beaches in spring and summer.

The "ancient" animal is the horseshoe crab (also called the king crab). It has survived as a kind of sea animal for more than 200 million years. Some people call it "a living fossil."

Named because its shell resembles a large horseshoe, the "crab" really is related to scorpions or spiders. Some horseshoe crabs are as much as two feet long, including the long, sharp spine (or "tail") at the back of the shell.

The crab usually stays in the ocean or in Delaware Bay. It prefers to remain 12 to 35 feet deep, getting its food on the sandy ocean bottom. It uses it legs to grind food and can eat only while walking.

From late May through June, a female horseshoe crab lays about 10,000 eggs in shallow nests in the sand. Birds gather immediately and eat most of the eggs. Those spared hatch in July or August.

Next time you see a horseshoe crab, think "ancient"—think of dinosaur days.

STRUGGLE IN A SWAMPLAND

There are no known stories of Indians actually battling a mastodon in what is now New Jersey. Indian legends tell of huge animals, however. Skeletons of the furry beast, as large as an elephant and having long curved tusks, have been found in the state. It is possible that a scene such as this might have occurred in New Jersey swamplands.

This artist has imagined a large band of brave Indians, trying to bring down a mighty mastodon in a marshy area. The arrows that they shot could not pierce the animal's thick, hair-covered hide. However, they could hope that the mastodon's struggles might make it sink in the mud. If that happened, the giant beast could be conquered.

INDIANS

MAGIC CARPET NO. 4

From cold and distant lands they traveled here,
O'er ice and snow, the sun their guide.
The first Lenape families found our land,
Then used it with respect and pride.
    Repeat Chorus (see page 9)

New Jersey's first residents were the Lenape Indians. Their ancestors came from what is now Siberia, halfway around the world from our state.

Our original people were not "savages" or "redskins." They were a noble, worthy people. They loved and respected the land. They built villages beside clear, clean streams. They had a good family life. Children were taught skills necessary for survival in a wilderness.

We "find" the Lenape in their poetic place names. It's easy to see many such Indian "reminders" on New Jersey maps!

65

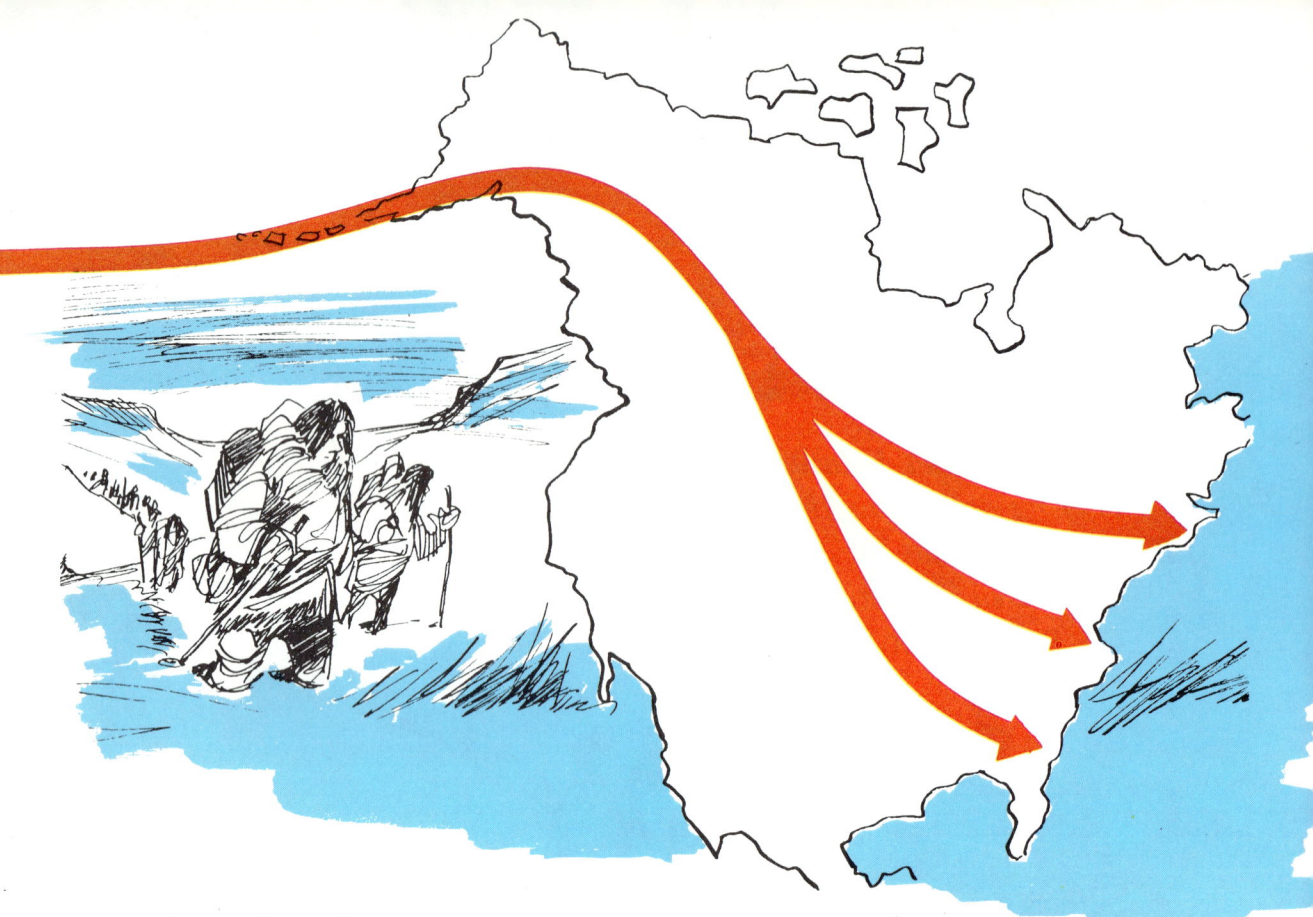

OUR FIRST PEOPLE

Long ago—about 12,000 years ago—the first people came to live in what is now called New Jersey.

Those first people were the *Lenape* (sometimes called Lenni Lenape) Indians. Many writers said Lenape meant "original" or "important." Now the word is thought to mean "ordinary people."

Nevertheless, they were our original people—the first to live here. They were important to our history.

No one knows exactly where the Lenape Indians came from, but it was from someplace in a distant land called Siberia. That is about 15,000 miles west of New Jersey.

Some kind of disaster struck Siberia—most likely horrible freezing weather. The Lenape left their ice-bound land. They headed east toward the sun, which they worshiped as their source of strength.

At the time, Siberia and Alaska were connected by open land. Later, rising seas covered the "land bridge." It no longer exists.

The journey of the Lenape was one that makes our minds tingle with excitement and amazement.

Try to imagine the tremendous courage of those original people! As grandfathers and grandmothers died, their grandchildren continued the walk until they became old and passed away. Then *their* children and grandchildren continued. That went on and on for hundreds, even thousands of years.

Each group, different as the centuries rolled on, walked across frozen seas and through deep snows. They fought off wild beasts. They faced hunger and suffering.

They walked through what is now Alaska and northwestern Canada, then turned south into what is now the western United States. Some headed toward Mexico. Other tribes traveled east toward the Atlantic Ocean.

Finally, after about five thousand years, the Lenape reached the Atlantic Ocean. Each day's sunrise made them sure they were home at last.

The Lenape Indians belonged to a larger group called the *Algonquians* (or Algonkians). Algonquians who lived throughout the eastern forests often are known as "Woodland Indians."

Many Algonquian tribes were fierce and warlike, but the Lenape generally were peaceful and friendly.

It is said that the Indians called New Jersey *Scheyechbi* (Shay-ik-bee), meaning "Land Along Water." Rivers, lakes and the ocean were necessary for the Lenape.

Until recently, it was thought that there were three Indian groups in our area (Munsee, Unami and Unilachtigo). **Archaeologists** now say there were only two—*Munsee* and *Unami*.

The Munsee lived in the northern part of the state, the Unami in the southern part. Their languages and customs were slightly different.

After they had lived here for thousands of years, the Lenape saw the great white sails of the explorers from Europe. The Indians welcomed the strangers.

Our written knowledge of our New Jersey Indians began with what explorers wrote, starting about 475 years ago.

The earliest known account came from an Italian captain, Giovanni da Verrazano. He wrote in 1524 that the Indians seemed "very glad" to see the newcomers.

Explorers wrote that the Lenape were good-looking, strong and much taller than Europeans. They had black eyes, black hair and "brass-colored" skin, according to one explorer.

Hail the Lenape! They might have thought themselves "ordinary," but those original people were important!

Imagine the feelings of the Lenape Indians when they saw the first ships that European explorers sailed into New Jersey rivers and bays. Remember, they had never seen a vessel larger than their dugout canoes. They certainly could not know that these ships had come from other nations. It is likely that the Indians thought the explorers were gods of some kind.

VILLAGES BY THE WATER

At first, New Jersey Indians were wandering hunters, following herds of wild animals. Some might have hunted huge mastodons. Some Indians lived in caves. One such cave has been found in the Kittatinny Mountains.

Soon the Indians found farming was a better way to live. They began to settle in villages.

Indians gave their settlements simple names, usually describing where the village was located. Examples would be Allamuchy, which meant "Place Within The Hills," or Cohansey, named for Indian chief, Cohanzik.

Lenape men and boys first cleared the land. Large trees were cut down by building a hot fire at the base. After several days, the fire burned through the tree trunk and it fell.

The best site was sloping ground on a riverbank. The stream gave clean water for drinking and for watering gardens. Fish were plentiful. Streams also were used for traveling in canoes.

After the land was cleared, the Indians dug or scraped the soil. Seeds were planted. Women and children tended the gardens, which were shared by all families. Food providers were honored in Lenape villages.

Indian houses, or wigwams, were simple. Thin green trees, called **saplings,** were stuck in the ground 10 or more feet apart. The tops of the saplings were bent together and tied with leather strips.

Other saplings were tied to the framework to provide strength and to provide a place to attach house coverings.

On the framework, the Lenape placed bark or skins of animals. Mud, clay and grass filled in whatever holes were found.

An entrance was left in the framework for a "door," covered by a leather skin in cold weather. There were no windows.

Every wigwam had a place for a fire in the center of the room. A hole was cut in the roof to let out smoke. You can be sure that enough smoke remained inside to make eyes water!

Around the fire, the Indians built

wooden benches along the walls. Families sat on these to talk, tell stories or to play simple games. Personal belongings were stored under the benches.

Family members slept on the benches at night. As families grew, smaller children slept on mats on the earth floor.

There were no tables or chairs. In winter, families sat around the fire to eat. In summer, they ate outside.

Lenape villages had several types of homes. Some were small, round buildings with a rounded roof. Some had straight walls, with a peaked roof. Others were long and rounded at the ends.

Every village had one or more "long houses." They were large, with peaked roofs, such as those on modern houses. Some of these buildings had several families, much like a modern apartment house.

One long house was the village community center. Important meetings and religious ceremonies were held there.

Indian villages would have appeared very simple compared to our towns, but they helped the Lenape to survive in the wilderness.

A great deal of experience was necessary for hunting in Lenape Indian times. Animals were found by the tracks that they left. Then a boy had to learn the skills needed to cast a spear when a deer or other animal was close.

FOOD AND CLOTHING

Villagers rejoiced when the Lenape hunters managed to down a deer with their bows and arrows or with a spear. A deer was valued because it meant new clothing as well as food. Animals were never hunted for sport.

Food came first; that was the chief reason for killing any animal. The Lenape carefully cut off the deer's skin and stretched the hide over a wooden rack to dry.

The deer was cut into pieces small enough for the hunters to carry back to the village. Small animals caught in traps also were skinned and taken to the village. The small skins were used too.

Nearly all Lenape food was raised in the village gardens. Mothers and daughters planted the seeds, using wooden sticks and sharp stones to dig the earth.

Corn was the main crop. It was used in many ways—as corn on the cob, corn meal mush, dumplings, cornbread, popcorn and even mixed with maple syrup as candy. Other main crops were beans, squash and pumpkins.

Fish were also an important part of the Lenape Indian diet. Some were speared or caught with hooks. Sometimes villagers all worked to place a fish net across a stream.

After the net was in place, most of the Indians then would walk downstream, scaring fish toward the net.

Some skilled fishermen also could catch fish by hand, without a net.

Indians stored food for the winter. Corn, beans and squash were dried and kept in baskets or jars. Fish was smoked and stored.

Some of the tastiest foods were berries and nuts. These grew in the forests or in the fields. Indians also ate several kinds of roots, leaves and plants.

Food was cooked in clay pots or wooden bowls. Meat and vegetables were cooked together to make a stew. Corn and beans cooked together were called **succotash**. Meat and fish were cooked on sticks.

Water, the main drink, came from clean streams. Water was carried and stored in clay pots and jugs. Shells were used as drinking cups.

When they had time, the Lenape Indians worked on the hides that had been stretched on wooden racks. The hides were scraped with shells, stones or sticks to make leather.

In warm weather, the Lenape wore few clothes. Women wore short, light skirts, with possibly a loose top. Small children generally wore no clothing. Men wore pieces of leather, called loincloths, hung from the waist.

Warm clothing for winter was made from the fur of deer, elk and beavers. Fur leggings covered legs. Men and women wrapped their arms in furs.

There were no shoes, but for long walks, or for winter, the Lenape wore moccasins. These they made from soft deerskin. Leather was cut to fit, then shaped and sewed. Soles were soft. Often the Indians added decorations of porcupine quills or colored shells.

No food or clothing could be bought. No wonder a deer meant a celebration!

FAMILY STRENGTH

The Lenape Indians believed in a strong family life. Every person was important to the health and safety of both the family and the tribe. Everyone worked, from the very young to the very old.

Women and girls farmed, made clothing and wove baskets. They made pottery, prepared meals and raised children.

Men and boys cleared the land, built houses and made canoes. Men were expected to keep weapons ready and to defend the village when necessary. They hunted and fished for food.

Older people made pottery, **wampum** beads and small tools. Younger children tended babies, carried water, picked berries and gathered firewood.

New babies were always welcomed in a village. Everyone knew that a baby would grow up to be another person who would share the many tasks of a family.

Little babies were strapped to a flat cradle board. Indians believed that this would help the baby to grow tall and straight. Babies were strapped to boards until they could walk.

The cradle board was easy to carry if a tribe went on a trip. During gardening season, the cradle boards were hung in the shade on nearby trees. At night, the cradle board became a crib.

Indian children did not go to school, but they spent most of their childhood learning what they would need to know in the wilderness.

Indian boys and girls went to "school" almost every day — not in a regular building but in "classes" that mothers and fathers taught. Children had to learn many things if they were to survive in the surrounding wilderness.

Their education for living came mainly from parents and grandparents. The teaching often was tough, but existing in a wilderness was not easy.

Girls were taught gardening, cooking, sewing and how to take care of children. Indian boys were taught to hunt, fish, make houses and build canoes. Boys were forced to run and jump to make their bodies strong and healthy.

Education was not just a matter of being taught how to work. Young Indians knew the value of their experiences in the gardens and in the forests. Whatever they did helped the family and the village. Everyone was *needed*.

Children had to learn the customs of their tribe. They were taught the proper way to dress, not only for everyday life but also for special occasions. They were taught to be patient and kind to one another.

By keeping the families happy and united, the Lenape tribes survived for a long time. They could depend on one another.

New Jersey's rivers and lakes were Lenape "highways," where Indians traveled in handmade "dugout" canoes. Some were as much as 40 feet long, big enough to carry two or three families or many warriors. Most canoes were "family size," about 12 to 14 feet long.

Making a canoe began by cutting down a big tree about three feet thick. The tree was felled by building a fire at the base. Red hot coals burned through the trunk and eventually the tree fell.

The trunk was cut to length, then hot coals were heaped on the section to burn away unwanted portions. As the coals burned down, the inside of the trunk was dug out with crude tools. Parts not supposed to burn — the sides and the bottom — were covered with wet grass or wet mats.

Good examples of dugout canoes can be seen in either the Paterson Museum or at the Bergen County Historical Society headquarters at River Edge.

LENAPE TRADITIONS

Much of what we know of our Indians was written by settlers. Their early writings often were filled with praise for the Lenape.

The Lenape believed in friendliness. They had no fences. Visitors were welcome. As proof, a pot of food always was cooking to be shared with travelers or hunters. Any visitor would be fed and given a place to sleep for the night.

Tribal traditions were passed on to younger children by skilled storytellers. Older men and women described happenings of the past, keeping alive knowledge of where a tribe came from and who its great people had been.

The storytellers told tales of hunting and stories about their gods. They told of important ceremonies that they remembered.

Storytelling was the main way of keeping traditions alive, since the Lenape had no newspapers, books or magazines. Some tribes also drew pictures on stone walls.

Every Indian boy and girl eventually had to prove that he or she was grown up.

Girls were required to spend time by themselves at about age 11 or 12. They were expected to think about when they would be wives and mothers. They often were asked to describe dreams that they had when alone.

To prove that he was old enough and strong enough to be a man, a boy went off into the forest alone at about age 10 or 11. He spent several days and nights in the woods. If he saw something special in a dream, it became his good luck symbol.

The Lenape painted their faces and

Lenape Indians married very young. A bride would be 13 or 14, her husband about 17 or 18 years old. Family approval was required, for each couple had to prove ability to take on new responsibilities. Men and women had to look outside their own villages for a mate. Wedding ceremonies were a simple exchanging of gifts. The man gave his bride a bone, signifying that he would provide meat and fish. She gave him an ear of corn, meaning it was her job to supply garden crops.

bodies for special festivals and ceremonies. They used colored clays, burnt wood and berry juices to make special colors.

Sometimes the Lenape wore masks at ceremonies to honor ancestors, to stop evil spirits or to show respect for the gods.

The greatest celebration each year was the harvest festival, early in the fall. It lasted for 12 days.

Harvest festivals were like our Thanksgivings, except that the Indians celebrated for longer than one day. They thanked their supreme god, named Manito.

Indian tribes gradually grew smaller after settlers from Europe took over the Indian lands. European diseases, especially smallpox, killed a great many Lenape.

Finally, there were only a few hundred Lenape Indians left. In 1758 a treaty provided that all surviving members of the tribe could live in a reservation in the Pine Barrens. It was one of the first Indian reservations in this country.

The reservation was called *Brotherton*. About 200 people came to live there, but life was extremely difficult. In the year 1802, most of the Lenape people moved to New York State to join relatives. Eventually, the Lenape moved to Oklahoma.

Brotherton has long vanished, but memories of when the Lenape were there live on. The area is now called Indian Mills.

Although there are several thousand persons in New Jersey today who are Indian or part Indian, not many are the Lenapes—the original people.

Yet we know the Lenape Indians were here. We know that they were an important, intelligent, friendly people. Indian names are found in nearly every part of the state. Their customs and traditions are remembered.

Hail to the Lenape!

When Indians became ill, "medicine men" were called to practice all their skills and traditions. Here a medicine man performs a ceremonial dance outside of a "sweat house" in which a sick patient is getting heat treatment. Water was poured over hot stones, creating steam, much as in a modern sauna. Medicine men also tried various kinds of herbs, plants, animal blood or bones, and other types of medicines. Such doctoring was simple, but it often worked.

What did our first people REALLY look like? Since there were no photographs in those days, we must rely on the way artists represented them. The two drawings at the top, showing an Indian warrior and a family group, are probably closest to the truth. Both were sketched nearly 350 years ago. The painting above and the head to the right, both done in recent years, show Mohawk-like scalp locks. It is most likely that New Jersey's Indians wore long, untrimmed hair.

76

COLONISTS

MAGIC CARPET NO. 5

When we were just a tiny colony,
Survival was a constant fear.
Our people struggled toward their greatest goal,
Of finding freedom's promise here.
    Repeat Chorus (see page 9)

Explorers hoped to find "The Indies" when they sailed westward from Europe 500 years ago. Instead they found a land that they called "America."

Our area between the Hudson and Delaware Rivers was settled by colonists from many nations — Holland, Sweden, England, Scotland, Ireland, Germany, France and elsewhere. In 1664, England gave us our name: New Jersey.

Life in colonial New Jersey was harsh. Everyone worked, from sunup until sundown. Disease and death were always near. It took courage to settle in a new land.

It's time to meet the colonists!

SHIPS FROM MANY LANDS

Land Ho!

That cry by a cabin boy, high on the mast of a tiny ship, thrilled the early explorers of New Jersey! Solid land was within sight, the first seen in many months.

Everybody knows of the explorer named Christopher Columbus, an Italian captain who sailed from Spain in 1492. He landed on islands between Florida and Cuba.

Columbus was looking for the "Indies." That's what India, China and Japan were called in those days. So he called the islands the "West Indies."

Since he thought he had reached "The Indies," Columbus named the native people "Indians." That mistaken name stuck with all of our original people.

Exploring was fearsome in those days. Most people thought the world was flat, and that a ship would fall off the edge. Sailors believed the ocean was filled with beasts that could swallow an entire ship.

But the explorers continued to sail. They were hoping to find gold and spices, the most valuable things of their time.

Explorers were the first to see New Jersey, other than the Indians. The explorers came from many lands—*Italy, Spain, France, Holland* and *England*.

Two Italian captains came first. They were Giovanni Caboto and Sebastian Caboto, who sailed off the coast of New Jersey in 1498. They claimed the land for England, for they were captains of English ships.

Then, in 1524, another Italian,

named Giovanni da Verrazano, sailed inside New York Bay and saw New Jersey. He was captain of a French ship, so he claimed the land for France. A great bridge across the lower New York Bay now honors Verrazano.

The first landings in New Jersey came in 1609. That year Henry Hudson sailed the *Half Moon* along all the Jersey Shore. He anchored his ship in Sandy Hook Bay and crew members went ashore. Later he explored the river named after him—the Hudson River.

Henry Hudson was an English captain, but as you might have guessed, he was NOT sailing an English ship! The *Half Moon* was flying a Dutch flag. Holland claimed part of America because of that English captain.

You will be reading about *Holland* and the "*Dutch*." People who came from Holland were called Dutch colonists.

Captains in those days sailed for whatever nations would supply ships and crews. Nations were willing to help because they hoped the explorers would bring back gold and other riches.

It took courage to sail on the ocean 400 years ago. Just because explorers hoped for wealth and fame did not make them less brave.

The explorers led the way. Soon other courageous people would leave their homeland to establish New Jersey's first **colonies**.

Crossing the Atlantic Ocean in colonial times required bravery. Imagine the trip. Your ship would be about 90 feet long and 25 feet wide. There would be about 120 people aboard — fathers, mothers and children. The trip from Europe would take about 9 or 10 weeks. Sometimes waves would be 30 feet high. In such stormy times, everyone would be crowded below decks. Land was a very welcome sight, you can be sure!

DUTCH AND SWEDES

New Jersey's first colonists were the Dutch and Swedes. The Dutch came here from Holland as early as 1630 and settled in what is now Hudson County. Within ten years, the Swedes and Finns founded New Sweden along the Delaware River in what are now Gloucester and Salem counties.

Dutch settlers called all of their settlement New Amsterdam. The Delaware River settlements were called New Sweden.

One of the first Dutch explorers to see our area gave it a great compliment. He wrote that it was "just like Holland."

He meant that he liked the good weather, rich soil, deep rivers and thick forests. Here a Dutch family could start a farm and live well.

The first Dutch families lived at what are now Hoboken and Jersey City. Across the river was the chief Dutch town, called New Amsterdam. New Amsterdam is now called New York. People still want to live near it.

At first, the Dutch lived on scattered farms. Then, in 1660, several families joined together to start Bergen, New Jersey's first town. They built a thick log wall to protect against dangers. Homes were inside the wall, gardens were outside.

Bergen is now just a part of Jersey City called "Bergen Square." New Jersey's first church and first school began in Bergen.

Even before 1660, the Dutch sailed up the Raritan, Passaic and Hackensack rivers and started big farms. They founded such riverside places as New Brunswick, Hackensack and Passaic.

The Delaware River area was wide open for any nation that wanted to establish a colony. Two Swedish ships sailed into the Delaware in March 1639. A few soldiers and colonists were

Dutch settlers always liked to live on streams, such as the Hudson, Hackensack or Raritan rivers. This scene of an early Dutch village shows several small homes, perhaps all occupied by members of the same family. Two ships are being built in the front part of the drawing. These will take farm products to New Amsterdam (now New York City). On the nearby hill, a windmill runs either a sawmill or a gristmill. Later, after 1660, Dutch families had to live behind tall wooden fences in case of Indian raids.

put ashore to start New Sweden, on both sides of the river.

New Sweden never really had a chance. Very few colonists came from the mother country. Among the settlers were Finns, who had come from Finland.

New Amsterdam decided to control New Sweden. It sent a fleet of Dutch ships and about 300 soldiers to the Delaware River in 1655. New Sweden surrendered all claims.

However, Swedes and Finns stayed on their farms. The Dutch were pleased, because they needed settlers. Sons and daughters of New Sweden's colonists soon married Dutch people. Few wanted to return to their old countries.

Some Swedish family names are still known along the lower Delaware River. The Swedish Church in Swedesboro has many Swedish records. Swedish names are found on headstones in the church cemetery.

Swedesboro is really an *English* name for a Swedish town. The Swedes called the place *Raccoon.*

The Swedes built the first log cabins in America. One of those cabins can be seen near the Hancock House at Hancock's Bridge.

The Dutch were fine farmers. They grew cabbages so big that they were called "Governor's Head" cabbages. Boatloads of vegetables and fruits from Dutch farms helped feed New Amsterdam people.

Dutch families often had 12 or more children. That is one reason why so many Dutch names are still found in New Jersey. Dutch names include Cowenhoven, Conover, and many names beginning with "Van," such as Van Doren.

Houses built by Dutch settlers 200 years or more ago remain, especially in Bergen County. You can easily recognize Dutch houses by the thick stone walls and the high, steep roofs.

The greatest Dutch contribution to New Jersey was a college started at New Brunswick in 1766. It was first called Queens College. Today it is Rutgers, The State University of New Jersey.

New Jersey's biggest colonist was Johan Printz, who was governor of New Sweden from 1643 until 1653. He kept the little colony going in spite of the fact that he received very little in the way of settlers or supplies from Sweden, his home country.

Printz was a huge man — more than seven feet tall! He weighed more than 400 pounds! Indians called him "Big Tub," but never to his face. Governor Printz was very harsh, both to his colonists and the Indians, but life in the wilderness was harsh, too. The giant governor returned to Sweden in 1653. Most of his family went with him, but one daughter remained in the colony to raise her family.

NEW JERSEY GETS A NAME

Four ships sailed up the Hudson River in August 1664. English flags flew from their masts. Dutch leaders in New Amsterdam knew that England had come to claim all the land where the Dutch and Swedes lived. The Dutch surrendered without firing a shot.

So the land between the Hudson and Delaware rivers became "English." That August the land also received a lasting name: *New Jersey*. It came from the Isle of Jersey ("Old Jersey) near England.

New Jersey's first English town was Elizabethtown. It was established in the autumn of 1664. The town's founders came from Long Island, where they had moved from Massachusetts.

Most of New Jersey's early English settlers had been in America for many years. They had settled first in Connecticut, Massachusetts or Long Island.

People from Connecticut founded Newark in 1666. They named their community after a town in England.

This etching, which was drawn in 1908, showed Dutch Governor Peter Stuyvesant surrendering New Amsterdam to England in 1664. Stuyvesant, who had a wooden leg, is on the white horse in the center. The English gave the name "New York" to New Amsterdam. The land to the west, across the Hudson River, was named New Jersey.

Other New Englanders settled Woodbridge, Piscataway, Middletown and Shrewsbury. All those colonists were seeking religious freedom and other liberties. They had not found such freedoms in England.

Meeting houses were the first buildings erected in any English town. Meeting houses were used for everything—church, town meetings, school and as a fort.

About 10 years after people had settled the eastern part of the colony, other Englishmen arrived at the Delaware River. These people were Quakers, a religious group.

Unlike most other English colonists, the Quakers came directly from England to New Jersey. They founded many southern New Jersey towns. They settled Salem in 1675 and Burlington in 1677. You can still see several fine old Quaker meeting houses in southern New Jersey towns.

More settlers were needed to help conquer the wilderness. People were invited to come to New Jersey. They were promised religious freedom and many other rights.

Settlers from other nations soon came to New Jersey. These colonists included Scots, Irish, Germans, French and others. The Dutch and Swedes remained on their farms or in their villages, along with the English. All lived under English rule. New Jersey had more different kinds of people than any other American colony.

At first, New Jersey was split into *two* colonies, called *East New Jersey* and *West New Jersey*. Each colony had a capital, Perth Amboy for East New Jersey and Burlington for West New Jersey. New Jersey was nearly 50 years old before it became one united colony!

The joining of East and West New Jersey took place on April 17, 1702. Now, every April 17, our state observes an official "New Jersey Day" to recall our state's real birthday.

Quakers first came to America from England in 1675. They sailed off Delaware Bay and started a village that they named Salem. It is now a fine town, proud of the fact that it was the first Quaker settlement in America. Philadelphia is often regarded as the Quaker beginning in the New World, but it was not founded until 1682. Old Quaker meeting houses are easy to find in southern New Jersey — such as the large brick meeting house (above) in Crosswicks or the tiny wooden structure at Seaville in Cape May County.

TOWARD A NEW WORLD

New Jersey's first settlers sailed here on tiny ships, whether they came from New England or from Europe. Since they could not bring much with them, they had to choose very carefully.

Men brought tools to aid in clearing the forests—axes, saws and hammers, and hoes. They also brought fruit trees and vegetable seeds. The colonists, it must be remembered, were mainly farmers.

Women packed cooking utensils, such as iron pots, frying pans and wooden bowls. Most carried spinning wheels and candle molds. Everything had to be useful.

Each colonist could bring a prized possession or two—an old family clock, pewter plates or silver spoons. A few, especially ministers, had precious books with them.

Each boy and girl might include a small toy or doll, although such things could be made wherever the family settled.

Cows, sheep, pigs and goats all had to be brought to New Jersey. There were no such animals here.

A voyage from England to New Jersey could take as long as three months. All food and water had to be stored.

Animals were put in pens on the decks. Often the waves crashed over them. In warm weather, trees and plants also were left on deck.

Below decks, the colonists suffered. Ocean waves poured streams of cold water on the people. Food was poor. Drinking water was limited. These were dreaded trips.

Nearing America, the colonists worried. Would they battle huge beasts? Would the Indians be savage? Would the soil be good?

The first sight of New Jersey made newcomers joyous. The forests were thick and green. The rivers were broad and clean. There was wonderful open space. This would be a land of opportunity!

The settlers found that the forests were filled with small game, such as rabbits, raccoons and opossums. They saw deer almost everywhere. Often they saw bears and wolves.

Wild geese and ducks flew overhead in great flocks. Wild turkeys gobbled in the trees. Many kinds of fish swam in the streams. Clams and oysters were plentiful in bays near the ocean.

Best of all, friendly Indians welcomed the colonists. They showed the newcomers such native plants as corn and beans. Some settlers were sheltered by Indians after landing.

New Jersey, the colonists knew, was a good place to be!

Colonists thought very carefully about what they brought. First they put aboard their small ships such necessities as fruit trees, tools and animals such as cows and sheep. Then came room for spinning wheels to make thread, axes, hoes or iron pots. Occasionally, someone brought something very special, such as a clock.

85

EAST AND WEST

New Jersey was two colonies from 1664 to 1702—East New Jersey and West New Jersey. People lived differently in the two regions.

People in the East New Jersey towns of Elizabethtown, Newark, Woodbridge, Piscataway and Middletown lived in small villages. They desired to be close to one another and near their meeting house.

West New Jersey people preferred larger farms, although some lived close together in Salem, Burlington, Trenton and other villages. People from the widely-scattered farms might see neighbors only at church services or Quaker meetings.

When they first landed, whether in East New Jersey or West New Jersey, the colonists built rough little houses, similar to Indian homes. A few colonists even lived temporarily in caves. In warm weather, many slept in the open on the ground after landing.

The first houses were made of logs, since trees were easy to find. Sometimes a man would build his cabin by himself or with the aid of his wife and children. Usually, neighbors worked together to "raise" a house.

The first houses had only one large room. It was everything—living room, dining room and bedroom. As families grew in size, older children slept in a loft above one side of the room. It was reached by a ladder.

Every house had a large fireplace in a corner or on the end of the building. It supplied heat, light, and a place to cook food. Keeping the fire alive was essential, since the colonists had no matches. If the fire went out, a boy or girl raced to a neighbor to "borrow" red hot coals.

During winter months, the entire family stayed close to the fireplace and its great roaring fire. Food would be cooking in an iron pot over the fire and bread would be baking in an oven on the side of the fireplace.

A candle or two might glow in the room. Candles had to be snuffed out when not needed. They were all homemade. Each candle required hard work.

On the table, places would be set with homemade wooden plates. Even forks and spoons were carved from wood.

At first, tables were just wide slabs of wood placed on logs. In time, a father, an older brother, or an uncle would make a real table and some chairs.

Families certainly had to be very close! They had to work together and cooperate for the good of everybody in the house and in the village.

The colony of New Jersey really was two colonies — East New Jersey and West New Jersey. The two small units were divided by a line — from about Little Egg Harbor to Delaware Water Gap. East and West New Jersey finally were united on April 17, 1702. East New Jerseyans preferred to live in small villages. West New Jerseyans wanted large farms.

East or West, life was much the same, since all colonists had to chop down trees to clear the land for farming, build their own log houses, raise all their crops, tend their animals and make their own clothes or anything else they needed.

87

LIFE WAS HARD

WORK! That was one word that everyone understood in colonial times.

Men and boys labored to clear the land for gardens and orchards. They cut down trees to build their own homes. Men and boys tended the gardens and took care of the animals.

Women and girls made clothes—and it was not easy! They sheared wool from sheep to begin the long process of making cloth.

The wool had to be combed, then spun and finally woven into a piece of cloth. The cloth might be dyed with different color berry juices.

Mothers then took the cloth and cut it to make dresses, suits or other clothing. Usually clothes were made too large, to last for several years.

Clothing was never thrown away. If a garment no longer fit, it was passed on to a small child or taken apart. Then it was cut and resewn to make another dress or shirt.

Women and girls made soap and candles. These were messy, smelly, tiresome jobs, but necessary.

No one could avoid work.

As the sun rose, a drummer boy went through the village, beating his drum to wake people.

Work began right after breakfast. Everyone had a job—spinning, weaving, cutting wood, tending cattle, making candles, pulling weeds or running the village mill.

The only day free from work was Sunday, but it was not a "day off." Sunday was kept for church services—several times a day. Ministers usually preached for two or more hours. If a boy or girl fell asleep, a church monitor would hit the sleeper in the head with the end of a long pole.

Sickness was common. There were few medicines. Death was always near. A few colonial people lived to an old age, but most adults died very young. Many children did not live to be as old as you are!

Despite the hardships, children had time for fun.

Boys went fishing and hunted for

Even before the sun rose, colonial villagers were roused from sleep by the pounding of the village drummer boy.

small game. Children gathered nuts and berries. Fish, game, nuts and berries provided family food, but getting them did not seem like work.

Children went on long hikes across wide fields and through deep forests. They skated or rode sleds in winter.

The evenings were fun! Families gathered in front of a huge log fire roaring in the great open fireplace. Some children were lucky enough to have a father or mother who told scary ghost stories!

Boys and girls were important. It wasn't fun to make candles all day long. It wasn't fun to saw wood all day long for the fire. But all work helped families survive in this new land.

The one word that all colonists understood was WORK. They labored to provide all things that they needed. This included growing wheat for flour, spinning thread for cloth and making leather from cow hides. Fishing helped provide food and gave a chance for fun. Still, at night there was always time to gather around the roaring flames of the fireplace.

FORGOTTEN COLONISTS

Many American colonists had no choice about coming to America.

They were black people from Africa. They were taken from their homelands by Europeans, forced aboard little ships, and brought to America as slaves.

Many black people died of starvation and neglect on the ships. When they reached colonial America, they were sold to work on farms.

The first Dutch settlers of New Jersey had slaves, both black persons and even Lenape Indians. During colonial days, Perth Amboy had a "market" where slaves were "auctioned," as if they were not human beings.

Some white Americans sought to aid slaves. The Quakers of southern New Jersey, for example, opposed slavery.

Nevertheless, in the year 1757, there were 3,981 slaves in New Jersey. Since the colony's total population was only 47,402 people, there was one slave for every 12 white people.

It was written in 1758 that nearly all of the houses in Perth Amboy "swarmed" with black slaves. When Samuel Finley, a minister and the president of the College of New Jersey

No Americans ever were treated more brutally than Africans, who were taken from their native lands, put in chains and brought here as slaves. New Jersey had thousands of slaves, often bought or sold at a slave market in Perth Amboy. Many black Americans can trace roots back 250 or more years.

died in 1766, he ordered that his six slaves be sold. Those six slaves included three children. Except for the Quakers, churches were not opposed to slavery.

Most slaves in New Jersey worked in houses, in barns or in fields. They were what today would be called maids, yard workers or farmhands.

Slaves worked long hours without pay. They were forced to live in crude little houses on the edges of fields. The only time they had off was part of Sunday, when they were sent to church. They had to sit in the balcony, away from the white masters.

Some slaves lived in the houses of their owners. They did most of the work, taking care of children, cooking meals and keeping the house clean.

There were masters who boasted about how well they treated their slaves. Dutch farmers said some slaves "even sat down to eat with the families."

If that could be considered good treatment, it was one of the few privileges that slaves had. These people were the forgotten Americans.

Very few black colonists were given any education. They could not seek new jobs, keep money or travel to another colony except with their masters.

When slaves finally were freed in New Jersey, many years later, they succeeded as well as people who had come here as free men and women.

Freed slaves drove stagecoaches, or worked as carpenters, bricklayers or shipbuilders. Some ran their own restaurants. Others taught school.

Many black people in New Jersey today belong to families that have been in this country for 200 or more years. They are proud that their ancestors were among New Jersey's early colonists.

About 150 years ago, some white people suggested sending all black people back to their native Africa. Blacks would be free.

Black people hated the plan. They said that their families had been in America longer than most white families had lived here!

They were Americans!

BLACK DOCTOR OF THE PINES

James Still was born in 1812 deep in the southern New Jersey Pine Barrens. He went to school for only three months, all before he was eight years of age. Yet he grew up to be one of the best loved and most respected men in southern New Jersey history.

He taught himself to read and write, studying at night in front of a blazing wood fire in an open fireplace. He also studied the plants and shrubs of the great pine forest outside his home, learning what might be useful in treating sick people.

Young James Still began using his knowledge and skills to cure ailing neighbors. His fame spread. People came to seek his aid. He helped them with medicines that he made himself from shrubs and herbs that grew nearby.

Hundreds of people declared that James Still had made them well. He never claimed to be a trained physician, but when he died in 1885 many people knew him and mourned him as "The Black Doctor of the Pines."

THE COLONY GROWS

Let us take a look at the colony of New Jersey in the year 1770. More than 100 years had passed since the English had taken over the land and given it a name.

The colony was growing. Children and grandchildren of the first families had become adults, married, and moved outward to start new towns.

The new families went westward from Newark to found Orange, Chatham, Morristown, Succasunna and other towns. New young families from Elizabethtown founded Springfield, Westfield, Plainfield and other places.

In southern New Jersey, people from the first towns of Salem and Burlington set up new villages, including Trenton, Camden and Bordentown.

Dutch families sought new land along the Hackensack and Raritan rivers, starting New Brunswick and Hackensack as important "Dutch towns."

By 1770, New Jersey's total population was about 100,000 people, less than the population of today's Elizabeth. It was substantial for colonial times, however.

Few people lived along the Jersey Shore. Middletown, Shrewsbury and Freehold were thriving towns, but all three were inland from the ocean. Small settlements were at Toms River, Tuckerton and Cape May.

In the early years there was very little industry. In about 1700, however, iron ore was discovered near Succasunna (named for an Indian word, "succasunny," meaning "black stone").

At first the ore was taken to Hanover. There it was made into iron bars formed to fit the shape of a horse's back. Horses thus carried the iron to New York for shipment to England.

Soon such "iron towns" as Dover, Rockaway, Hibernia and Ringwood sprang up. The iron-making furnaces ran night and day. Each furnace burned about 1,000 acres of woodland a year.

Southern New Jersey had iron towns, too. The best-known was Batsto, deep in the Pine Barrens, where wood was plentiful. Ore called "bog iron" was found in the beds of Pine Barrens streams.

Mill owners were very important people. Some towns had several mills—grain mill, saw mill, and in some places, a mill to make cloth.

Farmers sold extra crops in New York or Philadelphia. Both cities bought wheat, flour, vegetables, fruits, beef cattle and pork.

New Jersey, by 1770, had two colleges. The College of New Jersey (now Princeton University) was started in Elizabethtown in 1746. Queens College (Rutgers University) began at New Brunswick in 1766. New Jersey is the only state with two colleges that were founded before the American Revolution.

Although still small, New Jersey in the year 1770 was busy, exciting and on the move!

Life in a glassworks was extremely difficult. The furnaces ran 24 hours a day, seven days a week. Nearly everyone in town worked for the glass company, including little boys who were only seven or eight years old.

Workers were paid in "money" (called scrip) that the company printed. The money was worthless outside of the town, so it could only be spent in the company-owned store. Usually the prices in the company store were much higher than in stores outside of the glassmaking town.

It was said in the glass towns that "the more a person worked, the deeper he got in debt."

ANGER IN NEW JERSEY

New Jersey was one of 13 colonies. All 13 were close to the Atlantic Ocean, as the map on this page shows.

Most colonists were willing to be ruled by England, although, as you know, they had come here from England, Germany, Holland, Sweden, Ireland, France, Scotland and other nations.

England gave colonists a market for their products. It encouraged settlers to come to the colonies. Most important, English soldiers were needed to defend the colonists against possible enemies.

Colonial towns insisted that all men and older boys must serve in the local **militia** companies. Militiamen were volunteer soldiers who were supposed to be ready in case of attacks by Indians. Each militia company marched and drilled on the **village green**.

Still, in case of a real war, English soldiers would be very necessary to protect the colonies.

People who lived in America did not pay any taxes to England for nearly 100 years. Then, in about 1755, the colonists were asked to support English (or British) soldiers. In some colonies, people had to open their homes to provide rooms and food for British troops.

That caused bitter argument. New Jersey people became very angry. In 1757, England said it wanted to put 600 English soldiers in homes in Newark, Perth Amboy and Elizabethtown.

Instead, the New Jersey legislature built **barracks** for the soldiers. Five were constructed in Perth Amboy, Burlington, Elizabethtown, Trenton and New Brunswick.

Only one of the five barracks remains—the Old Barracks in Trenton. Many of you have visited there or will visit there.

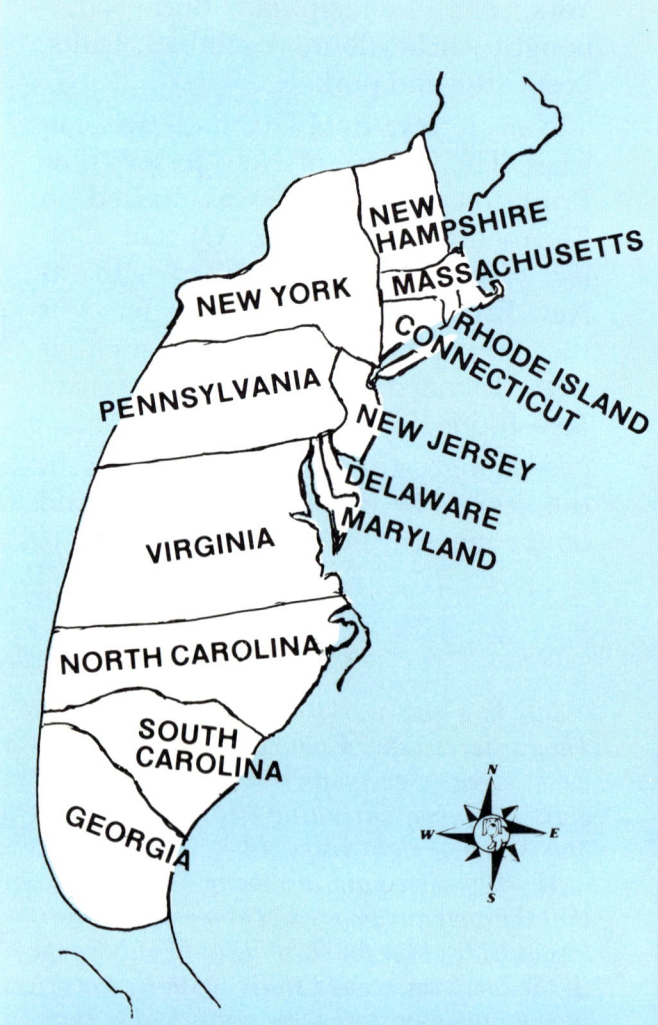

Right in the middle — that was New Jersey as the 13 colonies began to swing away from Great Britain. New Jersey people opposed taxes on stamps, sugar and tea, then signed the Declaration of Independence.

Then England decided to tax the 13 colonies. First it put a tax on sugar in 1764. A year later, England taxed stamps. Then, in 1767, colonists were asked to pay taxes on glass, paper and tea.

Each time that taxes were set, the colonists protested that this was *"taxation without representation."* The colonists meant that they had no say in deciding what were proper taxes. English citizens who lived in England had greater personal rights than American colonists.

England even chose the governor for each of the colonies. These were called "Royal" governors because they were appointed by an English king or queen.

The time came when colonists had to decide whether to continue to be ruled by England or to fight for freedom!

This troubled nearly everyone. Most people thought of England as their "home" country. Leading colonial citizens worked hard for a peaceful settlement that would guarantee them rights as Englishmen.

It did not work. War approached.

Those who decided to remain loyal to England and its government were called **Loyalists**. Those who decided to fight for independence were called **Patriots**.

Colonial days were nearly at an end. The American Revolution was near.

Many of you have seen the Old Barracks in Trenton, but certainly not as it appears here, when British soldiers lived in it. This Trenton barracks was ordered built in 1757 when Great Britain threatened to house soldiers in private homes. Five barracks were built. Those in Perth Amboy, Burlington, New Brunswick and Elizabethtown are gone.

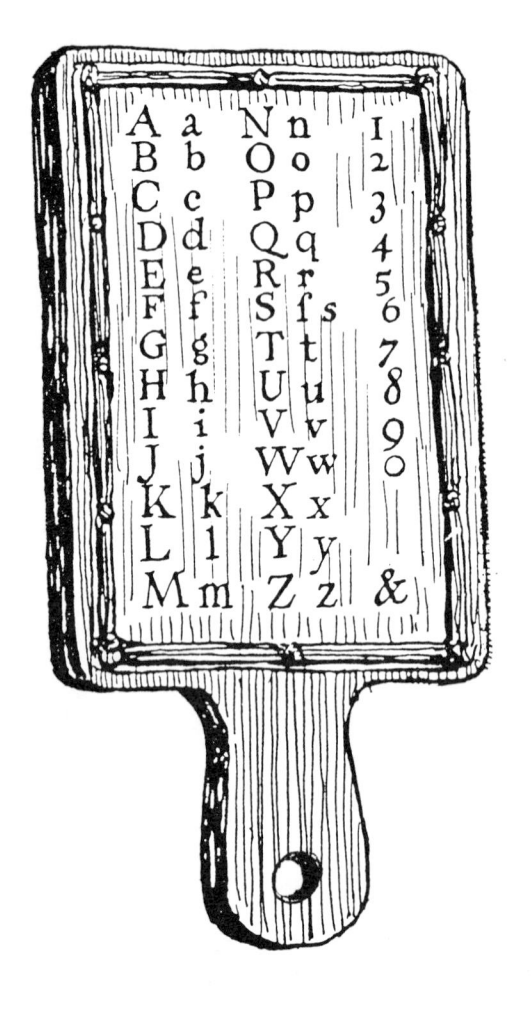

A		In *Adam's* Fall We Sinned all.
B		Thy Life to Mend This *Book* Attend.
C		The *Cat* doth play And after flay.
D		A *Dog* will bite A Thief at night.
E		An *Eagles* flight Is out of fight.
F		The Idle *Fool* Is whipt at School.

Education was very limited in colonial times. Most boys and girls, if they went to school at all, learned only simple reading, writing and arithmetic. Few girls went to school after about age 6, except in West New Jersey, where Quakers provided more educational opportunities. The alphabet was taught with a "Horn Book" (above), which looked like a modern wooden cutting board printed with letters or numbers. Reading was taught with Bible verses. "Play" was running or rolling hoops, but there was little time for fun.

He that ne'er learns his A, B, C,
For ever will a Blockhead be;

Afs	Bull	Cat

96

REVOLUTION

MAGIC CARPET NO. 6

♪ New Jersey played a most important role,
In seeking peace and liberty.
As Revolution's Crossroads it was known,
A part of U.S. history.
      Repeat Chorus (see page 9)

War! The 13 colonies signed the Declaration of Independence in 1776. New Jersey began to echo with the sights and sounds of war. Our state became the center of action.

Five major battles were fought in New Jersey. Washington spent three of the first four winters of the war here — twice in Morristown, once in Somerville. English troops were always near. New Jersey had its own Minutemen.

The American Revolution turned 13 colonies into one nation. It is important to know that the war was here — not far from your homes or your school.

97

THE WAR WAS HERE

The greatest years in our country's history were those between 1775 and 1781, when Americans joined to win their freedom from England. Those people wanted to be a new, free nation—The United States of America!

Once the war started, New Jersey became the center of the action.

New York was to the east. Philadelphia was to the west. They were America's most important two cities. Imagine living in the state between the two great cities as war began.

British armies and American armies fought often on New Jersey soil. General George Washington himself spent more than two full years in this state. That was nearly one-third of the entire war. He spent two winters in Morristown and one winter in Somerville.

Great battles were fought at *Trenton, Princeton, Monmouth, Springfield* and *Red Bank. That* Red Bank, by the way, was on the Delaware River, just south of Camden.

New Jersey had its own **Minutemen**. They were militiamen, who were excused from regular army service on their promise to fight for their country "at a minute's notice."

Boys often served with the Minutemen, carrying water and food to the soldiers. They ran errands and sometimes took important secret orders from one Minuteman commander to another. Some boys even carried guns.

INSTANT SOLDIERS

New Jersey's Minutemen appeared often during the Revolution. They fought in the battles of Trenton, Princeton, Monmouth, Springfield and elsewhere. The Minutemen were the "home guard" or "reserves."

They went into action quickly, alerted when wives or children raced into the fields to bring guns to the "instant" soldiers. The men would stop whatever they were doing and run to the nearby fight. Minutemen had no uniforms and wore their work clothes into battle.

New Jersey's most famous fighting men were the "Jersey Blues." They had been organized more than 100 years by the time of the American Revolution. The Blues had their own song, written by Minuteman Richard Howell. After the war, he became governor of New Jersey.

Girls and their mothers helped, too. They made food, sewed uniforms, knitted stockings and helped to bind up the wounds of soldiers hurt on the battlefields.

It was terrible to live in New Jersey during the Revolution. The sounds of gunfire and cannon shots often told that the enemy was near. That meant homes, fields, barns and even lives were threatened.

When Father or a big brother took a gun and dashed off, there was always fear that he might return wounded. Perhaps he might never be seen again!

Think of New Jersey as the *most* important state in the Revolution. It was called "Revolution's Crossroads" for very good reasons.

ROAD TO FREEDOM

America's greatest holiday is the Fourth of July, when we celebrate the fact that on July 4, 1776, the United States declared war on England in the Declaration of Independence.

From that day our nation became 13 **states**, not 13 colonies. The name "state" meant people no longer wanted to be English colonists.

However, actual revolution began long before that Fourth of July. You remember that colonists were very bitter about taxes on sugar, stamps, tea and other things.

When the College of New Jersey held its graduation in 1770, the graduates wore plain, homemade clothes. They refused to buy expensive clothes made in England. (The College of New Jersey is now Princeton University).

The most unpopular tax of all was the one on tea. Men in Boston, Massachusetts, disguised themselves as Indians in December of 1773, and dumped English tea into the harbor. When messengers on fast-moving horses brought word of that "Boston Tea Party" to New Jersey, crowds cheered!

Early in December 1774, the captain of the little ship, *Greyhound,* sailed off Delaware Bay into Cohansey Creek in Cumberland County. His ship was loaded with tea. He feared to take that cargo to Philadelphia. He hoped Greenwich people would not care.

Local patriots showed him that he was very wrong. On the night of December 22, many men disguised themselves as Indians. They rode into

Greenwich on horseback, piled the tea in the town square, and burned it. It was New Jersey's own tea party!

The Greenwich tea burners included the town minister and the brother of the sheriff! Richard Howell, who helped burn the tea, was elected Governor of New Jersey many years later.

Each of the 13 states sent delegates to Philadelphia in 1776 to draw up a Declaration of Independence.

New Jersey's five delegates were:
- Abraham Clark, a lawyer from Elizabeth.
- Frances Hopkinson, a well-known musician and poet from Bordentown.
- John Hart, a Hopewell farmer.
- Richard Stockton, a Princeton lawyer.
- The Reverend John Witherspoon, a Presbyterian minister and president of The College of New Jersey.

It took many months to prepare the Declaration of Independence. It was written mainly by Thomas Jefferson of Virginia. The Declaration was made public on July 4, 1776, but was not signed until August.

New Jersey was ready for independence. On July 2, delegates from all parts of the state adopted the first New Jersey Constitution. That beat the Declaration of Independence by two days.

Then, on August 30, New Jersey's first *state* governor was elected. He was William Livingston of Elizabethtown. Livingston was a lawyer who published very strong anti-British articles in the newspapers.

Bells rang throughout the new United States of America on July 4, 1776. This nation had declared its independence! One special bell sounded from the Cumberland County courthouse.

The historic bell is now in the lobby of a newer Cumberland courthouse in the same town. It truly is New Jersey's own Liberty Bell. The famous old bell also is shown on the county's official flag.

Revolution's Crossroads

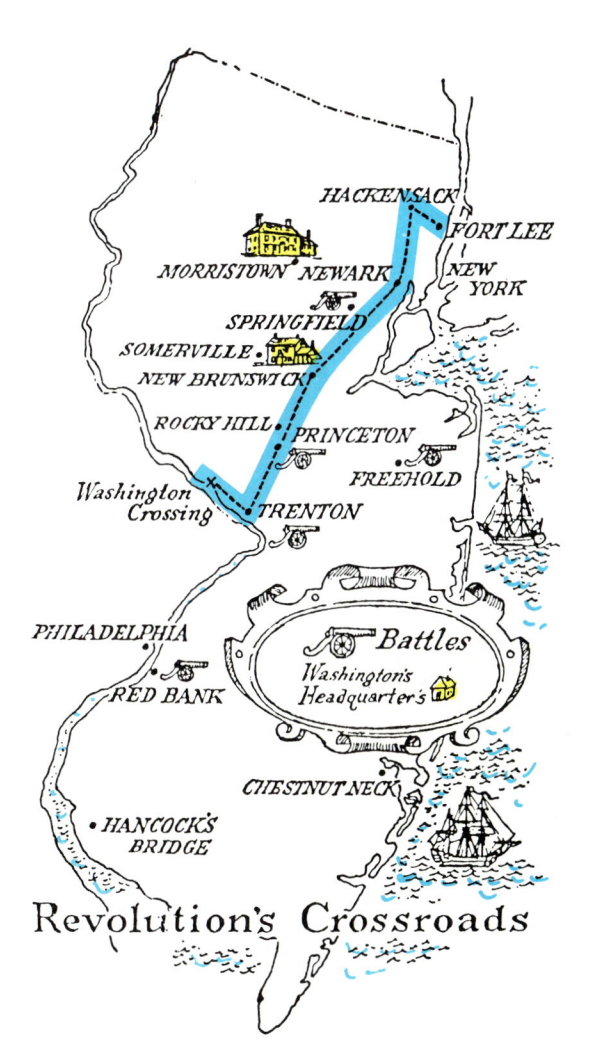

Here are places you'll read about in this Magic Carpet — important battle grounds, two towns where Washington spent winters and Chestnut Neck where a sea fight was waged. The blue line across the state is the retreat path of Washington's army in November and December 1776.

101

FROM GLOOM TO GLORY

Swarms of red-coated English soldiers marched off troop ships at Staten Island in early July of 1776. Along with the English were tough fighters from Germany, called **Hessians**. The **Redcoats** could be seen from Elizabethtown.

The English badly defeated Washington's army in August 1776, at Long Island and in New York City. Defeat seemed certain. American soldiers retreated hastily across New Jersey in November of 1776.

It was a time of awful gloom. Cold rains soaked Washington's blue-coated army. Word came that the invaders had taken Fort Lee on the Palisades on November 19. Great quantities of food, blankets and ammunition were captured at Fort Lee by the enemy. America was *losing* the war. The end seemed close.

Washington and his weary soldiers marched across New Jersey toward Trenton and the Delaware River. Before the Americans reached the Delaware River, Washington sent soldiers to seize all boats within 30 miles of Trenton, on both sides of the river.

Seizing the boats was a brilliant move. Americans crossed the Delaware into Pennsylvania and kept all the boats there. When the British reached the river, they could not find any way to cross.

Three weeks later, on Christmas night, 1776, Washington called together his 2,400 men. It was to be a Christmas that America will never forget. The general led the soldiers into boats at night and headed back across the icy Delaware River. They were on the way to attack the strong Hessian defenses in Trenton.

After landing at McConkey's Ferry, the American army crept toward Trenton as quietly as possible in the darkness. Soldiers were sick and miserable. Many were without shoes. They left bloody footprints in the snow. Sleet stung their faces.

The Hessians were asleep when the Americans smashed into Trenton early in the morning on December 26. The battle was short and sharp. The Hessians had 971 men killed or wounded. Washington's army had only four wounded men. The victory was one of the greatest in all military history.

Washington returned to his Pennsylvania camp, but only for a week. Then he and his army crossed the river once more. They again fought briefly in Trenton, then headed toward Princeton on January 3, 1777.

British soldiers fought bravely outside Nassau Hall on the Princeton college campus. But Washington's army was able to defeat the Redcoats. Gloom turned to hope!

The Americans were exhausted. They needed rest, food and the chance to spend a long winter in safety. Washington marched the army to Morristown in January 1777.

The Americans spent that cold winter in the hills, safely behind the Watchung Mountains and the Great Swamp. Hope returned.

The first desperate year was over. The terrible fears after the defeats at Long Island and New York were nearly forgotten. Trenton and Princeton were remembered. Perhaps this war *could* be won, after all!

The American Revolution ended more than 200 years ago, but units of "soldiers" work to keep it as a living memory. They are not in any army; they are club members whose hobbies are the uniforms, weapons and living conditions of soldiers in the years from about 1775 to 1785. They even spend winter weekends at encampments, where they live just as soldiers did long ago. At the encampments, they wear the same uniforms, fire the same kinds of rifles and eat foods cooked over open fires. Unit members really are historians, who do their studying by "being there" (at least in spirit) with the soldiers who fought in New Jersey.

CAT AND MOUSE

When spring arrived in 1777, Washington marched his army out of Morristown. They were headed for the Watchung Mountains near North Plainfield and Bound Brook. From the hills, the Americans could see British troops in the valley to the south.

The British commander at New Brunswick decided that he must get Washington's army out of the mountains. He decided to play what has been called "a cat and mouse game."

British soldiers would move toward the mountains, much as a cat might move its paw toward a mouse. Small battles, called **skirmishes**, took place at Spanktown (now Rahway) and Quibbletown (now Metuchen). The American "mice" would nip the claws of the British "cat," then dash back to the hills again!

The British quit the game. They boarded ships at Staten Island in June 1777, and sailed for Philadelphia. They did not *dare* march across New Jersey!

British soldiers reached Philadelphia, but American forts along the Delaware River kept English ships from bringing in supplies. Gradually, the British conquered the forts, one by one.

The Battle of Monmouth was fought on an extremely hot day. Temperatures rose above 100 degrees. That heat brought fame and a nickname to Molly Ludwig Hays. Tradition says that Molly carried pitchers of water to the soldiers. They called, "Molly, bring the pitcher!" or just "Molly, the pitcher!" She soon was called "Molly Pitcher." During the battle, Molly's husband William was injured. She dropped her pitcher, took his place at the cannon and fought bravely all afternoon.

One of the last forts to surrender was Fort Mercer at Red Bank in *Gloucester County*. British and Hessian troops attacked Fort Mercer fiercely on October 22, 1777.

Only a few hundred Americans were at the fort. The British force had about 1,200 men. Tradition says that the troops at Fort Mercer included black soldiers who were part of a Rhode Island regiment.

The battle at Fort Mercer roared for nearly an hour. When it was over, several hundred of the Hessians were dead or wounded. Fort Mercer had been held! Soon after, the fort had to be given up because of greater British strength and approaching winter, but the enemy had been delayed.

The English settled down in Philadelphia for the winter of 1777-78. Washington took his army to Valley Forge, north of the city. The Americans spent a very cruel winter there. They shivered in the cold and had little to eat. But they worked hard. They wanted to be ready to fight when spring came.

The strong, well-rested British army left Philadelphia in June 1778, and headed across New Jersey for New York City. Washington followed. He finally caught up with the Redcoats near Freehold in Monmouth County on a dreadfully hot Sunday—June 28, 1778.

Americans had never faced British soldiers on an open field. Usually the Americans fought from behind fences or trees. Could they match mighty British strength on an open field?

They could, indeed! The two armies fought all day. Neither side won, but the British had to flee to New York City during the night. It was amazing that the Americans had not retreated. They *were* as good as the British!

After the Battle of Monmouth, Washington chose Somerville for his winter camp. He stayed there, at the Wallace House, in the winter of 1778-79. Most of his officers and soldiers were stationed at Bound Brook, Somerville, Bedminster and Pluckemin.

That winter in Somerset County was quite mild and easy. The soldiers needed it. The war had been going on since 1775. They were tired.

105

MISERY AT MORRISTOWN

General Washington rode his big white horse through a heavy snowstorm when he entered Morristown on December 1, 1779. Cold winds whipped from the north. Another dreadful winter had begun!

Officers lived in homes in Morristown. Nearly 10,000 soldiers in Washington's main army stayed in tents or log cabins at nearby Jockey Hollow.

Most people think of Valley Forge as the place where the worst American suffering took place during the Revolution. Actually, the Morristown winter of 1779-80 was *much* worse!

There were 28 snowstorms between November and April. Snow was 14 feet deep in drifts. The Hudson River froze so solidly that horses and wagons could be driven across.

The soldiers suffered horribly at Jockey Hollow. Many wrapped their feet in rags. Few had warm coats. Most had no blankets. Many of them died during a January blizzard when heavy snow broke down tents in which soldiers were sleeping.

Very little food was available. Washington wrote that the soldiers "ate every kind of horse food but hay."

The General and Mrs. Washington stayed at a mansion owned by Mrs. Ford, the widow of an army colonel who had died in 1776. Mrs. Ford and her four children also continued to live in the mansion.

The Ford family used two bedrooms. General and Mrs. Washington had one room. About 15 other officers also lived in the house.

Everyone tried to keep warm in

Famed artist John Ward Dunsmore painted this scene showing Parson Caldwell handing out Watts' Hymnals at the Battle of Springfield. This was one of about 30 Revolutionary War scenes that Dunsmore painted in the 1920s. He carefully researched weapons, people, clothing and buildings to insure accuracy. Fraunces Tavern in New York owns several of Dunsmore's paintings.

front of a blazing fireplace in the huge kitchen of the Ford mansion. Sometimes there were nearly 25 officers—as well as the Fords—around the fireplace!

There were no battles that winter. The sickness and deaths from the bitter cold and the poor food were just as hard to endure.

Morristown was important. The British decided to attack it.

British and Hessian troops advanced toward Morristown on June 23, 1780. Lookouts spotted the enemy coming. A big cannon on the Watchung Mountains near Summit was fired to call Minutemen to arms.

American troops met the invaders at Springfield. The Battle of Springfield was much bigger than many other battles of the Revolution. More than 5,000 British opposed 2,500 American soldiers and about 5,000 New Jersey Minutemen.

The battle raged all day. British soldiers burned the church and most of the houses in Springfield. At day's end the invaders were in full retreat back to Staten Island. Morristown had been saved!

Springfield's hero was a minister, the Reverend James Caldwell. During the battle, American troops ran out of the wadding used to pack powder into the cannons.

The minister thought fast! He raced into his church and gathered hymn books. They had been written by a man named Watts. As Pastor Caldwell passed out the hymn books for soldiers to use as wadding, he yelled:

"Give 'em Watts, boys! Give 'em Watts!"

Watts made the difference. The cannons roared again! The British were defeated!

THE HOME FRONT

Nearly all New Jerseyans played some role in the American Revolution. That's how it is when war is so close that the sounds of battle can be heard!

The mountains of New Jersey were filled with iron forges that made guns and cannonballs for the American army. Forges in the Pine Barrens also turned out materials for Washington's men.

Ironworkers were important. They did not have to serve in the army if they worked in mines or in iron factories.

Also important were salt makers. The war cut off salt supplies from England. About 20 salt works were built during the Revolution along the Jersey Shore. The most important works was at Toms River.

Salt was badly needed. It was used to flavor food, of course. It was needed to preserve meat and fish.

Salt makers let sea water run into shallow bins. The sun dried away the water and left a rough salt. It was eagerly bought, even though prices were very high.

British troops destroyed the Toms River salt works in April 1778. It was a serious blow to American needs. The workers quickly rebuilt the works. It then operated until the end of the war.

Winning the war depended on more than fighting on a battlefield. Farmers worked hard in the fields to provide food. Even very young boys and girls worked. They pulled weeds or hoed corn.

Older girls and mothers sewed warm clothes for the soldiers. When ladies called on Mrs. Washington at Morristown, the general's wife was knitting a stocking for a soldier! The Morristown ladies knew that *they* too really should be home knitting.

Everyone worked! Everyone knew that *not* working could mean terrible defeat!

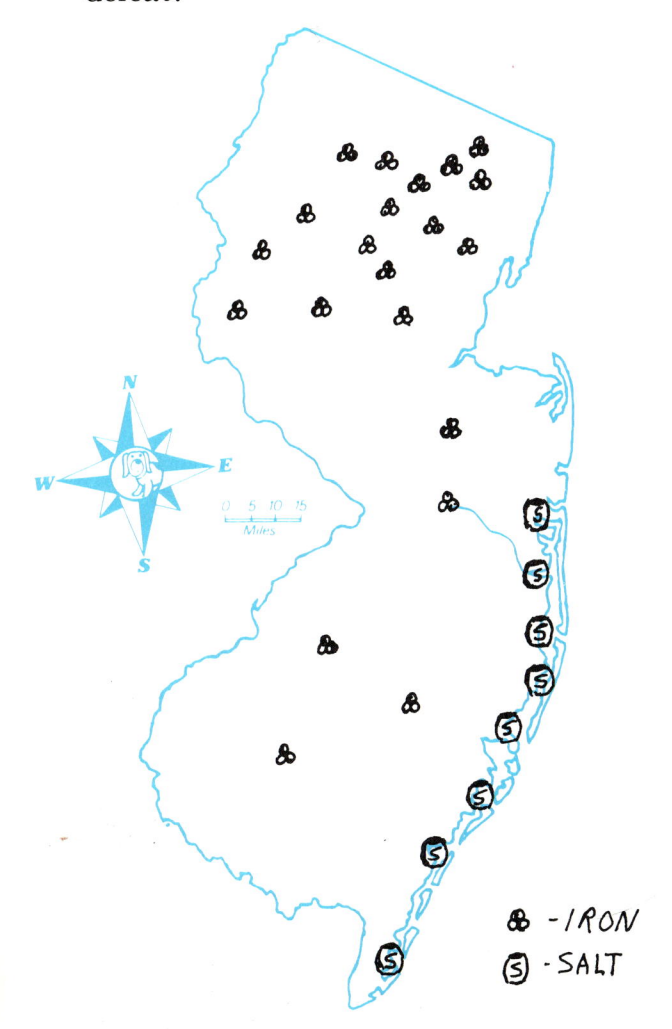

New Jersey's wartime ironworks were in both the mountains and the Pine Barrens. Salt makers were numerous along the Jersey Shore.

Rhoda Farrand of Morris County won fame as a knitter! When she heard soldiers at Jockey Hollow were suffering from frozen feet during the winter of 1780, she went into action.

Her son Dan hitched oxen to a hay wagon and put his mother's rocker aboard. Mrs. Farrand called for her daughters, Hannah and Bet, telling them to bring needles and wool.

As the wagon rolled through villages, Mrs. Farrand and her daughters knitted stockings. People rushed to see the strange sight. Mrs. Farrand called to them, "Knit stockings for our freezing soldiers at Jockey Hollow!"

Many of the ladies had meant only to look. Instead they slammed down their windows, picked up their own needles and wool, and went to work.

Soon after, wagonloads of newly knitted wool stockings were taken to the Jockey Hollow camp. Feet no longer froze in Morris County!

DIFFERENT KIND OF WAR

Big battles get most of the attention, but the Revolution involved many New Jersey people in seldom-remembered "little battles."

Hundreds of the "little battles" in New Jersey were called "skirmishes." Today we would call this kind of fighting "guerrilla warfare."

Usually the skirmishes took place without warning. British soldiers would clash with American soldiers or Minutemen beside the roadsides or in the woods. Skirmishes usually ended within a few minutes.

Sometimes soldiers were killed while they slept. Such actions were called **massacres**.

One massacre brought death to 30 Americans at Hancock's Bridge on March 21, 1778. Three hundred British Loyalists and Hessians attacked the house where the men were asleep. All of the Americans were slain.

Another massacre took place on September 28, 1778, at Old Tappan in Bergen County. Several hundred British soldiers attacked about 120 sleeping Americans. More than 50 Americans were killed.

Unusual "little wars" were carried on by daring New Jersey sea captains, called **privateers**. They owned swift-sailing boats. Some boats were only about 30 feet long.

Privateers kept their ships close to the Atlantic Ocean. Ports were at New Brunswick, Manasquan, Toms River, Barnegat Bay, Chestnut Neck, Tuckerton, Cape May and along Delaware Bay.

Privateers would hear of British ships sailing toward New York or Philadelphia. They would sail out on the ocean to attack the enemy. The British ships usually were loaded with valuable supplies, food or clothing.

Privateer captains wanted to fight the bigger British ships in the darkness. They hoped to be aboard enemy vessels before the surprised enemy could fight back.

Privateers brought captured ships back to American docks, where cargoes could be unloaded without fear of attack. The captured goods were sold. Many privateers made huge profits.

The British hated and feared the privateers at Chestnut Neck, near what is now Atlantic City. The British called the Chestnut Neck raiders a "Nest of Rebel Pirates."

A large force of British ships attacked Chestnut Neck in October 1778. On October 6, the village was burned to the ground. Several privateer ships were sunk.

Southern New Jersey Minutemen finally forced the British to leave Chestnut Neck, but the battle very seriously crippled the privateers.

Capt. Adam Hyler of New Brunswick was New Jersey's most daring privateer. He put cannons on his small ship and fastened long rowboats to the stern. He named his little ship the Defiance.

He chose his crew carefully, seeking men who were reckless but also able to row quietly and swiftly toward enemy warships.

One night in October, 1781, Hyler sailed the Defiance into Sandy Hook Bay to attack five large British ships. His men rowed silently in the darkness to surprise the British crews.

Within 15 minutes the Americans had overcome four of the enemy ships. Cargoes were taken into the rowboats and the British vessels were set afire. The fifth ship was not burned because women and children were aboard.

The Defiance triumphed over other English ships. However, in January 1782, a strong enemy force destroyed Hyler's ship, tied up at a dock near New Brunswick.

The skirmishes and battles by the privateers were not part of an organized plan. Yet the actions of these "guerrilla fighters" did much to cripple the British.

SIX REVOLUTIONISTS!

THOMAS PAINE: *His brave writings stirred Americans! He wrote: "These are the times that try men's souls! In this crisis, the Summer Soldier and the Sunshine Patriot will shrink from service to his country!"*

THE REV. PHILIP FITHIAN: *This young minister was a leader of those who burned the British tea at Greenwich on December 22, 1774. Some believe that he planned the burning! He joined the army as a chaplain and died in service on October 8, 1776.*

PHILIP FRENEAU: *This Monmouth County writer was called "The Poet of the Revolution." His poems about freedom helped make people determined to fight.*

TEMPE WICK: *One of New Jersey's best known women of the Revolution. In January, 1781, American soldiers were protesting because they had not been paid or fed. Three of them tried to steal Tempe's horse. She dashed off and, one legend says, hid the horse in her bedroom in the Wick farmhouse in Jockey Hollow.*

MRS. ANNE COOPER WHITALL: *A Quaker lady whose home was near the Red Bank battlefield. During the attack on Fort Mercer she continued to use her spinning wheel. When a cannonball whizzed by her head and hit the wall, she picked up the spinning wheel. She took it to the cellar—and went back to spinning! Later, she helped care for wounded soldiers, in both armies.*

OLIVER CROMWELL: *A black soldier from Columbia in Burlington County. He served six years in the 2nd N.J. Regiment and fought in many battles. He became a farmer after the war and died at age 106!*

WASHINGTON STAYED AWAKE HERE

People sometimes say that an old house is important because "Washington *slept* here."

A New Jersey boy who had learned about the American Revolution put it much better. He wrote about New Jersey that "Washington *stayed awake* here!" He was right.

Now that you know more about the Revolution, you will be "awakened" to go out to see New Jersey places connected to that war.

First, see the Ford house in Morristown, where Washington spent the winter of 1779-80. You can almost imagine that the general is still there!

Near Morristown is Jockey Hollow, where soldiers suffered dreadfully. Some soldiers' huts remind us of the terrible times of 200 years ago.

Washington's Crossing is worth a visit. Start on the Pennsylvania side. There you can see the beautiful painting of George Washington crossing the Delaware. Cross over to McConkey's Ferry House in New Jersey, where the Americans landed.

In Trenton, stop at the Old Barracks. It is much as it was on December 26, 1776, when Hessians were surprised by the American attack.

Anne Cooper Whitall's house can be visited at the Red Bank Battlefield in Gloucester County.

The Dey Mansion in Preakness, near Paterson, was where Washington and his officers lived during the summer and fall of 1780.

Monmouth Battlefield is now a state park. It is where troops fought in the hot sun of June 28, 1778. The Old Tennent Church on the hill near the battlefield was used as a hospital during the battle, as was St. Peter's Church in nearby Freehold.

The Hancock House at Hancock's Bridge, Salem County, was the scene of the massacre in March 1778.

The New Jersey Liberty Bell, which rang on July 4, 1776, is in the courthouse in Bridgeton.

The Wallace House in Somerville is where Washington stayed during the winter of 1778-79.

Many other Revolutionary War churches and buildings remain. Try to visit one or more.

Few American military events have captured the imaginations of artists more than the crossing of the Delaware by Washington and his troops on Christmas Day, 1776. The best known painting (below), by Emanuel Leutze, was not finished until 1852. He was not at the crossing, of course, but his aim was to show the danger and excitement of the affair. The drawings above, made much earlier, probably were more accurate, although it is not likely that the soldiers stood all the way across!

IMMIGRATION

MAGIC CARPET NO. 7

♪ We are a state of many immigrants,
Who came to look for life anew.
A common ground for all who brought their skills,
And found new hope and freedom, too.
    Repeat Chorus (see page 9)

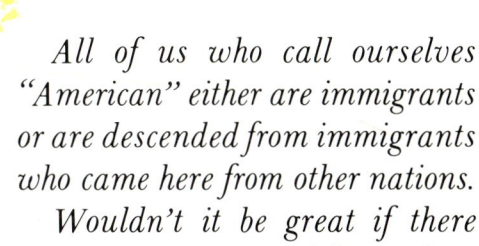

All of us who call ourselves "American" either are immigrants or are descended from immigrants who came here from other nations.

Wouldn't it be great if there could be a parade of flags of all nations that have sent people to New Jersey!

There would be hundreds of flags in line. Remember, some national flags have changed many times. Some colonial nations no longer exist. Many have different names. For every change, there would be a different flag.

Leading the flags would be our own United States banner — the flag that says that from many people we have become one nation.

115

NATION OF HOPE

People who lived in this country before the American Revolution felt that England was their ruler, even though many had come from other nations. Nearly all would have agreed that they were "Englishmen."

After the Revolution, people in the United States began calling themselves "Americans." They had won freedom. Land was plentiful and cheap. This was a nation of hope, where dreams could come true.

America was really a mixture of many nations. As you know, New Jersey's colonists included Dutch, Swedes, Finns, English, Africans, Scots, Irish and Germans. There were also a few Frenchmen and an occasional Italian or Spanish family.

In the year 1790, when the first United States Census was taken, New Jersey's population was only about 194,000 persons. Nearly eight per cent—about 14,000—of these were black persons descended from African ancestors.

The other New Jerseyans of 1790 had two things in common:

1. With few exceptions, they came from Great Britain or northern European countries.

2. Again with few exceptions, they worshiped in Protestant churches.

However, this nation had to look to other nations. The United States needed to expand its ability to manufacture products. America's first planned industrial city was started at Paterson in 1791.

America was growing. It needed skilled persons to set up and run the factory machines. It needed clever mechanics as well as strong men to dig the canals and to lay the tracks for railroads.

Expert glassblowers came to southern New Jersey from Germany. Experienced ironworkers arrived from Germany and Wales. Paterson's mills brought in machinists from England.

Then, in about 1830, a great new and different stream of **immigrants** began—Irish Catholics. They were "different" because earlier Irish immigrants were mainly Protestant. The "new" Irishmen had suffered from great poverty in their own land. America seemed to be the place where they could find opportunity.

Later, in the 1840s, another "new" group arrived. They were Germans who had been revolutionists in their country, fighting for the freedoms that Americans had won in our revolution. The German Revolutionists had lost. They had to flee their homeland.

The "new" Germans were mostly very well educated. They became leaders among Germans in this country. They also included many Catholics and some Jews. They settled in the cities, especially in Newark and Hoboken.

These Germans also founded more than a dozen new towns in Hudson and Bergen counties. Another group of Germans established Egg Harbor City in the pine woodlands of Atlantic County.

America was changing and expanding. It needed more people to keep the nation growing.

In 1860, there were only 109 Italians in New Jersey, only 44 persons from Spain and Portugal, only 31 Russians—and *NO ONE* from Poland, Hungary or Yugoslavia.

Soon—faster than anyone could have known—America would reach out to Italy, Greece, Spain and Portugal; to Poland, Russia, Hungary, Yugoslavia and other nations.

German and Irish immigrants swarmed into New Jersey in the 1840s and 1850s, fleeing hard times in their own countries. Germany was torn by revolution. The Irish were starving because their potato crops had failed.

To the left is shown a special ferryboat that took German immigrants from their ships to the Erie Railroad station in Jersey City. On the ferry's back, the word Eisenbahn means "railroad." Einwanderer means immigrant.

To the right are Irish laborers laying railroad tracks. When railroads and canals came to New Jersey in the 1830s and 1840s, thousands of Irish immigrants dug the canals and did the hard manual labor on the railroads.

AMERICA NEEDS HELP

Charles K. Landis, a Philadelphia lawyer, laid out a town in the Pine Barrens in 1861. He called it Vineland, and to make sure that crops would grow in the sandy soil, he sent to Italy for farmers.

Landis knew that Italians were very skilled farmers. He knew that only the most skilled persons could make the Vineland soil rich. The Italian immigrants quickly worked wonders in a region that settlers for 200 years had considered "barren."

America—and New Jersey—had fully awakened to the fact that people from lands other than Great Britain, Ireland, Holland, Germany and Sweden could be useful.

New Jersey sought more Italian farmers in 1880 when the state advertised in southern Italy that New Jersey's weather was like the warm sunny climate of Italy.

Elsewhere posters were going up in most of Europe, inviting families to leave their homelands to work in America.

The posters promised much: good jobs, cheap land, healthy climate and happy towns. Nearly every state sought immigrants. Railroads and steamship companies offered low transportation rates.

New Jersey, and the United States, needed the Europeans. Since there now were fewer people eager to come from northern Europe, the "invitations" went to southern and eastern Europe: Italy, Spain, Yugoslavia, Greece, Hungary, Russia, Poland, Czechoslovakia and other nations.

At the same time that America urged people to leave their homelands, great troubles struck eastern and southern Europe.

Powerful landlords turned people off farms where families had worked for a hundred years or more. Harvests were very poor in many nations. Homeless, starving people were everywhere, begging for work.

Conditions were worst in Russia, where the government killed thousands of innocent Jews, burned their villages and stole their valuables.

At first, a few daring persons left their villages and headed across the ocean to America. Some of those immigrants sent back letters and postcards, telling of good jobs in America.

Many, many thousands of people finally made the decision: *we must go to America.* They knew there was nothing for them in their native lands. Perhaps a person might make a fortune in America and be able to return home. Most wanted to earn enough to bring their families to America.

Imagine leaving home, to travel 3,000 miles away to a land that seemed as distant as the moon. Imagine selling or giving away every possession except what could be carried in one bundle or suitcase.

They were courageous people, and between 1890 and 1915, 16 million of them would head for America. They would become the ancestors of nearly *half* the people who now live in the United States.

This tide of immigration started slowly, but after the year 1900 more than a million people left southern and eastern Europe every year.

They streamed toward America. Many would find that their dreams could come true in New Jersey—a place most did not know existed when they left Europe.

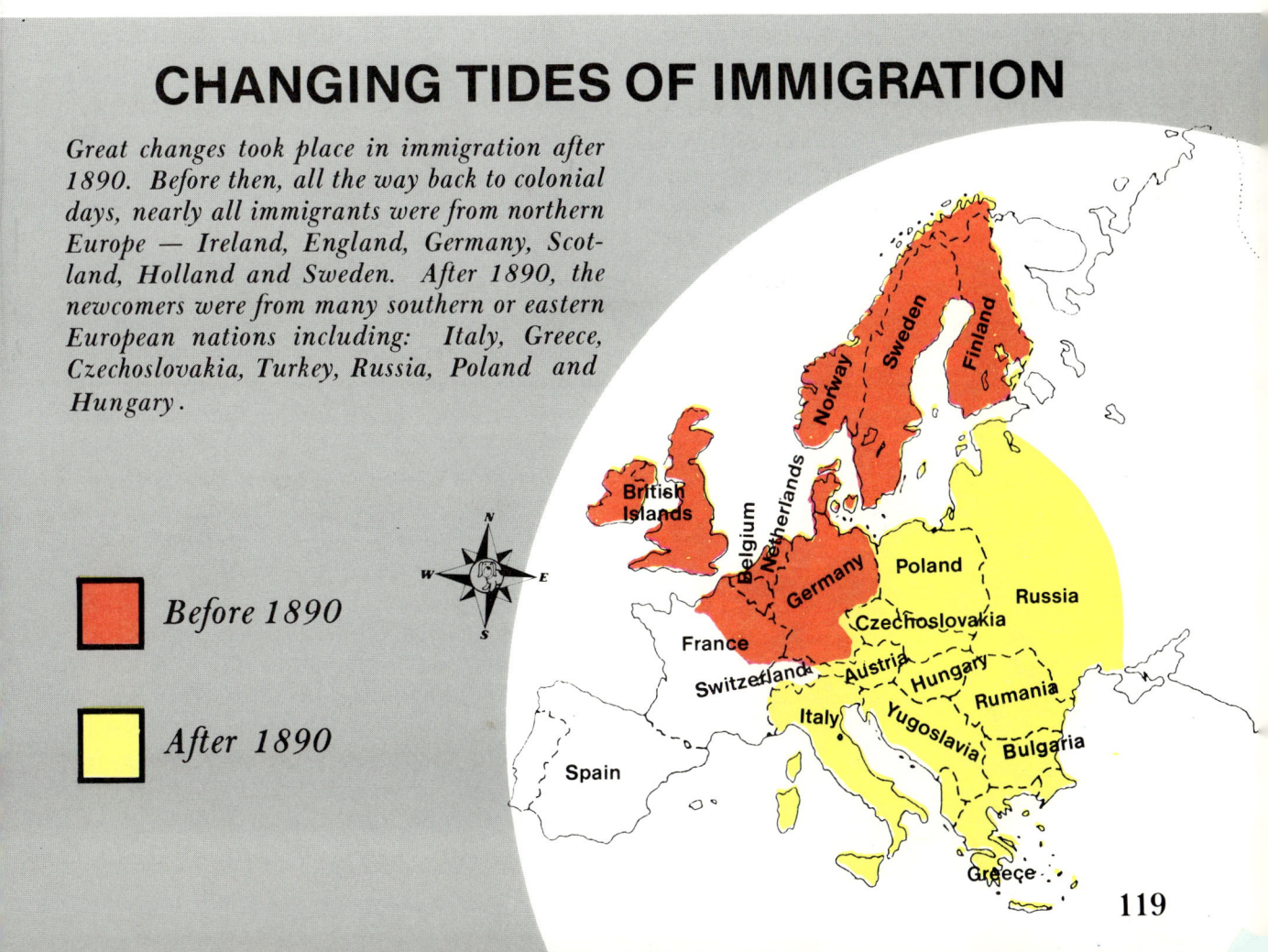

CHANGING TIDES OF IMMIGRATION

Great changes took place in immigration after 1890. Before then, all the way back to colonial days, nearly all immigrants were from northern Europe — Ireland, England, Germany, Scotland, Holland and Sweden. After 1890, the newcomers were from many southern or eastern European nations including: Italy, Greece, Czechoslovakia, Turkey, Russia, Poland and Hungary.

■ *Before 1890*

□ *After 1890*

HEADING TO NEW LIVES

Immigrants tearfully said their goodbyes in their European towns and villages. People remaining behind urged them not to leave, warning that there were snakes in Jersey City's streets and possibly even savage Indians in farm areas.

It was time to go. The immigrants walked out of their villages and headed for the port cities where they could buy steamship tickets. Tickets cost $30 to $40 each.

Most of the immigrants walked to the ports, sometimes as much as 600 miles away. Russian Jews often traveled by night, fearful that soldiers might arrest them. All travelers watched out for gangs of thieves along the roads.

Some headed for the ports in homemade carts or in crowded trains. Some from Greek or Italian coastal towns paddled small boats to the ports.

Port officials presented the first big stumbling blocks. Steamship officials gave the immigrants difficult mental and physical examinations. They did not care especially about the people. Rather, the companies knew that they had to pay return passage for anyone not admitted to America.

Finally the immigrants could go aboard their ships. They were herded down into the lower decks to **steerage**,

European immigrants left home carrying or wearing only a few possessions. Then they headed for ports to board ships to America. Some who lived near the Mediterranean Sea departed in sailboats or rowboats (left). Most walked, some traveling as many as 400 to 600 miles before reaching port.

Each person was examined at European ports before boarding ships. The voyage across the Atlantic Ocean was long and dreadful. Immigrants were crowded into small spaces below decks. Food was terrible. Bathrooms were scarce. Nearly all passengers became very seasick.

Immigrants usually had to stay below decks, away from fresh air and sunshine. However (as in the photograph to the far right), everyone gathered on the top decks as their ship neared Ellis Island. As many as 1,500 people might be on deck, eager for admission to America.

close to where the ship's steering gear could be seen.

It is difficult to even imagine what the voyages on the Atlantic Ocean must have been like.

The beds were steel cots, stacked high in bunk fashion. A thin mattress and a blanket might be provided for the iron springs.

Food was both terrible and scarce. Steamship companies counted on most passengers getting seasick. The fewer who ate, the greater the profits.

Two weeks in steerage meant sickness and despair. Many of the immigrants wondered why they had ever left home.

Occasionally, on calm, clear days, some of the immigrants went outside in special areas, hidden from first class passengers. The sea air revived their spirits.

Those with fond memories of the ocean voyages were usually small children when their families crossed the ocean. They were not likely to become seasick. On deck, ship crews fussed over the children.

Little boys and girls did not understand the great worry that hung heavily on their parents' minds—the fear that they might not be admitted to the United States.

The immigrants especially dreaded *Ellis Island*, where they would be tested for admission. The island lay in New Jersey waters, less than 1,000 feet from Jersey City.

At last, seagulls would appear. Land could be seen. Soon the *Statue of Liberty* (also in New Jersey) came into view.

Just to the north was Ellis Island. There, the immigrants would be tested for admission to America.

America! The promised land! So near—and yet so far away!

ISLAND OF TEARS

There it was: Ellis Island. This was the last testing ground before admission to America! Immigrants called it the "Island of Hope, Island of Tears."

One immigrant who came through Ellis Island said, "For one who passed by, everything was all right. For one who was detained or sent back, oh, that was awful!"

Ellis Island was built in 1892 to handle the great tide of immigrants coming to America. The first buildings burned in 1897 but new brick buildings were ready by 1900—just in time for the greatest waves of immigration.

The immigrants transferred from their steamships to ferryboats that carried them to Ellis Island. Once there, they moved quickly toward the inspection hall.

Every step deepened their fears. All Ellis Island workers wore uniforms—guards, doctors, questioners. That worried the newcomers. In their countries, uniforms meant cruel governmental power.

Pictures of people at Ellis Island show very few smiling adults. The fears were too great.

As the immigrants climbed the steps to the inspection hall, they were watched carefully. Inspectors looked for signs of limping, shortness of breath or poor eyesight. Anyone suspected of having physical troubles was put into a special line for further examination.

Every immigrant was tested for trachoma, a dreaded eye disease for which there was no cure at that time. Anyone with trachoma was certain to be returned to Europe.

The lines moved slowly toward questioners, who asked about 20 questions. Actually the questioning was very short, usually lasting only about two minutes. The questions were much the same as those asked in Europe before immigrants boarded the ships for America.

Only about two percent of all the immigrants failed either the physical or mental tests at Ellis Island. These were returned to Europe.

If two percent does not seem like

much, remember that about 16 million immigrants were examined at Ellis Island. That means that about 300,000 persons were not admitted to America.

Many families returned to Europe together if anyone of them was rejected. Some of those rejected committed suicide at Ellis Island rather than return home.

Actually no immigrant returned directly to his or her "home." The steamship company was required only to take a rejected immigrant back to the port where he or she had boarded a ship to America.

Remember that many people had walked hundreds of miles to get to the port. They had sold or given away nearly all of their possessions. Many had fled from villages that had been burned down.

"Going home" was a nightmare. Being admitted to the United States was a joy. No wonder Ellis Island was the "Island of Hope, Island of Tears."

Day after day the immigrants streamed ashore at Ellis Island. Often as many as 25,000 came in one week. The newcomers had few possessions, packed in old suitcases or wrapped in blankets or tablecloths.

They dreaded Ellis Island, knowing that it might be the end of their dreams. Even a gentle touch of a mother's shoulder brought fright to a family. Could this man in a uniform be saying, "You can't be admitted?"

Below, a woman is examined for trachoma, an eye infection. The examination was uncomfortable. Victims had to return to Europe.

Some were detained for additional mental or physical tests, but 98 percent of all immigrants passed. All persons who were rejected had the right to appeal (lower right). An interpreter was present if needed.

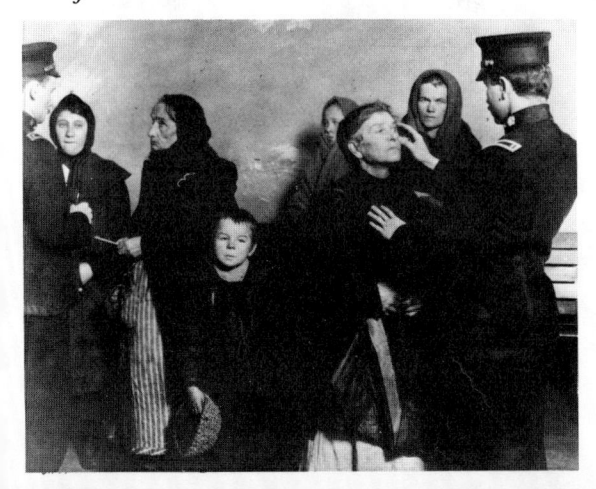

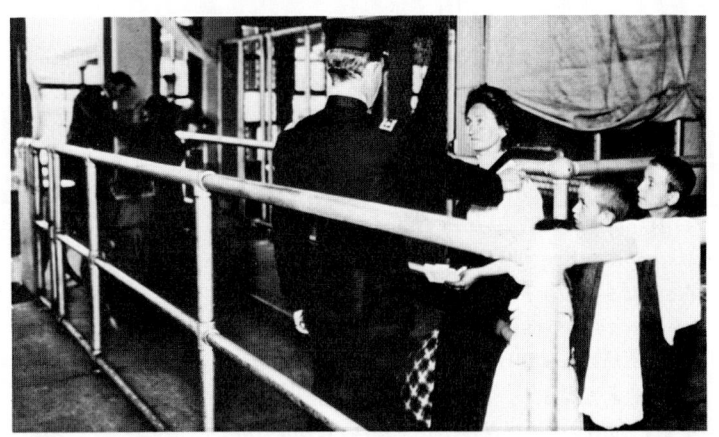

123

ANYTHING TO BE AMERICAN!

Getting through Ellis Island did not automatically make immigrants into "Americans." They still had to study United States history and government. They had to take a test. Finally, they had to swear that they would be faithful to their new country.

Joy filled their hearts, nevertheless, as they rode ferryboats away from Ellis Island. Some went to New York City, either to stay or to board trains. Most went to Jersey City or Hoboken, where "immigrant trains" carried them to distant states—or to cities and towns in New Jersey.

These new Americans, eager to work, mostly swarmed into the cities—Newark, Hoboken, Jersey City, Elizabeth, Trenton, Paterson, Passaic and Camden.

Immigrants took on the worst jobs in the oil refinery at Bayonne. They labored at the asbestos factory in Manville. They made handkerchiefs in Passaic, pottery and rubber goods in Trenton, silk in Paterson.

Others worked in the iron mines near Dover and Wharton. Many went to New Brunswick, Perth Amboy and Sayreville, to dig clay, make bricks and refine copper.

Some found careers as gardeners on the large estates in Morristown and Far Hills. The rose growers of Madison, Summit and Chatham found that immigrants made first-rate employees.

Leading the flag salute was a proud time for an immigrant boy or girl. It made the child feel genuinely "American."

Immigrant families wanted very much to be part of the life that they saw in the United States. Most tried to learn English, believing that it helped them get better jobs or to be more accepted.

Those who were older, from about age 12 and up, often went to night school to learn English. Staying awake in class after working 10 or 12 hours was very difficult.

Immigrant families tried to send children to school for as long as possible, although most boys and girls left school to work at about age 8 or 9. Some children never went to school at all, since entire families often worked in their homes at such jobs as rolling cigars or making artificial flowers.

Immigrant children shared one thing with colonial boys and girls — WORK! The difference was that immigrants were not working on their own family farms. The child above, for example, was laboring in a southern New Jersey cranberry bog. The boy below was one of hundreds of very young people who worked in southern New Jersey glass factories. Such use of child labor was common everywhere. The girls in the picture at the bottom, who would have been about 10 or 11 years old, worked in a Passaic County textile mill.

Each summer and fall, bands of immigrant Italian families headed for southern New Jersey fields to harvest everything from lettuce to cranberries.

In 1891, a noted town was founded in Cape May County to help Russian Jews. The immigrants cleared more than 650 acres of pine woodland, built homes and planted crops. They called their town Woodbine.

Woodbine was just one of several southern New Jersey towns founded to aid Jewish immigrants. Others were Alliance, Norma, Brotmanville, Rosenhayn and Carmel.

New Jersey's foreign-born population grew rapidly. More than a half million immigrants settled permanently in New Jersey, making it fifth among states in total immigration population. Since the state was so small, the large number of immigrants made New Jersey first in immigrants per square mile.

Life was not easy for immigrants. They often were cheated at the railroad stations, had their money stolen or paid for jobs that did not exist.

Many "old" Americans (those who had gotten to America first) disliked the immigrants.

These new people did not speak English. They ate "strange" foods. They danced and played differently from others in America. Their customs and churches were different.

Many immigrants went to night school to learn English. They worked all day in factories, then went to classes. They really wanted to be "Americans." Soon they were!

The story of immigrants—the "New Americans"—is important in American history. It also is the story of most of our own ancestors!

AND STILL WE COME

The great tide of new immigrants sweeping through Ellis Island slowed nearly to a halt about 75 years ago.

For one thing, a great war had broken out in Europe in 1914, called World War I. For another thing, some government leaders felt that too many immigrants were coming to the United States. New laws cut the numbers of immigrants to a very few people.

Those laws, which were unfair to many nations, were changed in 1965. Now a total of 250,000 immigrants can be admitted to the United States each year.

Our nation often has permitted large groups of special people to enter, even during the years when most other immigrants were kept out.

During the 1930s and 1940s, when millions of Jews were being killed in Germany, the United States allowed large numbers of German Jews to enter. Many of these **refugees**—as victims of injustice and terror are called—settled in New Jersey.

Large numbers of homeless European refugees came here in 1948. Then, special laws permitted thousands of Hungarians, Cubans, Vietnamese, Koreans and others to enter. All of them were fleeing from wars or injustices in their homelands.

Not all of New Jersey's "new" people come here from foreign nations.

Many families journey here each year from southern states. Thousands of people have come from Puerto Rico. Many people forget that Puerto Rico is part of the United States because people there speak a different language.

Most families move to New Jersey to escape poor living conditions in places where they grew up. All seek a new chance.

Scientists and engineers come here because the state has so many research laboratories. Most newcomers hope to find work in our thousands of industries.

Some families live here only for a short time. Such families would include those whose fathers are in the Army or Navy. Schools in Mercer, Burlington and Camden counties have many boys and girls whose fathers are at Fort Dix. Fort Monmouth in Monmouth County also is a center for Army families.

Most children of servicemen have lived in other states or other countries. Some of you might have been born in Germany, England or Japan. You can tell stories of foreign lands that can't be found in books.

Newcomers still see New Jersey as a

Vietnamese families escaping from their war-torn Asian homeland in the 1970s were called "boat people." They used any kind of boat to flee.

place of opportunity. That is true whether they harvest crops, work in factories, study in research labs or teach school.

Many people leave their homelands because they seek freedom and opportunity.

That search brought the first colonists to New Jersey. That encouraged people to come in the 1830s and 1840s to build our railroads and to dig our canals.

Hope brought more than 16 million immigrants to Ellis Island between 1890 and 1915. They came to work in our industries, to build our cities, and to construct our roads and bridges.

People fleeing poverty and injustice always have believed that the United States—and New Jersey—are places where they might get a chance to improve themselves.

New Jersey has more than 100 nationality groups represented in our population. Some of our ancestors have been here for more than 300 years. Some of our families might have come in very recent years. Here are a few representations of national groups in our state. Some are performing at their national festivals. Some are walking on city streets. Look at the faces; they represent the variety that is the major story of our state and our nation. Look at the street. Signs on shops of "new" immigrants are side by side with signs on stores owned by people of earlier national groups. We are all part of a great story — the story of a nation founded by immigrants and forever changing because of cultures added by newcomers.

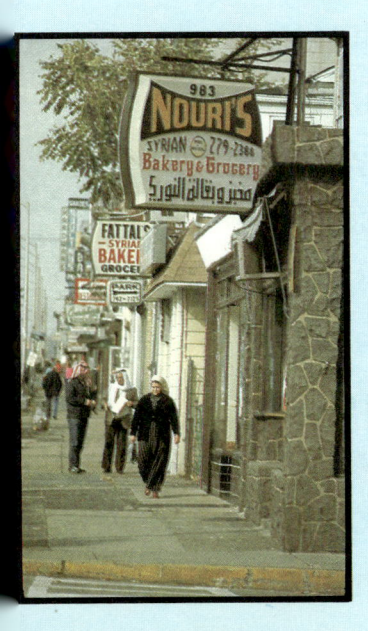

PERCENTAGE BREAKDOWN OF FOREIGN BORN NEW JERSEY RESIDENTS

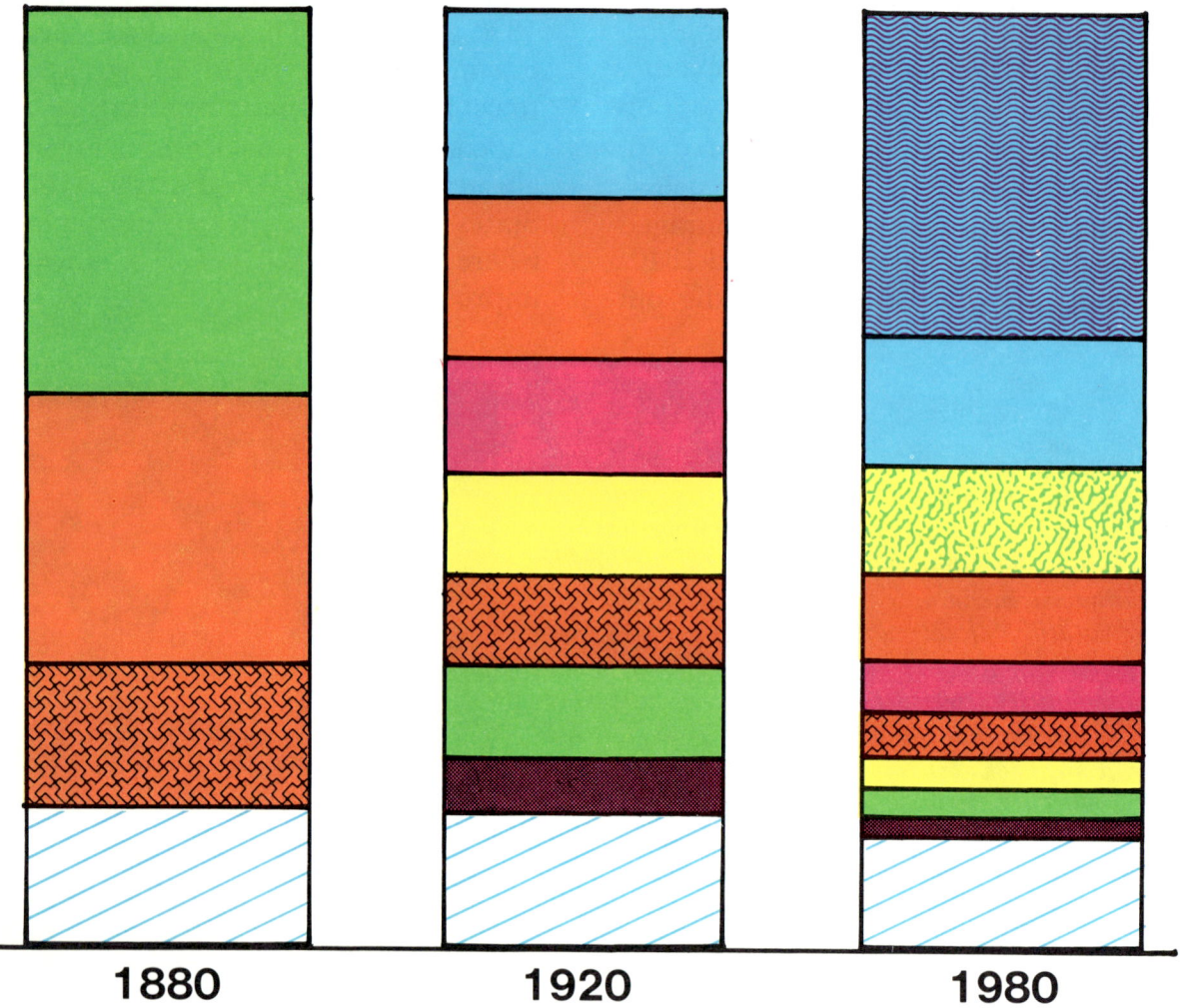

1880   **1920**   **1980**

POPULATION 7,168,000   7,836 SQ MLS

Irish and Germans led all immigrant groups in New Jersey 125 years ago. Today, very few immigrants come to our state from those nations.

That is one of the things that you note quickly in the bars above. The varied blocks represent people from other nations as counted by Census takers in 1880, 1920 and 1980.

Notice that Italians, not shown at all in the 1880 bar, were number one in 1920 and second in 1980. Latin Americans, not found in either previous census, were first in 1980 by a big margin.

One showing remains about the same: OTHER. That means that we always have had, and likely always will have, small numbers of persons coming to New Jersey from a great many nations.

- ASIAN
- BRITISH
- EASTERN EUROPEAN
- GERMAN
- HUNGARIAN
- IRISH
- ITALIAN
- LATIN AMERICAN
- POLISH
- OTHER

128

NEW JERSEYANS WHO LEFT HOME

New Jersey's story is not just a matter of people coming here to make our state great! People from New Jersey have helped change America and the world, too.

Pike's Peak in the Rocky Mountains was named for explorer Zebulon Pike of Mercer County.

The first Stetson hats worn by Western cowboys were made in Orange, N.J.

The first of the famous Colt revolvers was made in Paterson by Samuel Colt. Western fighters used it.

Gold was discovered in California in 1848 by James Marshall of Lambertville, N.J.

Cornelia Hancock of Hancock's Bridge, Salem County, became a famous nurse during the Civil War.

The first American to explore what is now Los Angeles, California was Robert Stockton of Princeton.

Clara Maass, a young nurse from East Orange and Livingston, gave her life in Cuba in 1901 to help prove that mosquitoes carried yellow fever.

Paul Robeson of Princeton and Somerville, first noted as a champion athlete and brilliant scholar at Rutgers, became known as one of the world's great singers.

Daniel Burnet of Newark was the first President of Texas in 1845. Texas was an independent nation then.

Grover Cleveland, who was born in Caldwell, became the 22nd *and* 24th President of the United States.

Woodrow Wilson, Princeton University President and N.J. Governor, became the 28th President.

Alice Paul of Moorestown for many years was a national leader in the fight for women's rights.

Two New Jerseyans were U.S. Vice Presidents — Aaron Burr, Newark, and Garrett A. Hobart, Paterson.

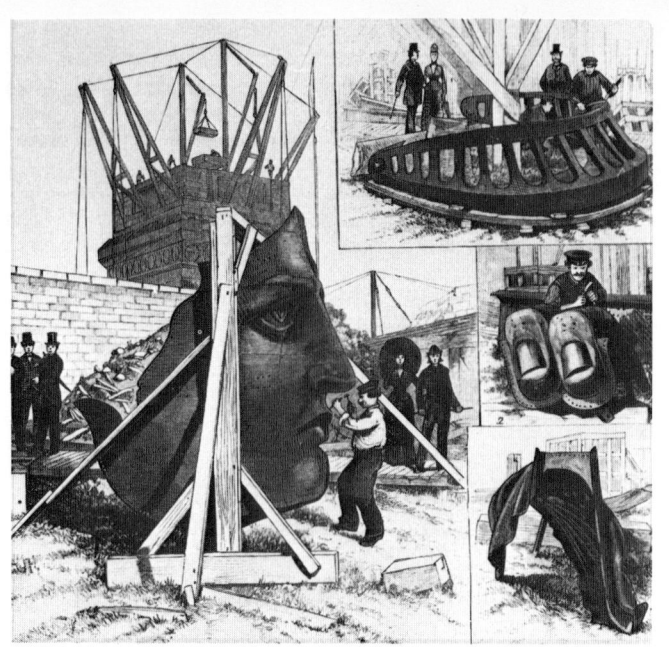

We always think of the Statue of Liberty as a giant — and she does stand 151 feet tall on a stone base and pedestal that add another 154 feet in height. Yet she really is made of pieces. A way to show that is to go back to the 1880's, before she was finished and sent to America from Paris. To the lower right is her forearm and torch, about 35 feet long, exhibited at Philadelphia in 1876. Her head (above) was shown in Paris in 1878. Above (left), Miss Liberty's iron skeleton was visible as she was being erected in Paris in 1884. To the upper right, toes, face and other parts were seen on the island where the statue was completed in 1886.

TRANSPORTATION

MAGIC CARPET NO. 8

New Jersey on the go, a busy state,
From stagecoach to the modern jet.
Our products travel through our docks and ports,
To world-wide destinations set.
   (Repeat Chorus, see page 9)

Walking, horseback, wagons... stagecoaches, steamboats, trains... canal boats, trolleys, cars... buses, trucks, ships... subways, planes, rockets.

Note all of those — and realize that each is (or was) a type of transportation that has moved New Jersey people for the past 350 years. Can you think of more ways to travel? (Come to think of it, we did forget bicycles!).

Our state always has been a transportation hub. Nearly every kind of vehicle ever made has played a role in New Jersey history. There is no better place than our state to learn about ways to get from here to there!

131

STATE ON THE GO

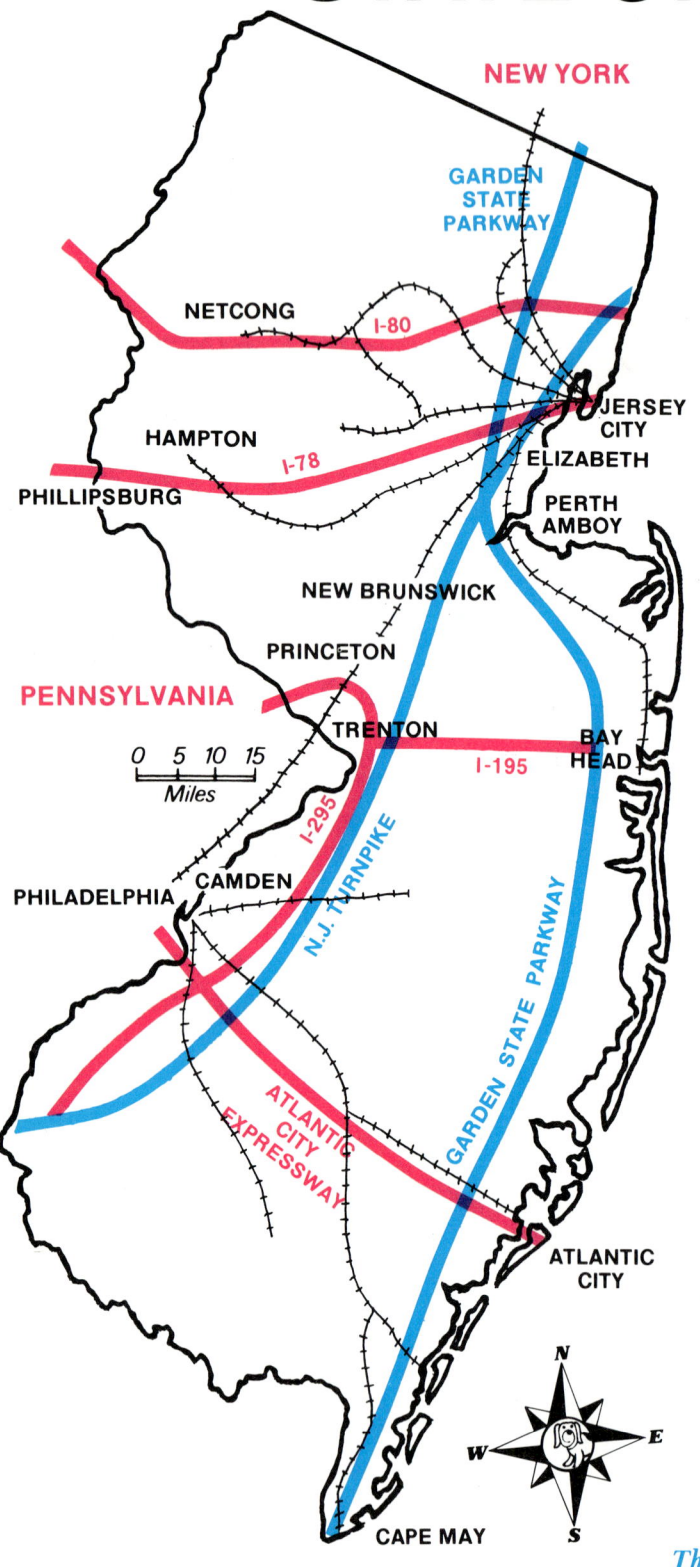

Transportation *always* has been the name of New Jersey's game—and always will be.

The reason is easy to understand. Two deep, wide rivers—the Delaware and the Hudson—are on either side. Both are natural **harbors**.

New York City grew beside the Hudson River, to the east. Philadelphia rose beside the Delaware, to the west. New Jersey was in the middle, able to serve both.

Colonial travelers crossed New Jersey often on the way between New York and Philadelphia. Washington's army traveled through the state many times, to keep the British troops from controlling the two big cities. New Jersey's role as a "pathway" thus began very early.

Today, New Jersey is the busiest travel area in the United States. Millions of people move into, across or over our state every day—by automobiles, buses, trains, boats, planes, bicycles, motorcycles, helicopters, ships and on foot.

All kinds of products move into and out of our state, carried by freighters, oil tankers, trucks, trains and **cargo** planes.

Giant ships each day enter or leave world-famed ports at Elizabeth and

This map shows New Jersey's major roads and railroads. Thousands of smaller roads connect with the big highways. There are also several lesser railroads in the state.

Newark. Cargo is shipped in and out of ports at Camden and Salem.

Hundreds of thousands of trucks move constantly across our highways. Trains carry heavy products. Tankers and barges bring materials to oil refineries and chemical plants.

Let's talk about some good things and some bad things in our state's transportation story.

New Jersey people own about five million automobiles. That is good—except that our roads always need repair. That costs great sums of money.

Our state leads all others in railroad tracks per square mile. Again, that is good—except that fewer and fewer people ride on trains. There are not as many trains as when your father and mother were your age.

Transportation is a big, exciting story. It has been vital throughout all of our history.

It is vital today. If our state and nation cannot move people and products safely and inexpensively, the United States will be seriously crippled.

The handsome ship (top) near Camden is only one part of our state's varied transportation story. Most important are highways. One of the busiest intersections on the N.J. Turnpike (above) is Exit 14 near Newark. The graph (below) helps prove how important automobiles are to New Jersey. Each column shows the number of cars per 1,000 persons. We top the U.S. average and lead New York and Pennsylvania.

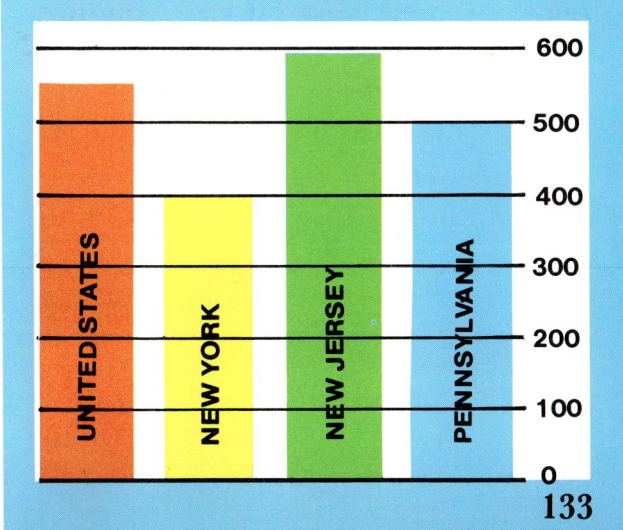

133

ROADS WERE ROUGH

Travel was so important in colonial New Jersey that some of the colony's first laws in 1673 ordered that roads be built to connect all towns.

One important road, started in 1681, connected Burlington and Salem, two Quaker towns. Another, finished in 1684, ran across New Jersey from Burlington to Perth Amboy, then the two capitals of the colony.

Rough roads went westward from Newark to Morristown and beyond to the iron mines in western Morris County. In 1697, a road was started between Cape May and Burlington. It took ten years to finish that highway.

Few roads ran to the Jersey Shore. There were no vacationers in colonial days. The only reason for going to the seashore then was to get fish, clams or oysters.

A few sandy roads were cut through the Pine Barrens. They were merely narrow lanes over which lumber, iron and glass could be brought to villages outside of the woodland.

Every colonial road was crudely built. All were very curved, winding in all directions. They followed narrow Indian paths or wound along the easiest routes over high hills.

There were no colonial road taxes. Instead, the law said all men could be "warned out" to build or repair roads. They received two days "warning." If a man did not show up for the work, he was heavily fined.

"Warned out" road builders usually did not work very hard. Consequently, all highways were muddy messes after spring rains. Ruts were baked hard in the hot summer. Travel was quite easy only in winter, when horse-drawn sleighs whizzed over packed-down snow.

Governor William Franklin knew how bad the roads were. He traveled them often. He wrote in 1766 that New Jersey roads were "seldom passable without danger or difficulty."

Crossing streams created problems. At first, travelers sought shallow places in the rivers. This was called "fording." A crossing place was called a "ford."

Early travelers had problems until ferries were started or bridges built over streams. People on horseback could ride across, and if the river was deep and wide, the horse swam. Those on foot hoped to find shallow places where they could wade to the other side.

Rough little bridges were built over small streams as early as 1690. They were just a few logs thrown lengthwise, wide enough only for one small wagon. Such bridges washed away in high spring floods.

Wide streams were crossed on ferries. These were large flatboats, pushed along with long poles. Ferries ran regularly across the Hudson River to New York before 1670. To the south, an important ferry connected Philadelphia and Cooper's Ferry (now Camden) in 1688.

The first colonial travelers walked or rode horseback. Wagons were difficult to build. The earliest ones were nothing more than heavy boxes with solid wooden wheels. Teams of huge oxen pulled the carts.

Few colonists ventured very far from their own villages in the early years. It was just too slow, too tiresome and too costly.

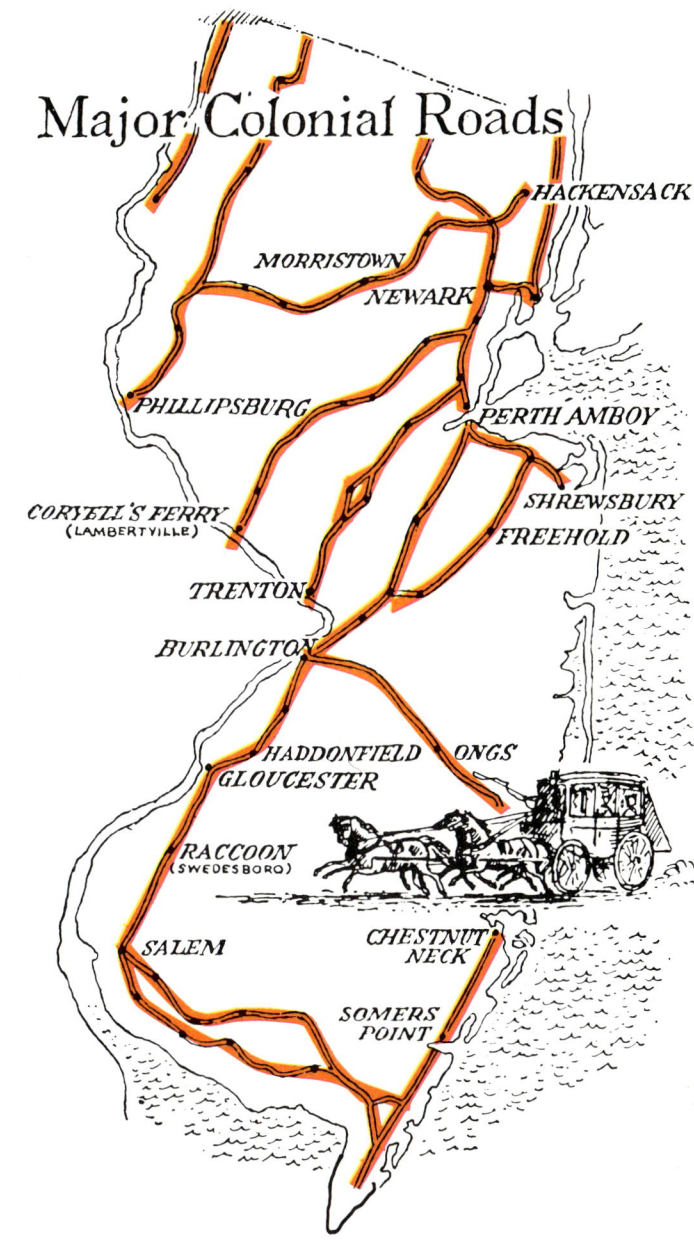

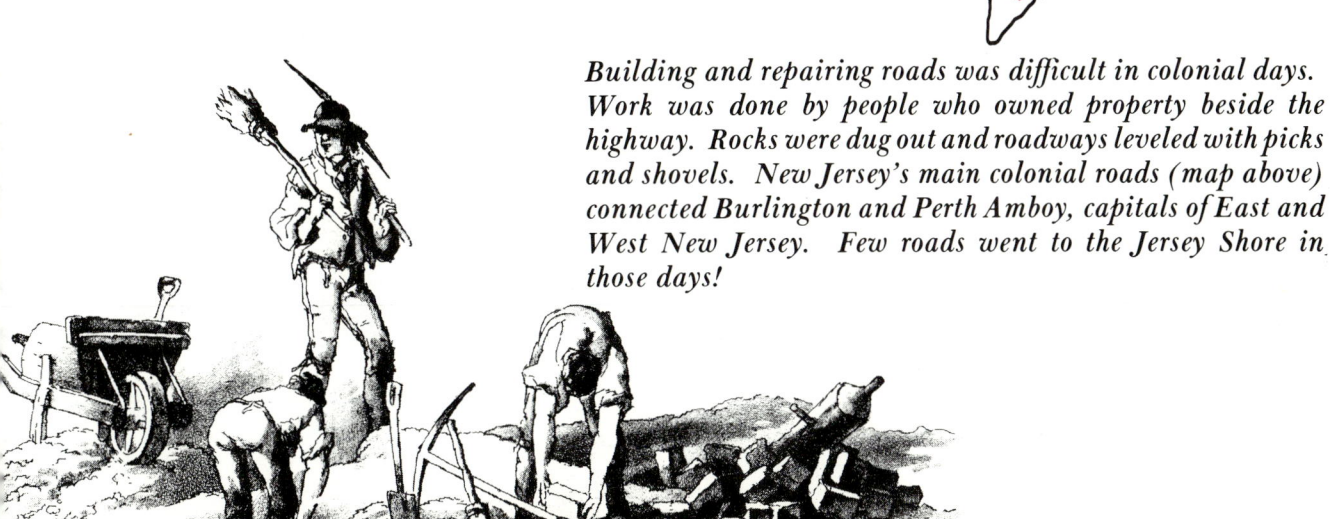

Major Colonial Roads

Building and repairing roads was difficult in colonial days. Work was done by people who owned property beside the highway. Rocks were dug out and roadways leveled with picks and shovels. New Jersey's main colonial roads (map above) connected Burlington and Perth Amboy, capitals of East and West New Jersey. Few roads went to the Jersey Shore in those days!

SPEED FOR TRAVELERS

Travelers heard astonishing news in 1766. A new stagecoach company promised to speed passengers from New York to Philadelphia in two days!

Five years later, operators of a "Flying Machine" (a stagecoach) boasted that they could take travelers from New York to Philadelphia in 1½ days. That promise amazed the colonists.

New Jersey by then had about 65 small towns and about 35 villages. About 100,000 people lived in the colony, all close to roads.

Roads were as poor as ever. Each spring, "repairs" consisted of throwing large stones or tree trunks into the muddy lanes. Only a few roads had occasional wide spaces where wagons could pull out to let other vehicles pass.

Riders feared their stagecoaches might upset on the awful roads. In especially bad places, coach drivers yelled, "Gentlemen to the right!" or "Gentlemen to the left!" Riders leaped from one side of the coach to the other to keep the vehicle from tipping over.

Large rivers still were crossed on ferries. Even a new road built in 1766 from Newark to Paulus Hook (now Jersey City) followed the old practice. Stagecoaches met ferries on the Passaic and Hackensack rivers.

Two long wooden bridges were built over the Passaic and Hackensack rivers in 1795. The Passaic River bridge was 492 feet long, the Hackensack River bridge was 980 feet in length. That speeded up traffic, but only a bit. Stagecoach passengers had to wait for the ferry at Paulus Hook.

The slow travel caused passengers to depend on the colony's many

Every villager loved to hear the call: "The stage is in!" Children watched in awe as the driver slammed brakes on the wheels and reined horses to a stop. Passengers got off for a meal or to stay overnight. A tavern was the center of everyday village life. It was the place to see glamorous strangers, to talk and to attend social affairs. Town government met in the tavern.

Haddonfield's Indian King Tavern, built in 1750, was one of New Jersey's finest old colonial inns. It has been preserved as a State Historic Site. Tavern rules (below) had to be strict. Very few beds were available. "Five to a bed" was not unusual.

Rules of This Tavern

No more than five to sleep in one bed
No Boots to be worn in bed
Organ Grinders to sleep in the Wash house
No dogs allowed upstairs
No Beer allowed in the Kitchen
No Razor Grinders or Tinkers taken in

taverns. These really were like modern hotels. Colonial laws required that every town must have at least one tavern for the convenience of travelers.

Taverns were the village centers. Town meetings and court trials were held there, as well as social events. Visitors stopped for meals or stayed overnight.

Taverns had wonderful names, such as the *Rose and Crown* in Elizabeth, the *Half Way Home* in Bergen or the *Black Horse* in Perth Amboy. The *White Hart* and *Red Lion* were in New Brunswick and the *Sign of the College* was in Princeton. Haddonfield had the *American House* and Bound Brook had the *Bull's Head*. Repaupo's pride was the *Sign of the Seven Stars*.

Brightly-colored signs hung over each tavern entrance. As a stagecoach was about to pull in, the driver blew a huge horn to announce his arrival. As the horses slowed in huge clouds of dust, villagers raced to the scene.

Stagecoach passengers were exciting people. They told of new laws. They might announce the death of some great colonial person. Sometimes a traveler even left a New York or Philadelphia newspaper. This was exciting, since there were no newspapers published in colonial New Jersey.

Travelers crossing the state often arrived in Jersey City or Burlington just as the ferryboat pulled away from the docks. They had to stay overnight.

Since the ferryboat owners also ran the dockside hotels, passengers believed the owners sent boats off early on purpose. They usually were right!

TOLLS AND PIKES

Old ways could not be sufficient in a growing state. By the year 1800, it was plain that some new way of road building had to be found to keep increasing New Jersey traffic from being slowed to a halt.

The colonial method of "warning out" men to maintain roads always had been a failure. In 1800, rapid changes in New Jersey made "warning out" a hopeless thing of the past.

The state's population had pushed over 200,000. That is not much in today's world, but it was a lot of people in 1800.

There were other changes that affected road traffic. Trenton had been made the state capital in 1790. Factories had been built beside the Paterson Falls in 1791.

The big breakthrough came in 1801, when a private company was organized to build a **turnpike** from Elizabeth to Springfield, Morristown, Succasunna, Newton, through Culvers Gap and on to the Delaware River.

A turnpike was a highway that charged each user a toll. Every few miles, the road was closed off by a gate, called a "pike." When a traveler paid the toll, the pike was "turned" (opened). Hence the name, turnpike.

That set off a "rage for turnpikes." About 30 were built between 1801 and 1835. Most were in northern and central New Jersey, the areas of heaviest traffic.

Turnpike surfaces were mostly dirt and gravel. The turnpikes were wider than the old colonial roads. The 25-mile-long Trenton to New Brunswick Turnpike, for example, was 36 feet wide.

Incidentally, that long section of Trenton-New Brunswick toll road cost $65,000 to construct. It would cost at least $50 million to build 25 miles of a modern toll road.

The first turnpike surfaces really were only small improvements. They were still muddy in spring and dusty in summer. The chief virtue was that

One unusual traveler in turnpike days was the "drover." He gathered sheep, pigs, goats, cattle or other animals that his neighbors wanted to sell. He herded them, or "drove" them, to city markets. People knew when a drover was on the way. Great clouds of dust rising above the herd could be seen, even from miles away. When the drover reached a "pike," he paid a toll. Twenty sheep cost six cents.

Drovers were on the road for many days and nights. At nightfall, they herded the animals into special pens in tavern yards. Travelers refused to sleep in the same room with drovers. They claimed a pig or sheep herder smelled like his animals. They were right!

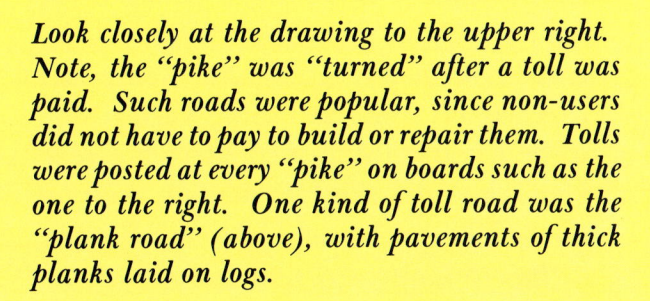

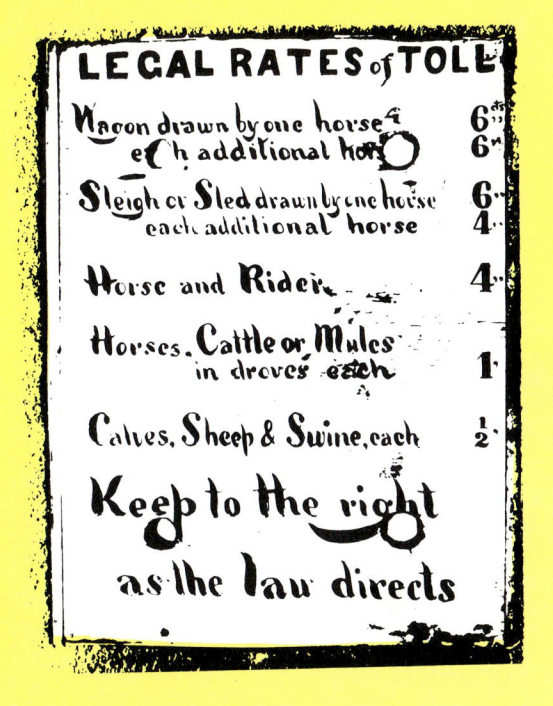

Look closely at the drawing to the upper right. Note, the "pike" was "turned" after a toll was paid. Such roads were popular, since non-users did not have to pay to build or repair them. Tolls were posted at every "pike" on boards such as the one to the right. One kind of toll road was the "plank road" (above), with pavements of thick planks laid on logs.

the roads usually were quite straight.

Turnpike users grew hopeful in 1850, when imaginative builders began constructing roads that used three-inch wooden planks atop a dirt and log base. Most of the plank roads were built in southern New Jersey. They helped to make Mt. Holly and Camden transportation centers.

Called "plank roads," the wooden surfaces were quite smooth—or until the planks began to rot. Travelers were fairly happy to exchange tolls for comfortable rides.

Turnpikes of all kinds lost popularity before 1860. People did not like to pay tolls, especially for rotting wood surfaces or dirt surfaces that were deep mud in rainy weather.

During the great popularity of turnpikes, between 1801 and 1860, many wanted to avoid tolls. They drove their wagons or horses on old back roads. Such a traveler would "shun the pike." One back road from near Summit to Madison is called "The Shunpike" in memory of "shunpiking" days.

139

ALONG THE TOWPATHS

Water always was (and still is) a major means for New Jersey travel. In colonial days, much-used rivers were called **thoroughfares**. Long after the American Revolution, rivers provided the easiest means of transporting farm products.

Between 1800 and 1840, Bergen County farmers carried vegetables to New York in boats. Hunterdon County wheat growers hauled their grain in wagons to New Brunswick, where the wheat was loaded in ships. Cumberland and Salem county farmers sent steer and hogs to Philadelphia on barges.

Water travel was not possible everywhere, especially in northern New Jersey areas where the swiftly-rushing, dangerous mountain streams could not be used to move people or products.

Then, between 1825 and 1835, a means was found to bring profitable waterways to the Bordentown-New Brunswick flatlands and to the northern mountains. The age of **canals** came to New Jersey.

Canals are man-made "rivers" connecting important towns and large bodies of waters. Canals take boats across the land by means of "locks," which are huge water-tight "boxes." Water levels can be changed in a lock, raising or lowering canal boats between natural bodies of water.

New Jersey had two canals. One, the *Morris Canal*, went through mountain land in the northern part of the state. The other, the *Delaware and Raritan Canal*, was dug through the central part of the state.

The Morris Canal was the dream of George Macculloch, a Morristown school teacher. One day, while fishing on Lake Hopatcong, Macculloch imagined that the lake could provide water for a canal westward to Phillipsburg and eastward to Newark and Jersey City.

A company was formed to build the Morris Canal between Phillipsburg and Jersey City. The canal was easier to imagine than to build. Vessels had to be lifted a total of 914 feet between Newark and Lake Hopatcong, then let down 760 feet to the Delaware River.

Thirty-four locks had to be built on the 90-mile-long Morris Canal. Locks were not by themselves enough to conquer the sharply rising slopes.

Engineers cleverly built "inclined planes," which were like small railroads. On hills too steep even for locks, boats were put on rails and towed up the plane to where the land leveled off and water could be used again.

Inclined planes and locks slowed the barges. It took five days to travel from Jersey City to Phillipsburg.

The Morris Canal took six years to complete. Every foot was dug by men or mules. When it was finished, the canal brought coal to factories. It also took New Jersey products to markets. Northern New Jersey boomed.

Results were even more spectacular in the central part of the state, where the Delaware and Raritan Canal route was across level ground. It was easy to construct, with only 14 quite small locks and no inclined planes. The D.&R. Canal linked Bordentown and New Brunswick, by way of Trenton and Bound Brook.

The D.&R. Canal operated until 1932. Much of it, including some old locks, can be seen between New Brunswick and Princeton. Some of its wooden locks and gates are still in place.

These days, people love to paddle canoes on the D.&R. Canal. Many enjoy fishing from the old canal towpath. The canal water is also used by some towns along the route.

Very little is left of the Morris Canal. A small portion can be seen near the reconstructed village of Waterloo. Another part is at Saxton Falls State Park. A high dam in Hopatcong State Park is a reminder of canal days.

The canals have passed into history, but they were amazing while they lasted.

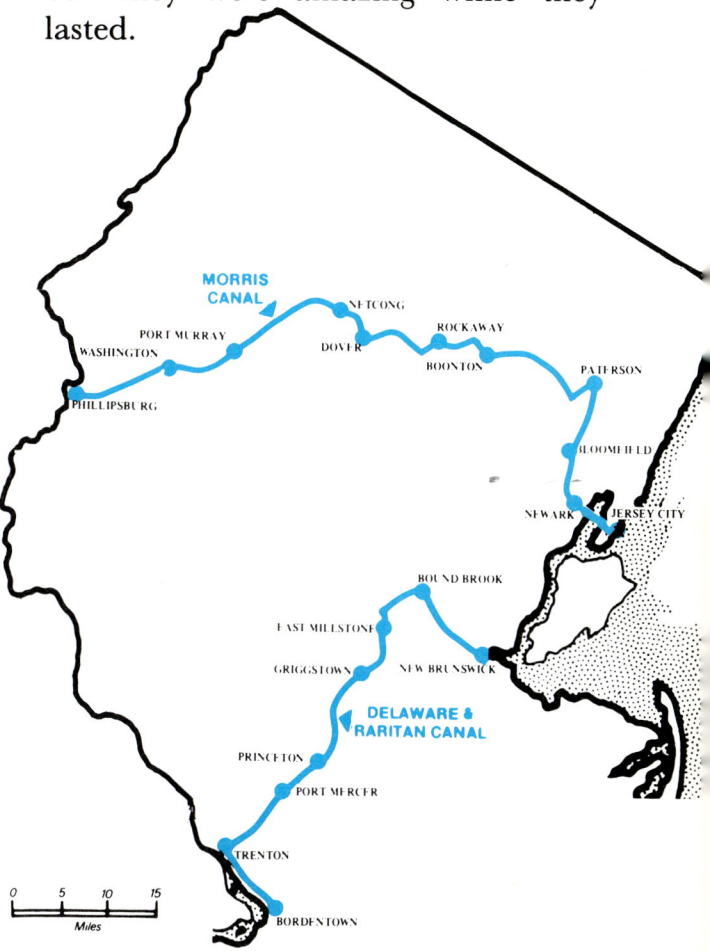

This painting of the Morris Canal shows action at the inclined plane near Wharton. When a barge reached a plane, the mules were unhitched. Then, as you can see, the barge was put in a "cradle" and towed up the inclined plane. The map above shows the routes of New Jersey's two canals.

141

RAILROAD TRACKS

The story never seemed to change. New advances in stagecoaches, in roads, in turnpikes or in canals did not keep up with traffic.

New Jersey was growing fast by 1830. Rough country roads, turnpikes and slow-moving canals were not satisfactory.

Steam was the powerful answer.

Steam power had come to our state and nation in 1786, when a Trenton gunmaker named John Fitch sailed America's first steamboat between Burlington and Philadelphia.

John Stevens of Hoboken heard about the steamboat. He was sure that if steam could move boats, it could also drive land vehicles. In 1812, the state legislature gave him this country's first steam railroad charter (or permission) to build a railroad.

Most people thought John Stevens was crazy. Imagine people riding behind a smoking, snorting locomotive! He kept insisting that everything and everybody could move faster in cars pulled by a steam engine.

Stevens made America's first steam locomotive in 1826. He ran it on a circular track on his Hoboken estate.

John Steven's sons finally made their father's railroad dream come true. In 1832, they ran New Jersey's first railroad train from Bordentown to South Amboy.

Every town wanted a railroad. Tracks began to reach outward to nearly every part of the state. New Jersey grew rapidly beside those expanding railroad lines.

New villages sprang up in former cow pastures or forests. Old villages became towns. Towns grew into cities. Ever-bigger factories, using steam power, were built beside the tracks. The trains brought in coal for the factory steam engines.

This was America's first steam locomotive, planned and built by John Stevens in 1825. It was an experimental run to prove that a steam engine could drive a vehicle. Stevens called it a "steam wagon." The 16-foot-long "wagon" sped along at 12 miles an hour — a bit faster than a horse could run.

142

The first small locomotives burned wood to make their steam. Trains sometimes stopped if the wood supply ran low. Then the train's fireman broke up wooden farm fences or cut down nearby trees to get the locomotive running again.

Bigger locomotives were necessary. Several Paterson companies began making locomotives. Soon the locomotive makers switched fuel from wood to coal. For a short time, Paterson made more locomotives than any other city in the United States.

The first railroads naturally were laid out mainly between New York and Philadelphia. Then, in about 1860, tracks were in place from Hudson County to Pennsylvania's coal mines.

Southern New Jersey's first important rail line was finished in 1854 from Camden to the Jersey Shore. It was called the Camden & Atlantic Railroad.

Builders of the Camden & Atlantic decided to end the tracks at a village on Absecon Island, where there were only 30 tiny houses. The railroad builders changed the village name to Atlantic City. It quickly became America's leading vacation town.

Huge railroad yards and stations were built in Hoboken and Jersey City in the 1850s and 1860s. These were the closest places to New York City, the best market in the world for products brought in by railroads.

A new group of travelers began. They lived in towns within about 25 miles of New York or Philadelphia. These people rode trains to their jobs in the cities and were called **commuters**.

Railroads also encouraged vacation travel. Special trains carried people to the Jersey Shore or to northern New Jersey lakes, usually for one-day "vacations." These were called "excursion trains."

Railroads were the supreme way to travel for nearly 120 years, from about 1840 to 1960. However, in the last 30 years, railroads have become less popular and less used.

Trucks, buses and automobiles have taken away most of the railroad traffic. Some railroads no longer carry passengers. Some rail lines have disappeared entirely.

Railroads of today are far from dead—but they are in very serious trouble.

This newest of trains, fully automated, could operate without humans if necessary. It runs from Lindenwold in Camden County to Philadelphia. Tickets are sold by machines. Train doors open and close automatically.

RUBBER-TIRED WORLD

The first New Jersey automobile began chugging over the roads about 85 years ago. They were really only little "buggies" (as horse-drawn carriages were called) with gasoline engines instead of horses. Naturally, they were called "horseless carriages."

Driving was a real adventure in the early days. Automobiles had no tops to keep out the rain or windshields to stop the wind. Goggles kept dust out of passenger's eyes. Riders wore long coats (called "dusters") to keep dust and mud from spoiling their good clothes.

Engines were noisy and not dependable. Tires blew out every few miles. When people drove more than 50 miles, they carried six or more "spare" tires for the long trip!

Roads were as terrible as ever. Automobiles became stuck in thick mud. Sharp stones exploded rubber tires.

No wonder many horse drivers yelled at automobile passengers: "Get a horse!"

New Jersey was the first state to improve roads for automobiles. History was made in 1912 when our state became the first to pave a road with concrete—at New Village in Warren County.

Increasing numbers of automobiles chugged over the roads in the 1920s and 1930s. Pavements had to be widened. Some roads were widened to three lanes, then a few were made into four-lane highways. Traffic lights were installed at dangerous road intersections.

During the 1930s, New Jersey built the first "cloverleaf" exits on main highways. A cloverleaf permits cars to leave very busy routes in gradual circles. New Jersey also installed the first "jug-handle turns." These highway pulloffs allow drivers to cross main roads on traffic lights.

Today, our state's two best-known roads are the New Jersey Turnpike and the Garden State Parkway. Both were built during the 1950s.

The Turnpike takes drivers between the George Washington Bridge in Bergen County and the Delaware Memorial Bridge in Salem County.

Traffic circles such as this make it easier for vehicles to enter or to leave superhighways. The cartoon to the right calls to mind the fact that New Jerseyans own about 5 million cars — nearly as many as there are in all of the continent of Africa.

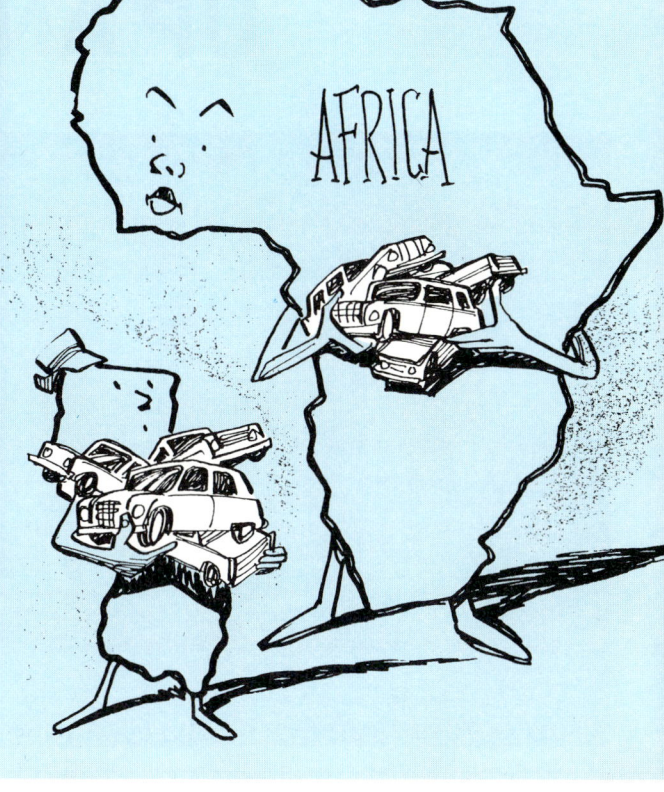

This important north-south road, 132 miles long, carries millions of cars, trucks and buses across the state every year.

People headed for the Jersey Shore know the Garden State Parkway. It is 156 miles long, running all the way from the New York State border to Cape May.

Both the Turnpike and the Parkway are toll roads. Another important toll road is the Atlantic City Expressway from Camden to Atlantic City.

New Jersey also has many miles of interstate highways. These roads have been built with U.S. government funds. They connect states or cities. Some New Jersey "interstates" are Routes 78, 80, 287, 280, 195 and 295.

There are no tolls on the interstates. People in all states pay taxes to maintain these national roads.

All of us now live more and more in the automobile age, especially as towns outward from the old cities get new residents and new industries.

New Jersey has more automobiles—about 5 million—and more licensed drivers per square mile than any other state. Often traffic chokes to a standstill—even on the interstates—because too many cars and trucks are on the roads.

Automobiles are great—but their fumes pollute the air, their engines use precious gasoline and highways cost tremendous sums of money. If driven carelessly, automobiles also can cause death or horrible injuries.

Someday some of you might work on ways to make automobiles more comfortable, safer and cheaper to drive. Anyone who does, will contribute to future happiness.

UP AND AWAY

One of the state's busiest smaller airports is at Morristown. It centers on the quite small control tower (above). Many company-owned planes are based at Morristown Airport. It is busy, but it could fit in one corner of the Newark International Airport (below). This is one of the world's best-known and fastest-growing facilities.

Long ago, you remember, New Jersey people thought they were "flying" when their stagecoaches "sped" from New York to Philadelphia in "only" two days.

Now we easily can go from Newark or Philadelphia to Florida in less than two hours!

The difference is jet planes. Jets whisk us from New Jersey to California in about five hours or take us to distant Hawaii in about ten hours. Some jets can fly around the world in about one day!

Newark International Airport is one of the world's most modern and busiest airports. All kinds of planes use the Newark runways, including the biggest of passenger planes and huge cargo planes that carry freight.

Newark Airport, completely rebuilt since 1973, is one of the fastest-growing air terminals in the United States. About 25 million people fly in or out of the terminal each year.

Perhaps you have been at Newark International Airport to see some one fly away to California, Puerto Rico, Chicago or even to a foreign nation. The terminal is always filled with people. Many passengers are thrilled, for their journeys might be "once-in-a-lifetime" visits to a faraway place.

Many artists, actors, writers, politicians, educators and business people use Newark Airport. A trip to California is no more unusual for them than a trip to the nearest city is for us.

Planes fly out of Newark Airport for other nations. Special long runways are needed for such flights. New Jersey people leaving for overseas also can go to Kennedy International Airport in New York or Philadelphia International Airport.

Airport terminals move people rapidly. Tickets are readied at the long counters. Luggage is quickly carried on or off the planes.

Newark Airport is only one of several New Jersey airports. Other major airports are at Teterboro, Trenton, Camden and Atlantic City.

Atlantic City's Bader Field handles well-known people. Famous singers, musicians, comedians and others fly in to entertain visitors to the city. Leaders of government, including Presidents of the United States, have come through the airport to speak before big conventions in Atlantic City.

New Jersey has about 75 airports. Only a few are large. Some are little more than a runway in a grassy field, where only small planes can land. Some, as "home bases" for business planes, are very busy. A good example of a lively small airport is the one at Morristown.

If jet planes can take passengers around the world in less time than it took to go from New York to Philadelphia in colonial days, who can tell how far and how fast you and your children will fly in the future?

Up, up and away! America's first balloon voyage, from Philadelphia, ended in Deptford in 1793. Helicopters give us traffic reports and carry busy people to appointments. As for jet planes, they soar to world-wide destinations.

147

DOCKS FOR THE WORLD

If you walked along the docks at the seaports in Newark and Elizabeth, you would see coffee and bananas from South America, cameras and TV sets from Japan, shoes from Spain and dresses from Taiwan. You would see automobiles being unloaded from Japan, Germany, Italy, France, Sweden and other nations.

You might see boxes containing textiles from England, pocketbooks from Hong Kong, olive oil from Italy and meat from Australia. You might see cartons of spices from India, cigars from Puerto Rico, cheese from Switzerland and hams from Poland.

American-made products are also on the docks, to be shipped to other countries. You can see products from nearly every state—ready for shipment to London, Stockholm, Tokyo, Rotterdam, Naples and other great **ports** around the world.

Each day, heavily-laden ships come off the Atlantic Ocean and head for New Jersey ports. A few dock in Hudson County. Some head up Delaware Bay to ports in Camden, Salem and Philadelphia.

Most of the incoming ships are on course for Newark Bay, heading to or from the huge Newark and Elizabeth ports.

When a ship is in port, crews swarm aboard to unload the incoming cargo or to load outgoing shipments. Crew members are called longshoremen—short for "along the shore men." Longshoremen use machines and cranes to speed their work.

Most shipping is now done in containers. These are large truck or train bodies, brought to the ports by trucks or trains. The containers are packed at factories so that loading and unloading is faster and safer at the ports.

The Elizabeth port, one of the most modern in the world, was designed especially to handle containers and to use modern machinery.

Foreign vehicles are landed at Newark and Elizabeth. As many as

Seaports at Camden (above) and at Elizabeth/Newark are the busiest, but the state has several other smaller ports. Newark and Elizabeth (right) specialize in "container" shipments. Each container, the size of a truck body or train car, arrives at the docks locked, ready to be lifted aboard ships.

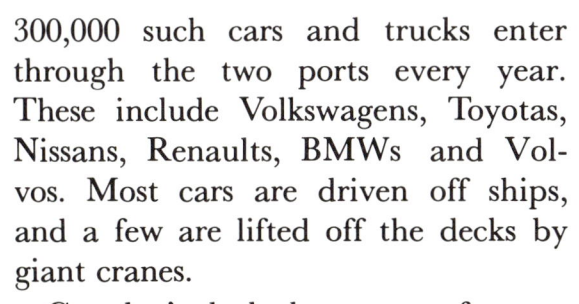

300,000 such cars and trucks enter through the two ports every year. These include Volkswagens, Toyotas, Nissans, Renaults, BMWs and Volvos. Most cars are driven off ships, and a few are lifted off the decks by giant cranes.

Camden's docks have room for special freighters or cargo ships. Interesting products handled at Camden include fertilizers, leather, licorice, food and other goods needed in southern New Jersey.

New Jersey's newest port is at Salem, where development started in 1982. This small port benefits farmers in the southern part of the state because it can handle such crops as soybeans.

Probably the least-known port in the state is the Military Ocean Terminal in Bayonne. It is the largest military shipping center in the world!

The Military Ocean Terminal's docks are jammed with tanks, weapons, trucks, food and everything else that soldiers or armies need. Thousands of army families ship their furniture and automobiles through the terminal.

Another important part of shipping is oil, brought to refineries on **tankers** built to carry petroleum. There are heavy shipments of oil to refineries on the Arthur Kill (Union County) or in Gloucester County on the Delaware River.

The great ships come and go, day and night, bringing to our shores what our nation needs and carrying away what our nation wants to sell. New Jersey ports help to keep our state and our nation great.

Imagine riding one of these old-time ferries across a river such as the Hudson, Delaware, Hackensack, Passaic or Raritan. Animals and humans crowded aboard the little wooden craft.

OVER AND UNDER

Crossing rivers always has been most important to New Jersey people. Early travelers simply waded across the streams in a shallow spot. Then, ferries were started at Hoboken, Jersey City, New Brunswick, South Amboy and Camden.

New Jersey's first really good bridges were not built until about 200 years ago. They were made of wood or stone. Heavy railroad trains later made it necessary to construct iron bridges, set on strong stone pillars.

The Hudson and Delaware rivers always presented the greatest challenges.

For more than 250 years, vehicles could cross from New Jersey to Philadelphia or to New York only on large ferryboats. Trains each day carried thousands of people to and from the ferry docks at Hoboken, Jersey City and Camden.

Some of northern New Jersey's passengers were helped in 1909, when a railroad tunnel was finished from Hoboken to New York. Another railroad tunnel was finished in 1910, allowing trains to run directly into the heart of New York City.

Then, in 1926, bridge building came to the front. That year, the Benjamin Franklin Bridge was opened between Camden and Philadelphia.

Five years later, in 1931, the great George Washington Bridge—a mile long—began carrying vehicles between Fort Lee and upper New York City.

Three other big bridges were built at about the same time between New Jersey and Staten Island, which is part of New York City. These were the Bayonne Bridge, Goethel's Bridge (at Elizabeth) and Outerbridge (at Perth Amboy). Bayonne Bridge is one of the world's longest steel arch bridges.

The Delaware is a river of bridges between New Jersey and Pennsylvania or Delaware. Twenty-five bridges cross the Delaware. (Eleven of them charge tolls.)

The longest Delaware River bridges are the Walt Whitman Bridge at Camden (named for the famed poet) and the Delaware Memorial Bridge at Deepwater in Salem County. The Memorial Bridge takes New Jersey Turnpike traffic over the river to Wilmington, Delaware.

There are many important bridges within New Jersey, itself. Four bridges go over the Raritan River near New Brunswick. Many large bridges cross the Passaic and Hackensack rivers.

Increased traffic between New Jersey and New York led to truck and automobile **tunnels** under the Hudson River. The Holland Tunnel, from Jersey City to New York, was opened in 1927. The Lincoln Tunnel, connecting Weehawken and New York, began receiving traffic in 1933.

Bridges and tunnels eliminated ferryboats on the Hudson and Delaware rivers. All stopped running more than 25 years ago.

These days, bridges and tunnels are very crowded with traffic. Vehicles have long waits every morning and every evening at bridge and tunnel toll booths.

Traffic planners have announced a "new" idea to cope with the traffic lines in northeastern New Jersey. There now are ferryboats back on the Hudson River.

Once many New Jersey bridges were wooden, covered by a roof. The only one of those remaining in New Jersey (far left) is the historic covered bridge at Sergeantsville. These days, great, graceful bridges span our widest streams. The first such modern bridge across the Delaware was the Benjamin Franklin Bridge from Camden to Philadelphia (left). It was opened in 1926. To the right is a tower of the famed George Washington Bridge from Fort Lee to New York.

151

Faster! We must go faster! People always have exclaimed that. Horseback riding beat walking and wooden carts. Stagecoaches of 1755 were called "Flying Machines." America's first steamboat, run on the Delaware in 1786, seemed a miracle.

Turnpikes were an improvement but John Stevens made this country's first railroad locomotive in 1825 to prove there was a better way to go. Canals, opened in 1831, moved products well, but steam railroads were faster after 1834.

Big ferries across the Delaware and Hudson rivers made river crossings easy by 1860. Electric trolleys were great in the 1890s. Automobiles were sensational after 1900. A railroad tunnel under the Hudson eased travel in 1909.

So, we have "sped along." Airplanes made us feel as free as birds. Tunnels and bridges seemed to speed automobile travel. Superhighways were built to move traffic fast. Overhead, jet planes fly faster than the speed of sound. Yet, automobiles often creep along in awful traffic jams. Faster! We have cried that for 350 years. Are we REALLY getting anywhere?

INDUSTRY

MAGIC CARPET NO. 9

*Our state has every kind of industry,
It's varied as from A to Z.
We're leaders in our nation's growth 'n' pow'r,
And research is our specialty.*
　　(Repeat Chorus, see page 9)

Look on can labels or boxes. Look at addresses on truck bodies. Look in the Yellow Pages. Find out where things are made.

You'll be amazed at how many New Jersey places pop up, giving clues to the extent of products made in our state. As a starter, look on a Campbell Soup label.

We'll look now at industry in the Garden State from earliest times. Many people think "industry" means only factories. It really means how people earn livings. It includes sports, office work, entertaining tourists, farming and dozens of other kinds of jobs that New Jerseyans have.

153

INDUSTRY MEANS WORK!

Industry is much more than big factories or oil refineries.

Industry really means the work that people do.

Factories are the **manufacturing** industry. New Jersey also has a *research* industry, *farm* industry, *tourist* industry, *entertainment* industry, *service* industry and other kinds of industries. All are important.

You have just learned about New Jersey transportation. Roads, bridges, shipping, railroads and other types of movement make up the *transportation* industry.

About 3½ million people work in New Jersey industries. Many have jobs that did not exist when your parents were your age. Industries are always changing.

Two good examples of jobs created by new industries would be the *casino* industry in Atlantic City and the Meadowlands *sports* industry in Bergen County.

More than 40,000 people work in the casinos, although the first was not even opened until 1978. Building the casinos created many thousands of new jobs for people in the *construction* industry.

About 4,000 new jobs were created after the Meadowlands racetrack and football stadium were opened in 1976. The basketball and hockey arena started operations five years later. New Jersey's sports industry is very real—and don't forget the big salaries paid to players!

Actually, the casinos and the Meadowlands Sports Complex are themselves only parts of New Jersey's huge tourist industry. Some believe that **tourism** is our largest industry, especially at the Jersey Shore. Millions of visitors enjoy our beaches, boardwalks and casinos. They spend billions of dollars every year. This makes thousands of jobs from Sandy Hook to Cape May.

BIG BUSINESS

This is fun. It is also big business, as part of a huge recreation industry in New Jersey. Workers build the amusement parks, stadiums, casinos and other places where people play. Ticket sellers, ushers and many others are employed to keep a recreation area going. Finally, but just as importantly, we pay our admissions to have fun.

Our state government invests a great deal of money each year to attract visitors to our recreational spots. A special government agency, the New Jersey Division of Travel and Tourism, works to tell people both in and out of our state about all there is to do in New Jersey. You have probably heard or seen their radio and television commercials. Colorful brochures and useful maps are other ways the office "sells" New Jersey. Your class can write to the New Jersey Division of Travel and Tourism at CN 826, Trenton 08625.

Manufacturing is still important in New Jersey, although many of our automobiles, cameras, TV sets, radios and other products are made in foreign nations. It actually costs much less to make a TV set in Japan and ship it to New Jersey.

You might wonder about the words "farm industry." Remember, farmers sell their crops. Many farm fruits and vegetables are used in New Jersey factories to make soups, pizza sauce, ice cream and hundreds of other food products.

Many movies are made in New Jersey. That gives people jobs in what is called the *entertainment* industry.

More and more New Jerseyans work in *service* industries. These are the offices, stores, gas stations and other businesses established to serve the public. None of these manufactures any product.

New Jersey always has had industry. Let's go back to colonial days. Then we'll travel through industrial changes to the present.

Turn the page—and we're off!

This seems more like work! It can be as varied in our state as a skilled Lenox China sculptor (top left) or people running a machine to pack cookies (above). Much of our state's work these days is in "high tech" industry (left), requiring great skills and much study.

BARTER AND TRADE

Industry was very much a part of colonial times. At first, families did nearly all their own work, although they did cooperate to build houses and barns or to lay out and fix roads. They exchanged *labor*, not money.

Soon they began to trade products. If a farmer grew more than enough wheat for his family's use, he might exchange some for a piece of furniture made by a neighbor. A person without an orchard might exchange a day's work for five baskets of peaches.

This system of payment, called **barter**, was industry on a very simple basis.

Elizabeth colonists started in 1664 to make leather from the skins of cattle that had been killed for food. Turning cattle hides into leather was called *tanning*.

When Elizabeth's tanners made more leather than their small village could use, they offered the extra supply for sale. Orders came in, even from miles away. A new kind of New

"Do-it-yourself" was the motto in colonial days. Mothers and daughters made nearly everything used by the family, including soap and candles. Every candle was made by hand (left), usually on spring days when it was cool outside. Apple cider was made in the fall by men and boys (above) with the apples crushed on a horse-powered grinding wheel. The most important colonial industry in New Jersey was making iron. Forges, such as the one on the right, were small. There were many in the colony, some of them started as early as the year 1675.

Jersey industry had begun—*selling* a village product in other colonies.

New Jersey's first important colonial industries were iron and glass. Iron making began at Tinton Falls in Monmouth County in 1675. Then, about 25 years later, colonists discovered iron ore at Succasunna in Morris County.

Workers began digging iron mines in the New Jersey Highlands, especially near Dover. Each iron furnace needed three things: fuel, to melt the iron; fast-running streams, to turn the wheels of the iron factories; and iron ore. The Highlands had all three, since wood from the forests was used for fuel.

Iron furnaces also started in the southern New Jersey Pine Barrens in the 1750s. There was plenty of pine wood, of course, and water. The iron ore was "bog iron," a soft iron "mud" found in stream bottoms.

Incredible amounts of wood were used by the iron industry. Each furnace required 1,000 acres of wood every year.

Southern New Jersey was also the location for another vital industry. America's first successful glass factory was started in Salem County in 1739 by a man named Caspar Wistar, a Philadelphia button maker.

Wistar did not know how to make glass. He sent to Europe for experienced glass blowers. They made glass by melting nearby sands, using hot wood fires. Many Wistar employees founded glass works in other parts of New Jersey and in other states.

The most famous colonial glass family was named Stanger. Seven of the Stanger brothers blew glass for Wistar until 1775, when they opened their own glass furnace in Glassboro.

Iron continued to be a big industry until about 30 years ago. Now, there are no iron mines operated in New Jersey. The "bog iron" works are just crumbling memories. Iron ore can be brought in from other nations cheaper than it can be dug in our state.

It's another story with glass. The Wistar works are gone, but southern New Jersey's big glass industry owes its start to the colonial pioneers.

157

OUT OF THE SMITHY

America's first planned industrial town was Paterson. It was established in 1791 because many of our nation's leaders believed that the United States must manufacture more of its own products. Until then, most goods used by Americans were made in foreign countries.

New Jersey had about 150 towns and villages by 1791. Every village had a blacksmith. His work place was called the "smithy." The blacksmith was a one-man factory. He made all kinds of iron things—horseshoes, "tires" for wooden wagon wheels, hinges, axes and many kinds of tools.

Paterson was founded on a different plan. Using power from the nearby thundering, 70-foot-high falls, the scheme was to operate several large mills. These would make cotton cloth, machines and other products needed by people in the growing United States.

Skilled mechanics were brought to Paterson from Scotland and England to set up the mills. America did not have such skilled persons.

Paterson did not prosper immediately, but within 30 years it was on the way to becoming a mighty industrial center.

A man named Thomas Rogers made a small railroad locomotive in Paterson in 1836. He shipped it to Ohio. By 1860, Paterson was the leading locomotive building town in America.

Other towns also turned to industry. Factories sprang up wherever there was water power.

Newark, Rahway and Burlington made shoes. Newark, Plainfield and Burlington manufactured clothing. Orange was noted for hats. Potteries opened up in Jersey City, Burlington and Trenton. Bricks were made along the Hackensack and Raritan rivers. Newark and Elizabeth shipped out leather products.

Railroads and canals speeded industrial development in the 1830s and 1840s. These new means of transporta-

During colonial days, little children, often eight years or younger, learned a "trade" (carpentry, furniture making, etc.) by watching their fathers or a neighbor at work. Often a boy was "apprenticed" to a tradesman. He worked hard, getting only a room and food. In turn, he learned to draw plans, use tools and make products.

tion brought in coal from Pennsylvania. Factories began to use coal-fired steam engines. Manufacturers did not have to rely only on waterpower.

Iron-making towns thrived beside the Morris Canal. Deep in the Pine Barrens at Batsto, workers turned out iron water pipes for Philadelphia. Southern New Jersey glass factories grew larger.

Lumbering was important, thanks to New Jersey's thick forests. All kinds of lumber were made—planks, beams and boards. Towns along the Jersey Shore and Delaware Bay made fine wooden sailing ships.

More and more people turned from farming to factory work. Since they worked very long days, they had to live close to their jobs. Factory towns soon became cities.

Water power was still important, but steam became industry's main driving force. Thanks to steam power, new towns rose beside the railroad tracks.

Recreation became an industry quite early. New York City people came to Jersey City, Hoboken and Bayonne before 1800. Camden was a favorite fun place for Philadelphia people in the 1830s and 1840s. When a railroad reached Atlantic City in 1854, the Jersey Shore's tourist industry began to boom.

By 1860, New Jersey—and all of America—had changed.

New products were being made. Increasing numbers of people depended on factory jobs rather than farm work. Most people stopped making their own clothing, tools, furniture and other goods.

Factories, not farms, ruled the nation.

This is where big-time industry began in America. Here, the "Great Falls of the Passaic" plunge downward 70-feet. Look at the fast-moving water at the foot of the falls. That means POWER. In 1791, a group of people decided to use that power to run the machines in large factories. They founded a town and called it Paterson. It was the first planned industrial town in all of the United States.

159

TIME FOR TINKERS

Few people noticed young Seth Boyden when he arrived in Newark from Massachusetts in 1815. Even his wife thought he was only a dreamer.

Boyden loved to **tinker** with new ideas. In 1819, he made America's first "patent leather," a shiny kind of leather that is still used. He gave that idea away, and in 1826 made this nation's first malleable iron, which was very easy to shape into products.

Boyden tired of anything, once he knew the secret of making it. He gave up his iron to make the first locomotive that could climb hills. He helped to make the telegraph work. He made his own lenses for a telescope. He experimented with strawberries until he grew berries so large that one could fill a coffee cup.

He gave his discoveries away and died poor. No wonder he was nicknamed "the Uncommercial Inventor!"

New Jersey had many "tinkers" like Boyden. They stumbled on discoveries, often not knowing the true value of their finds.

America was changing, thanks to the tinkers. However, other things were happening, too.

When Paterson brought in mechanics to build factories and machinery, owners of cotton mills asked mechanics' wives to operate mill machines.

Female workers were important. Skilled women were available in 1838, when New Jersey's first silk mill was opened in Paterson. The town soon was called "America's Silk City."

Other New Jersey towns made **textiles**. Large cotton mills were opened in Gloucester City in 1844 and at Millville in 1856.

People wanted silk and fine cotton cloth. They also badly needed rubber overshoes if they wanted to use the muddy streets and sidewalks.

New Jersey's first rubber maker opened his New Brunswick factory in 1839, where workers made 1,000 pairs of rubber overshoes every week. Very soon, there was competition from new Trenton factories.

So many new factories were being built and cities were expanding so fast that demands for bricks zoomed. It was said that cities had "a red look" because of the new brick buildings.

Taller buildings required new kinds of iron beams. A huge Trenton mill

The Trenton Iron Company (above), opened in 1845, was one of New Jersey's earliest big factories. It was started to make rails and other products for railroads. Other towns had similar big factories — Paterson, Phillipsburg, Dover, Camden and High Bridge, for example. Men and boys worked in the iron mills. Textile mills, or places to make clothing (as in the drawing to the right), often were started nearby to employ women and girls.

started making America's first iron beams in 1854. Some of the beams were used in the U.S. Capitol building.

Trenton's reputation as an iron center attracted a famous bridge builder named John Roebling in 1849. He won national attention in 1854 when he constructed a long railroad bridge at Niagara Falls.

Roebling's iron works later planned and built many great bridges—the Brooklyn Bridge, the George Washington Bridge, the Verrazano Bridge, as well as others known throughout the world.

Industry grew steadily. However, most factory products were based on discoveries that tinkers or blacksmiths might accidentally make in their shops.

The age of the tinker was about over. A new kind of person, led by Thomas A. Edison, set out seriously to invent new products.

161

NEW JERSEY'S WIZARD

One of the world's greatest industrial stories began in 1870, when young Thomas Alva Edison came to Newark from Boston. Before Edison died in West Orange in 1931, his remarkable mind had completely changed the way people live.

Born in Ohio in 1847, Edison had only about three months of regular schooling. He began work as a telegraph operator at age 17. At first he was really only a tinker, much like Seth Boyden, trying to improve telegraph instruments.

Edison's great career really began in 1876. That year, at age 29, he established the world's first research laboratory in Menlo Park in Middlesex County. Edison promised to turn out "a major invention every six months or so."

His first important invention at Menlo Park was the phonograph. It was an accident, actually, since Edison really was trying to invent a way to record telegraph messages. His phonograph, invented in 1877, was the "father" of today's record players and tape recorders.

Edison's most vital discovery came in October, 1879, when he perfected the world's first successful electric light bulb. It gave light for 40 hours.

Edison had to invent other products

Thomas Edison was invited to the White House in 1877 to show his new phonograph. Soon, people everywhere loved his invention — some listened in their homes (above). In public, others heard music at early "juke boxes" (right).

162

to make his light bulb useful. He found a way to get electrical power into homes. He invented switches, sockets, even a meter to measure electrical use. After that, he devised small electrical motors used to run machines.

By the time of Edison's electrical inventions, many people believed few new factories would be built. There was little space left beside railroad tracks, where steam-powered factories could be located.

Electrical power freed industry from coal and from railroads. Since electricity was carried through wires, factories could be built anywhere. Industrial buildings could be taller, because the small electrical motors to run machines were very light.

Edison moved his laboratory to West Orange in 1887. His most important discoveries in West Orange were movie cameras and projectors.

Eventually, Edison patented 1,040 inventions, far more than any other person in history. Less than a half dozen of his inventions were made outside of New Jersey.

Imagine a world without electricity, record players, radios, television and movies. True, Edison did not invent radio and television—but neither could work without electricity.

No wonder Thomas Edison was called "The Wizard of Menlo Park." He *should* have been called "The Wizard of New Jersey."

LIGHT'S BIRTHDAY

Early in the evening of Sunday, October 19, 1879, Thomas Edison turned on the current leading to his latest electric bulb. He had done exactly the same things a hundred times before, but earlier bulbs had failed or had been made of materials far too costly for most people to afford.

Others were also trying to invent a practical light bulb. The important word was practical — something that could be sold cheaply and would not be dangerous.

On that October Sunday in 1879, Edison used a piece of thread, hardened in an oven, as the filament. The filament is the bulb's part that actually gives the light. If it worked, an inexpensive bulb could be manufactured.

The light continued to glow. Edison and his associates scarcely dared breathe as it burned for an hour, then two, and on through the night and all next day. It lit up the laboratory for 40 hours before it burned out.

Edison had won! His practical light bulb finally had been born!

163

INDUSTRY GETS BIG

Joseph Campbell packed his first canned tomatoes at Camden in 1869. Isaac Singer manufactured his first sewing machines at Elizabeth in 1873. Raritan Copper Works opened a huge refinery at Perth Amboy in 1895.

You will ask, how are tomatoes, sewing machines and copper related?

All of them were among the industrial giants that ruled New Jersey work for nearly 100 years. In time, nearly one million people would work in the state's thousands of factories.

We now will look at manufacturing from about 1880 to 1960, eighty years when factories were in the era of their greatest production.

As factories became larger, they employed great numbers of **immigrants** who came to America between 1890 and 1915. Since most factories were located in cities, close to where workers lived, the cities grew larger and larger.

Joseph Campbell's Camden tomato factory became so huge that by 1950 Campbell's Soup Company made 10 million cans of soup every day during tomato season. More than 6,000 people worked on the canning lines. Thousands of southern New Jersey farmers sold tomatoes to the company.

Singer Sewing Machine Company workers turned out more than two million sewing machines annually at Elizabeth by the year 1880. That production level continued for another 75 years.

By 1915, several Middlesex County copper works produced more than half the copper made in all of the United States.

There were other huge industries. In 1899, Camden attracted a company named New York Shipbuilding Company. The company (always called "New York Ship") made ocean liners, battleships, aircraft carriers, submarines and other vessels. By 1950, it was one of the world's biggest shipbuilders. By 1960, it was out of business.

When war began in Europe in

Many huge companies that once operated in New Jersey are going, but Campbell soup is still made in Camden. The rich, red tomato paste, with half the water removed, is cooked into tomato soup. Then it is put in cans. Customers who buy the condensed soup need only to "add water, heat and serve."

1914, the United States was cut off from chemicals made in Germany. New Jersey chemists set out to discover Germany's secrets. Their efforts made the state the biggest producer of chemicals in this country.

Historians say that the time from about 1875 to 1950 was the "smoke stack" era. It was said that smoke pouring from factory stacks was the sign of prosperity.

The prosperity was more than smoke. It was also a matter of brains. New Jersey industries attracted people with imagination and skill. As the world changed and people wanted different products, New Jersey industry kept pace.

New Jersey workers earned the reputation of being able to make anything—machines, chemicals, paint, gasoline, automobiles, toys, airplane engines and thousands of other products.

They made light bulbs, medicines and some of the world's first plastics. They made paper, jewelry and dynamite. They made giant bridges, handkerchiefs and fine china. They made radios, televisions and tape recorders.

New Jersey industrialists proudly boasted that "if it's made anywhere, it is made somewhere in New Jersey."

The period of giant factories began to change in New Jersey about 25 years ago. Strict laws were passed to control air and water pollution. Big industries—such as the shipbuilders—moved to other parts of the United States.

Distant countries paid lower wages to workers. Japan and other nations began making our clothing, radios, TV sets, cameras and many other things that we use every day.

Industry was transformed. If the legendary Rip Van Winkle had fallen asleep in New Jersey 25 years ago, dreaming of industry, he wouldn't believe his eyes when he opened them today!

Thirty-five years ago, the doll heads shown above were just a few of the 1½ million made annually in a Trenton factory. Now the doll maker is gone. Also gone is the giant Camden shipbuilder that could turn out vessels such as the Savannah, shown below sliding down to the Delaware River in 1959. It was the world's first nuclear-powered cargo ship.

165

WE MAKE IT!

Factory production has gone down in New Jersey in recent years, although about 750,000 men and women still work in manufacturing.

Consider some of the facts:
- A factory in Jersey City makes spaghetti by the mile—hundreds of miles of it every week.
- A coffee plant in Hudson County roasts enough coffee every day to make millions of cups.
- Millions of Band-Aids are made in New Jersey.
- New Jersey bakeries turn out a million loaves of bread every week.

Glass factories in Cumberland County turn out huge quantities of bottles every day.

Automobiles are made in Edison and Linden.

New Jersey refineries make about 600,000 barrels of gasoline every day.

About 1 million Little League bats are made each year in Kearny.

Spaghetti, coffee, bread, bottles, automobiles, gasoline, Little League

New Jersey industries produce some of nearly everything that is made in the United States. These pages are just a sample. Nearly one million aluminum bats are made in Kearny each year. Many firms make spaghetti and other pasta. Above, an inspection makes sure that not even a speck of dust remains on one of the hundreds of thousands of automobiles made here. On the opposite page, you can see a bit of the modern "high tech" industry, along with a view of the huge oil refinery at Linden. Not least of all, New Jersey is home to one of the largest flag makers in the world.

bats: all made in New Jersey. That's just a tiny start, too! Manufacturing goes on.

Keep in mind that our state is the fifth smallest. But New Jersey is:

First in making medicine.

Second in producing chemicals.

Fifth in making rubber and plastics.

Sixth in turning out scientific and medical instruments.

Seventh in food products! *Seventh* in making china and glass. *Seventh* in producing leather and leather products! *Seventh* in making clothes.

Ninth in making paper, cardboard and boxes.

New Jersey's industrial story is tremendous. One way to understand it is to see what is made near where you live. Ask your parents or neighbors where they work. Ask what they make.

Look for New Jersey place names on can labels or on boxes. Look for New Jersey addresses on the side of trucks. Look at advertisements in magazines and newspapers. Find New Jersey products.

Manufacturing is not all "big." Did you know that all M & M candies are made in New Jersey?

Manufacturing is a big, exciting, interesting world. And, some day, it is where many of you will work.

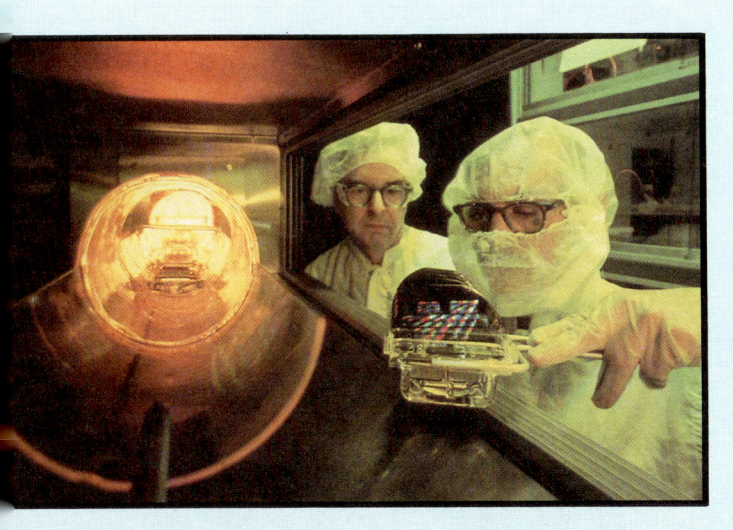

167

HOUSES OF MAGIC

Suppose that someday you could fly to the moon, live to be 150 years old and have a TV receiver only as big as a dime?

None of these is impossible. Scientists in New Jersey's hundreds of research laboratories may find the way. They are exploring the mysteries of space. They seek products to make living more enjoyable. They even study the secrets of life itself.

New Jersey has about 500 research laboratories. They employ more than 85,000 men and women.

A magazine article once referred to New Jersey's research laboratories as "Houses of Magic." Some of their discoveries *do* seem like magic!

You know that little radio that you use to hear rock stars or ball games? It depends on a marvelous discovery called the transistor. It was developed in New Jersey.

When your grandparents were your age, radios and TV sets were very large. There were no spaceships. The power to run a spaceship would have made it as heavy as a railroad train. It could not have been lifted into orbit.

Because transistors are tiny, radios now are very small. Spaceships, using transistors, are light enough to be blasted off.

The transistor is almost magic. Many scientists believe it is one of the greatest inventions in all history.

The transistor was patented in 1947 at Bell Laboratories in Murray Hill, New Jersey. This is one of the world's greatest research laboratories. Hundreds of scientists work there. Bell Laboratories also has research centers in Holmdel and Whippany.

A few of the other great national companies with large research facilities in New Jersey are Exxon, DuPont, Johnson & Johnson, Ciba, Mobil, RCA, Hoffman-LaRoche and Sandoz. Remember, these are just a *few*.

Nearly every area of New Jersey has research laboratories. Some are large.

Research is hard, constant work. Time after time, even thousands of times, experiments are performed without success. Then, sometimes when not expected, a mystery is solved.

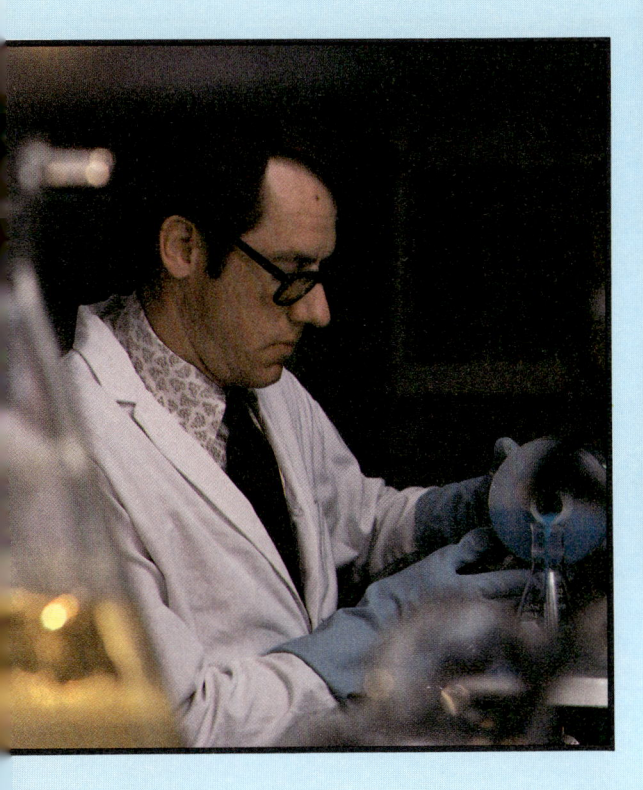

Imagine actually having the thrill of visting one of New Jersey's research laboratories! You would hear of the thoughts, the planning and the care that must be given to all experiments. Few visitors see the lab interiors, however. Scientists often work alone. They must concentrate. Often their work is highly secret.

Most are quite small. Scientists study many things: How to cure illness. How to make travel easier and safer. How to make vegetables grow better. How to improve TV pictures. How to make food better.

One huge southern New Jersey research establishment at Pomona, near Atlantic City, is the National Aeronautics Facility Experimental Center—called NAFEC for short.

NAFEC scientists study all kinds of flying problems. Their experiments make air travel safer.

Many great medicines and vitamins have been developed in New Jersey pharmaceutical laboratories. There is still much work to be done in the hope to make all of us live longer and healthier lives.

Many of New Jersey colleges and universities have major research programs. Rutgers is known for its research in medicine. Dr. Selman Waksman, one of its noted professors, invented a "wonder drug" called streptomycin.

Princeton University carries on many research programs. Some deal with space exploration. Princeton scientists also study such things as nuclear power, health and air travel.

The Armed Forces operate giant research laboratories in our state. One of the great military electronics research centers is at Fort Monmouth near Eatontown.

There probably is a research laboratory within 10 miles of your home or school. Perhaps you know a man or woman who works in one. Wouldn't it be great if a researcher could visit your school to tell you more about his or her work!

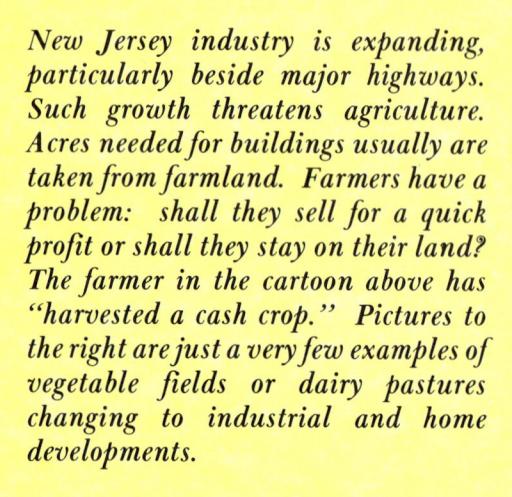

New Jersey industry is expanding, particularly beside major highways. Such growth threatens agriculture. Acres needed for buildings usually are taken from farmland. Farmers have a problem: shall they sell for a quick profit or shall they stay on their land? The farmer in the cartoon above has "harvested a cash crop." Pictures to the right are just a very few examples of vegetable fields or dairy pastures changing to industrial and home developments.

AGRICULTURE

MAGIC CARPET NO. 10

*We're proud to live within our Garden State,
Where farming means variety.
Crops and dairy products meet our needs,
In both the home and factory.*
   (Repeat Chorus, see page 9)

Look around New Jersey. This year's corn field often becomes next year's site for office buildings or condominiums. Farmland is disappearing.

Yet our state still has about 850,000 acres of farm land. These are acres that produce vegetables and fruits, acres where cows and chickens are being raised, acres where horses are kept and flowers are grown.

It is not easy being a farmer, in New Jersey or anywhere else. Some people DO stay on the farms. They stay in business by using marvelous machines and by using their brains.

THE BEST OF FARMERS

New Jersey still has about 850,000 acres of farmland, in every one of the 21 counties. About one-sixth of the state is farmland.

Is there *really* farming in New Jersey? That is a fair question. Consider some quite amazing facts:

- New Jersey is second among all states in harvesting *blueberries* and third in producing *cranberries* and *spinach*. It is fourth in *peaches* and *asparagus*, fifth in *snap beans* for canning or freezing and fifth in *tomatoes* for sale in markets.
- New Jersey farmland has the second highest value per acre in the United States.
- New Jersey still has large numbers of *milk cows*, *pigs*, *beef cattle*, *sheep* and *chickens*.
- Raising of *horses* has become a very important New Jersey activity.
- Vegetable fields and orchards still flourish, especially in southern New Jersey.

In New Jersey, only one person in 100 workers labors on a farm. Yet what would we do without farmers?

Farms give us food. Food is as necessary as anything in our lives. Farms also give New Jersey beauty. Our "picture postcard" areas are farmlands.

If you live on a farm, you probably know how hard the work is. You have probably pulled weeds or helped to clean out barns. Farming is never easy.

Most people, if they had a choice, would probably rather live on a farm. They would have clean air, open spaces and lots of good fresh food!

Imagine using the most expensive farmland in the United States to grow vegetables or to raise chickens and cows.

Imagine preferring to work long, hard days when a real estate buyer might offer to make you a millionaire by purchasing your valuable farm acres.

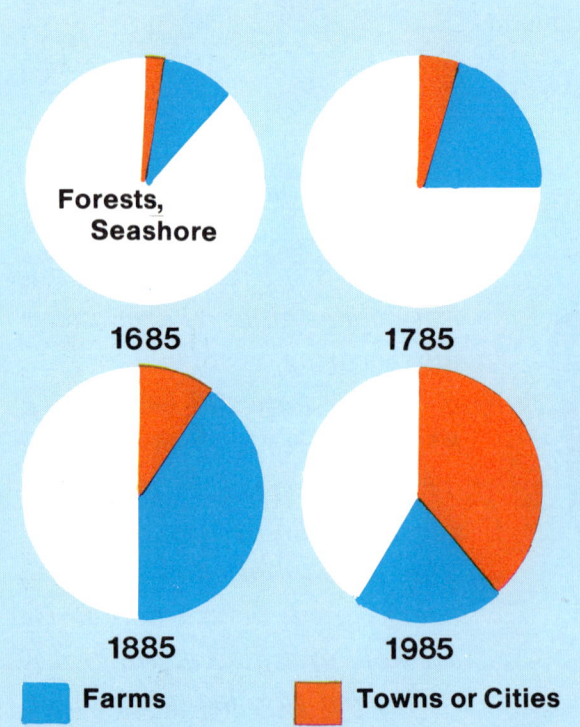

Most New Jersey land in 1685 was unused wilderness. By 1785, farming was becoming important. It was even more important in 1885, although towns were growing. In 1985, towns, cities and industries were using up much once-open land.

The temptations to sell are very high. Each year thousands of farm acres are sold to builders who put up office buildings or homes.

Fortunately, New Jersey still has more than 9,000 farmers who have chosen to remain on their land. They stay in business by using their brains, muscles, good sense and imaginations.

They use unusual new machines to plant seeds, to harvest crops and to tend their animals. Many use computers. New Jersey's farmers are as up-to-date as any in the world.

Staying on the farm involves risks. Weather can be too cold—or too hot. There can be too little rainfall—or too much. Insects can ruin crops, birds can eat seeds at planting time, diseases can strike.

Cheers, then, for those who stay!

New Jersey's agricultural land has been shrinking steadily for the past 20 years. Superhighways push across acres that have been farmland for more than 200 years. Home builders and industries follow those highways, seeking land.

Farm acres have risen sharply in value—up to $50,000 or more per acre near the highways. Many farmers could have taken the quick "cash crop" but have decided that they like to be farmers in spite of the problems.

If anyone asks whether we are really "The Garden State," show them this beautiful vegetable field at Great Meadows, in Warren County. Long, hard hours are required to keep a field in this condition. Fertilizer must be applied, weeds controlled, and, above all, the rows must be irrigated during rainfall shortages.

TIME TO SPECIALIZE

Colonial farmers worked extremely hard, but at least they did not have to worry about having enough land or how to sell their crops.

Once the colonists cut down the forests, they had more than enough acres for their vegetables, fruit trees and livestock.

One cow supplied milk, butter and cheese for a family. Four or five hogs provided meat for a year. A half dozen sheep supplied enough wool for family clothes. Ten trees gave ample fruit. One acre supplied vegetables for a family.

Farmers raised their own grain and hay to feed their cattle. They grew flax to make cloth.

Colonial farmers all started from scratch, however. Nearly all their seeds, fruit trees and animals had to be brought to this country from other nations.

Farmers grew careless about the land. They knew very little about fertilizing the soil. If their soil was ruined by too much harvesting, they simply moved to a new area.

Then, about 125 years ago, changes came. Larger factories became more numerous. Cities grew up around the factories. Young men and women left the farms to get better wages in the factories.

Farmers had to **specialize**, partly because they had less help and partly because people in the new cities provided good markets for farm crops. City families bought "Jersey" fruit, vegetables and milk or eggs. "Jersey-grown" became a famous measure of quality.

Some farmers raised only cows or chickens. Some specialized in sheep or hogs. Others grew only vegetables or fruit.

"All-purpose," or "self-contained," farms—where farmers grew everything that they required—have disappeared. Today's farmers specialize in only one or two types of products for marketing.

That kind of farming can create problems. Specialized farmers must buy other farm products. If they raise only chickens, they must buy chicken feed and additional harvests from other types of farmers.

New Jersey farmers have constantly changed their ways of planting and harvesting.

TODAY'S FARMER

Pumpkins! Thousands of luscious pies could be made from the harvest in this field! Or, if carving jack-o'-lanterns appeals, this field could supply pumpkin faces enough to light up a good-sized town or city!

This Morris County pumpkin grower is a specialist. His harvest time is in October, when the crop is ready for Halloween. Harvesting also supplies enough pumpkins for Thanksgiving Day pies.

Specialization keeps many farmers in business. A few grow Chinese vegetables for sale in nearby cities. Some grow special flowers or fruits. Specialization can be risky if the weather turns bad or if the market for the speciality disappears.

For example, when people began to build factories and home developments on what had been farmland, they needed evergreens, flowers and shrubs to beautify their properties. Nearby farmers grew them.

Another example of farm change is the great increase in New Jersey horse farms. Balancing that, the total of chicken farms has dropped sharply.

New Jersey farmers face competition. Forty years ago, New Jersey had 35 to 40 farmers specializing in rose growing. Farmers from other states began to ship in roses and sold them cheaper than New Jersey growers. Now only two rose growers are left.

Farm specialists must always be on the lookout for changes in public desires. If the farmer can forecast what people will eat—and can get his crop harvested in time—he is sure to succeed.

A typical farmer of 200 years ago (above) raised nearly everything that his family needed. He did not sell to others, although sometimes produce was traded. In the picture below, taken in 1922 at Swedesboro, farmers were loading their vegetables on trains for sale in Philadelphia.

COWS AND CHICKS

When we think of farms, we usually think first of cows and chickens. Perhaps that is because the farmers that we see on TV usually milk cows or collect eggs.

Milk and eggs are important in the New Jersey farm picture. Yet neither is nearly as important as when your parents were boys and girls.

New Jersey has about 35,000 cows, such as these on a Sussex County farm. Most New Jersey milk cows are black and white Holsteins. Such cows produce large quantities of milk. Once there were more than 160,000 cows in the state. Dairy farms slowly are being sold, often for industries or home developments.

EGGS FOR SALE

Here are some of the half billion eggs laid each year by New Jersey hens. The largest egg producer in the state is in Warren County. There are about one million chickens in that one location!

Many poultry farms have 30,000 or more chickens. New Jersey farming goes out beyond the hen "houses" and the fields. For example, the egg farmer has to have the product processed and sold. This is called "agribusiness," a combination of the skills of farmers, processors and sellers.

For most of our state's history, cows and chickens played the biggest roles in our Garden State's agricultural story.

In 1955, New Jersey had 160,000 milk cows. They produced more than 500 million quarts of milk each year!

That same year, the state's chicken farmers had 18 million hens. These laid 2.7 billion eggs each year! New Jersey was the leading egg producer in the United States.

Now let's see what has happened in about 30 years.

There are still slightly more than 35,000 milk cattle in the state. If cows were people, that would make quite a city.

Those 35,000 cows—*one fifth as many as in 1955*—produce 250 million quarts of milk a year, about half the production of 1955. The chief reasons for the higher output per cow are better food and better care.

That's a lot of milk. It could provide about seven quarts of milk a day for every fourth grader in New Jersey. Fortunately, there also are lots of adults to help drink it!

Additionally, New Jersey industries also use a lot of the milk to make ice cream, cheese, yogurt and butter.

Let's switch from cows to chickens. The changes have been dramatic since 1955.

Many chicken farms have been sold to housing developers. At the same time, many doctors have said that eating too many eggs might cause problems in blood circulation or for the heart.

People ate fewer eggs. Soon, New Jersey had far too many chickens and far too many eggs. Prices fell very low. Many chicken farmers were ruined.

Now there are about two million hens in the state. Most of them are White Leghorns, a fine egg layer. Those Leghorns produce nearly 500 million eggs every year.

Several huge farms in the state each have more than 30,000 chickens. *Salem, Cumberland, Warren, Hunterdon* and *Monmouth* are leading chicken counties.

Most chickens spend nearly all their lives in cages. They are fed and given water by automatic machines. Their eggs roll out of the cages and are collected by other machines.

Chickens are down, but not beaten. A half billion eggs would make some omelet!

FRUIT IN THE BASKET

Nothing is more delicious than ripe New Jersey peaches—unless it is tasty New Jersey apples, blueberries, strawberries or cranberries.

Fruit orchards are found in most parts of the state. Blueberries and cranberries grow best in southern New Jersey, thriving in sandy soil that once was thought to be worthless.

Peaches give New Jerseyans a chance to boast. Our state is the fifth biggest grower of peaches in the United States. Our farmers each year pluck about 80 million pounds of fruit from 1.3 million peach trees.

Warm winters, spring frosts and early summer hailstorms are hazards for peach growers. After blossoms survive spring frosts, as they usually do, fruit appears. The first New Jersey peaches are picked about July 10, the last in late summer.

Our peaches have wonderful names: *Early East, Sunhigh, Jerseyland, Red Haven* and *Rio-osogem.* "Jersey" peaches deserve to be famous.

Apples also must survive frosts and hailstorms. The earliest varieties are picked in late June. Our real apple harvest comes in the autumn. Cool weather and crisp apples seem to go together!

New Jersey orchards yield about 80 million pounds of apples every year. Think of all the pies that could make! *Red Delicious* is our best-known apple variety.

Gloucester County is the main county for both peaches and apples. Other leading fruit counties are *Monmouth, Burlington, Atlantic, Cumberland, Salem* and *Camden*. Apples and peaches probably are picked not far from where you live.

Blueberries! A perfect name for a perfect fruit! These berries are native to the New Jersey Pine Barrens.

Cultivated blueberries are bigger and sweeter than wild varieties. The luscious fruit is harvested on big areas in Atlantic and Burlington counties. One blueberry grower in Atlantic County harvests more than five million pints each year.

Our state ranks second among states in growing cultivated blueberries. Michigan is first. About 20 to 25 million pints of blueberries are picked each year in New Jersey.

Cranberries are New Jersey's reminder that Thanksgiving Day is almost here. The rich, red cranberries are almost as much of a Thanksgiving symbol as the turkey.

Indians picked and ate cranberries. The fruit was not really cultivated until about 135 years ago. Cranberries grow in damp bogs in Ocean, Atlantic and Burlington counties.

Once cranberries had to be harvested by hand. Now marvelous machines must be used to help in the picking. So many cranberries are grown in New Jersey that our state ranks third. Only Massachusetts and Wisconsin harvest more.

New Jersey grows other fruits—especially *strawberries* (about two million pounds a year). Our farmers also produce *grapes, pears, currants* and *quinces*.

Peaches, apples, blueberries, cranberries, strawberries and pears: New Jersey is a regular *fruit bowl*!

The "fruit bowl" is closer than you know! Some farmers permit visitors to "pick-your-own," with prices being a bit lower than in a market or store. You do the work—but you also have the fun!

It's harvest time in the Burlington County cranberry bogs. Unusual machines, shown here, are run through the bogs. Cranberries are shaken loose from bushes and float atop the water. Other workers, using long, wide boards, push the floating red fruit toward waiting trucks. They really are "rounding up" cranberries!

ASPARAGUS TO ZUCCHINI

Every year, on or about March 1, farmers in southern New Jersey begin planting onions and spinach in their rich earth.

Some of those same farmers are in the fields as late as early December, harvesting the last spinach leaves.

In between, they plant and harvest almost every kind of vegetable from asparagus to zucchini.

Vegetables are a healthy part of the New Jersey farm story. You have eaten some—*sweet corn, tomatoes, asparagus, lettuce, onions, sweet peppers* and many more.

People want vegetables grown on nearby farms. Thus, about 50,000 acres of New Jersey farmland are used to grow vegetables. A football field is about one acre in size.

Most New Jersey growers sell to the "fresh markets." These are where we can buy vegetables soon after they are harvested, rather than canned or frozen. About 80 percent of our state's produce is sold in the fresh markets.

Fresh markets include roadside stands, supermarkets and the "farmers markets" that are found in most cities. Vegetables and fruit are brought directly from fields or orchards to the farmers markets.

Small vegetable farms of one or two acres still exist near cities and towns. These farmers stay in business because shoppers want vegetables to be as fresh as possible. They are willing to drive to the farm to buy farm harvests.

Some farmers grow special kinds of vegetables—used in Oriental foods, in "health foods" and for gourmet cooking.

Sweet corn is the state's biggest vegetable crop. *Tomatoes* are next, followed by *sweet peppers, lettuce* and *spinach*.

Twenty years ago, a huge portion of southern New Jersey tomatoes, beans and other vegetables went to nearby canning factories or freezing plants.

That situation has changed greatly. Most of the canning plants have closed. The largest, Campbell's in Camden, now buys most of its tomatoes from other states.

There still are some big canneries, however. Some make sauce for spaghetti or pizza. Some use tomatoes for soup. Others put spinach, beans or corn in cans. An important factory in Cumberland County freezes and packs vegetables.

Vegetable farmers use unusual machines to plant in the springtime and to harvest when the vegetables are ready. Machines pick corn, har-

SUMMER'S RICHES

There is nothing quite like summer harvest time in southern New Jersey. Workers and machines swarm into the great vegetable fields, gathering vegetables of nearly every kind and shape. Harvests are huge — look at those beans (left), pouring down a chute! Baskets of peppers pile up on trucks (right). Corn is a special New Jersey treat, plucked while it is still wet with the morning's dew. There are always tomatoes, picked by the thousands and sent off to market for your enjoyment and mine.

vest beans, dig potatoes and even pluck tomatoes.

Most of New Jersey's vegetables come from *Cumberland, Burlington, Gloucester, Atlantic, Salem* and *Monmouth* counties.

Vegetable growing is hard work. Seeds or plants must be in the ground at exactly the right time. The soil can't be either too cold or too warm. Harvests begin in May and June, just as the sun starts to get hot.

Fields must be **irrigated** in dry weather. Some years, however, the fields get too much rainfall. That is dangerous. It might flood the acres or wash out tiny plants or seeds. If too much rain comes at harvest time, vegetables rot in muddy rows.

Some years, prices are so low that farmers lose money. Insects and plant diseases are always difficult foes that might strike at any time.

So, next time you bite into a tasty vegetable, give thanks to New Jersey farmers whose labor brings us the riches of the fields.

TO RIDE AND TO RACE

When your grandfather and grandmother were your age, nearly everyone thought horses would not be useful much longer. It seemed automobiles, trucks and tractors would make horses almost unnecessary in our country.

The horses fooled everyone!

Now there are far more horses in New Jersey than there were when even your *parents* were boys and girls!

A hundred years ago, horses pulled wagons, carriages and streetcars. They pulled plows and hay wagons in the fields. Nearly every family owned at least one horse.

Horses in those old days were absolutely necessary. Today's horses are kept for sport or pleasure.

Horses began their "comeback" about 60 years ago. New race tracks were built in Monmouth, Camden and Atlantic counties. Farmers near the tracks began to breed and raise *thoroughbreds*, as racehorses are called.

Other New Jersey farmers raised *standardbreds*, the horses that pull little two-wheeled carts in trotting competition at race tracks.

Thoroughbred and standardbred farms are huge in New Jersey. One in Atlantic County covers 3,500 acres! Several others are more than 1,000 acres in size.

The raising of race horses has increased greatly since 1976, when the new Meadowlands Race Track was opened at East Rutherford.

There are many kinds of horses in New Jersey other than the thoroughbreds and standardbreds. Non-racing horses belong to people who ride for

New Jersey has nearly 60,000 horses galloping across our state. Many of them are very valuable, such as these trotters performing at the Meadowlands Race Track. Other horses are raced with riders in the saddle. This is called thoroughbred racing. Race horses are important, but most New Jersey horses are used personally for riding in fields or on bridle paths in woodlands.

pleasure in their own fields or along bridle paths in parks.

Here are some of the recognized main breeds being raised in New Jersey:

Thoroughbred, Standardbred, American Saddlebred, Appaloosa, Palamino, Arabian, Half Arabian, Morgan, Crossbred Pony, Pinto, American Quarter Horse, Paint Horse, New Jersey Bred Hunter, Welsh Pony, Shetland Pony and the *Trotting Bred Pony.*

That totals 16 different official breeds. There are also many kinds of "crossbred" horses and ponies that are not officially registered.

It is easy to get information on all the breeds listed above. Some reference books might tell you that most of these breeds are found "mainly in the West." Plenty of each can also be seen in New Jersey!

Farms where horses are raised are beautiful. Long rows of white fences run beside the roads. Behind the fences, the valuable horses feed. When the spirit moves them, they race one another just as frisky children might do.

Horse farms are especially wonderful in the spring. That is when newborn foals stretch their long, spindly legs as they stand up beside their mothers. The foals soon learn to trot. Then they race their mothers across the pastures.

Big horse farms have their own practice tracks. Horses work out every day, preparing for races. All owners of thoroughbreds look forward to racing on New Jersey tracks.

Some horse farms were dairy farms not long ago. Owners began to raise horses when running dairy farms proved to be too expensive.

Many horse shows are held in New Jersey every year. Some feature horse care by boys and girls as well as riding competition for young people.

When the automobile first appeared about 85 years ago, people laughed at the feeble little cars and yelled, "Get a horse!"

More and more these days, people are saying, "Get a horse!" But they don't mean it the same way!

OLYMPIC RIDERS

The "Horse Capital" of the United States is at Gladstone in Somerset County. That is where the official United States Equestrian Team has been training since 1962.

The Equestrian Team stable headquarters is in a stable that cost $1 million to build about 80 years ago. It would take about $6 million to replace the structure today.

About 30 horses are permanently stabled at the farm. Some of the riders are young high school students who live nearby. The Equestrian Team represents the United States in the Olympics. It also travels to many nations to take part in riding competitions.

FARMING FOR BEAUTY

New Jersey has many farmers who stay in business by growing or raising very special crops or unusual animals.

Some farmers grow only flowers. Some sell full-grown trees. Some tend sheep, goats or pigs. A few keep bees to make honey. Some plant fields of lawn grass to be sold as squares or sod. Others are **ornamental** farmers.

New Jersey's flower farmers are special. Three kinds of flowers each bring growers more than one million dollars annually—*chrysanthemums, geraniums* and *poinsettias*. A greenhouse full of red poinsettias at Christmas time is a marvelous sight.

Flower farmers raise some of their blooms in fields. Most of the growing takes place in heated greenhouses, however. This is why *roses, orchids, carnations, chrysanthemums, poinsettias* and other flowers are available in winter when it is freezing cold outside.

"Ornamentals" are a major farm "crop." These are grown in field **nurseries**. There are about 1,000 nurseries in the state. Monmouth County is tops in ornamental growing.

Ornamentals are the shrubs, bushes and trees planted to make houses and business buildings look more attractive. Putting the ornamentals in place is called "landscaping."

Ornamentals include many flowering shrubs. *Rhododendrons* and *azaleas* are special favorites. There is a big demand for small evergreens such as *yews* or *junipers*. Many kinds of full-sized shade trees are grown and transplanted onto lawns.

One important New Jersey ornamental tree is the *American holly*. This tree grows wild in the state, but holly growers take good holly varieties and make them better.

The world's largest privately-owned American holly orchard is at Millville. The orchard is so famous that Millville calls itself "The Holly City of America!"

There are farmers who provide

BUSY BEES

Take another look at the little honeybee that you see buzzing in the blossoms. That bee is a main reason why we will have fruit. Many fruit growers either have their own bee hives or bring hives to their orchards or blueberry plantations during the blossoming season.

If the bees did not pollinate blossoms, there would be no fruit harvests. Bees are a very important part of nature's plan. They are seeking food to store in their hives. As they take nectar from the blossoms, they also fertilize (or pollinate) the flowers. The nectar is carried back to the hives. As this is stored, it becomes honey. That's another sweet gift from the bees.

Honeybees are not "natives" of New Jersey or the United States. The first bees were brought to our country from Europe in 1638. Now there are about 4,000 beekeepers in the state. Most of them keep bees as a hobby, but a few are in the business of taking hives to fruit farms when needed.

"instant lawns"—of *real* grass, not Astroturf or other artificial "grass." "Instant lawn" farmers are called sod growers.

New Jersey sod is used to get big league baseball and football fields ready for games. Many players like "real grass" better than the artificial surfaces.

A few farmers keep goats, sheep or pigs. There are about 15,000 sheep and lambs in the state, mostly in Hunterdon County. If you are lucky, you might visit a farm where the sheep's wool coat is being sheared (cut).

It may surprise you to know that about 45,000 hogs are raised in our state. Most are on Gloucester County farms.

Some New Jersey farmers raise cattle to be sold for beef. Another New Jersey specialty is raising valuable breeds of cattle. These are called "prize cattle," worth thousands of dollars each.

Fruit, flower and vegetable farmers depend on bees. Without bees, blossoms cannot make fruit. Where there are bees there is also honey. Some farmers sell that tasty product. There are about 4,000 beekeepers in the state.

Bees are so important that special hives of them are brought on trucks to orchards or blueberry fields. The bees leave the hives to pollinate blossoms, then return to the hives.

So, farmers find many ways to stay in business. Farming is much more than plowing the earth, milking cows or gathering eggs!

As more and more homes and industries have been built in farm areas, demands have risen for ornamentals. Flowers, grown in a heated greenhouse (above), have become a fine business for some farmers. Other farmers cultivate large fields filled with chrysanthemums and other flowers. There are also good markets for shrubs and trees to decorate the outsides of houses and office buildings. Below, a shipment of live trees, each about 20 feet tall, is being placed aboard a truck. Occasionally a giant New Jersey evergreen is cut down and taken to New York to be put up and decorated as Radio City's famous Christmas tree.

USING THEIR BRAINS

These days, anyone who stays in agriculture must "farm with his head."

That means the farmer must think about what to grow, how to grow it and how to market what his farm produces. As you know, his harvest might be milk, eggs or wool; horses, flowers or honey; fruit, vegetables and many, many other things.

Successful farmers must stay up to the minute. They must use computers. They must buy strange-looking (and expensive) machines to harvest their crops. They must study ways to get the freshest possible products to market.

New Jersey farmers work on some of the highest priced farm acres in the United States. There can be little allowance for waste or inefficiency.

Think first of farm machines.

There is a machine that, when driven over a row of asparagus, senses which tender stalks to cut. It's hard to do, even by hand.

Nothing is more important to vegetable and fruit growers than water. If rainfall is normal (about 45 inches a year in New Jersey) there is no problem. Many times, however, there are long drought periods, when crops could die. Then, irrigating equipment such as this is rolled into the fields, turned on, and plants survive. Truly, it "rains when skies are blue!"

Another machine plucks delicate tomatoes from vines without crushing the tomatoes into useless mush.

Giant machines pull up bean plants, shake out the dirt, separate the bean pods from the stalks and then toss the pods into a truck.

There are mechanized pickers of cucumbers, blueberry harvesters with long, sensitive steel fingers and sweet corn pickers that have fierce-looking snouts.

A heater in the cabs of the machines provides comfort on cool spring days. Air conditioned cabs protect against the summer sun. Thus machine operators can work longer days and long seasons.

Machines are just one part of farming with the head.

Scientists work constantly on new varieties of fruits, vegetables and flowers. They seek plants capable of withstanding diseases and insects. They try to find plants that will ripen earlier. Early harvests mean money.

Many farmers are making use of computers.

Computers keep track of many details—how much milk each cow gives or how many eggs each chicken lays, when to plant and when to expect ripe fruit. Computers keep track of feed, fertilizers and seeds. They check which products are profitable and which are losers.

All farmers are conscious of energy costs. If a barn loses heat, ways must be found to insulate it. If a storage shed gets too hot, fruits and vegetables might perish. The shed must be insulated.

Some farmers use solar energy. A greenhouse in Allentown (Monmouth County) depends solely on solar energy. It is the largest solar installation in the eastern United States.

Another greenhouse, in Piscataway, runs almost totally without humans. A computer regulates lighting, temperature and moisture. Flats (or boxes) of plants are moved on automated belts.

"Old fashioned" farmers do not survive in New Jersey. Our agricultural people are as up-to-date as space voyagers!

A VERY SPECIAL BEAN

Imagine a vegetable that is used in foods, paints, chemicals, soap, marshmallows and linoleum! It is the soybean, New Jersey's number one vegetable. About four million bushels are harvested every season with machines such as the one in this picture. Soybeans are a big, big story for New Jersey farmers.

Soybeans are most valuable because they have a high protein content. One cup of mashed soybeans equals an adult portion of meat. The beans also are used in margarine, cooking oils, salad dressing and mayonnaise. Many Oriental recipes use soybean sauce. Soy "milk" is a substitute for people allergic to cow's milk.

One bushel of beans makes six quarts of soybean oil, the most valuable use of the vegetable. The oil is used in foods and for industry. Soybeans can be ground to make flour. They can also be processed into meal for animal food.

To market we go! The pride of New Jersey farmers, is the pleasure of the state's consumers! Summer months mean a rich and varied harvest for sale at roadside stands and city supermarkets. Remember too, the milk we drink and perhaps our favorite spaghetti sauce started out on a New Jersey farm!

188

CITIES

MAGIC CARPET NO. 11

*Our cities are important to our state,
Providing work and leaders, too.
So many opportunities we see,
In all the things our cities do.*
    (Repeat Chorus, see page 9)

Sometimes people think cities are not as important as they used to be.

Many people have left the cities, heading out along the highways that lead away from Newark, Paterson, Camden, Trenton and other cities. Each morning and night automobiles jam "country" roads as people head for work.

New Jersey has a higher percentage of people living in city areas than any other state. Ours is really a city state. It is true that our older cities need lots of fixing up. Cities are worth the attention of every person in New Jersey.

Cities are not just little dots on a map! The dots are really more like the centers of cities.

It is hard to say where a city such as Camden ends and where neighboring towns begin. The same is true with Trenton, Newark, Jersey City, Paterson, Elizabeth and other large cities. Sometimes the neighboring towns have grown into cities themselves. Often those places were once part of the "dot" in the circle.

The "City Line" is really several cities that overlap. The point is that most New Jersey people live near the straight line that extends from Bergen County's George Washington Bridge to the Ben Franklin Bridge in Camden County.

These days, other "circles" are growing along the Garden State Parkway, the N.J. Turnpike and the interstate highways. New Jersey's "City Line" is growing wider and wider.

THE CITY LINE

Five out of every seven New Jersey people live within about 20 miles of the center of a city.

Draw a line between the George Washington Bridge at Fort Lee and the Walt Whitman Bridge at Camden. This is the center of what has been called a great **corridor**. On the map to the left, we have widened the corridor to 10 miles on either side of the Fort Lee to Camden line. That widened corridor, which we call the "City Line," cuts through all New Jersey counties with the most people.

The "City Line" goes through or within a mile or two of Newark, Elizabeth, Woodbridge, Trenton, Camden, Jersey City, Hamilton and Paterson, New Jersey's largest cities.

So many people live within the "City Line" that visitors often think New Jersey is just one big city along the New Jersey Turnpike!

Our cities and neighboring towns *do* run together.

It is hard to say where Newark ends and East Orange, Kearny and Belleville begin.

It is not easy to know where Camden and Cherry Hill are separated.

A stranger would think that Jersey City, Bayonne and Hoboken are one big city.

Trenton, Ewing, and Hamilton fade into one another.

The "City Line" is in place mainly because of New York to the east and Philadelphia to the west.

Highways were built very early between those famous city neighbors of ours. Naturally New Jersey cities grew beside the heavily-traveled routes between New York and Philadelphia.

Let's look at our cities.

Let's see what they are and how they came to be.

WHAT MAKES A CITY?

What makes a city?

Is a city merely tall buildings, many stores and movie theaters?

Is a city only heavy automobile traffic, honking horns, busy factories and crowded sidewalks?

We must ask such questions about cities in New Jersey. Ours is the most **urban** state in the United States. This means that far more of us live in city regions than in farm areas.

The word urban is very important to our state. Urban can be thought of as human beings living closely together. That is the main clue to the question: What makes a city?

More than anything, a city is people—people who live there all the time and people who come each day to work, to study or to exchange ideas. The word city comes from old Latin words meaning "citizen" and "place."

There are "old cities" and "new cities" in New Jersey.

Old cities include such places as *Newark, Jersey City, Paterson, Elizabeth, Trenton* and *Camden*. Once, these were called the "Big Six." They were the leading New Jersey centers.

Later we will talk about the "old cities"—what made them great and some of the reasons that they have declined.

New cities have risen rapidly in the past 25 years, growing as people have moved away from the "Big Six." These new cities have replaced cow pastures or vegetable fields.

Many people think that all cities are nearly ruined, as in the picture to the right. Some parts of every city are "blighted," which is the name for an area on the downslide. However, an example of a city that is turning itself around is Hoboken, shown above. New York City commuters have found it a convenient place to live. These residents have rebuilt many of Hoboken's old houses and stores.

Cities can be—and should be—exciting and wonderful.

Throughout most of history, cities have been the places where great ideas have been dreamed and carried out. Great museums and libraries are in cities. Most of New Jersey's colleges and universities are in or near cities.

Most of your families live in or close to a city.

Think about the city where you live or the one closest to you. What makes it worthwhile? What makes living in a city difficult? Is there anything YOU or your class can do to help make cities better?

Perhaps you live quite far from the center of a city. You may think that cities are not your concern. *That is not true!*

Perhaps your father or mother work in a city. What happens to that city should be very much their concern.

Cities are *necessary*.

City people buy the products that industry turns out—no matter where the factory is located.

Farmers very much need city people as markets for their fruits, vegetables, milk and eggs.

Everyone benefits from exchanging of thoughts and ideas in city offices and city universities.

Most of all, think of cities as *people*, not traffic or tall buildings or "downtown."

Cities are all kinds of people—parents and children, old and young, rich and poor.

Can we forget the cities?

Can we forget *people*?

GROWING PAINS

Railroads created New Jersey's cities. They brought in coal to power steam engines that ran factory machines. Factories grew larger and needed more workers. Railroads brought in **immigrants** to work at the machines.

Immigrants were very poor. They had to live within walking distance of the factories. Areas surrounding the factories became cities, crowded with more and more people.

Most factory owners also wanted to live very close to their industries. Some lived next door or on the same block.

Growing factories needed money. Big banks and insurance companies, with money to lend, located mainly in the cities.

Wealthy factory owners and other business leaders could afford to live away from the cities—in "the country." Trains carried them to and from city businesses. They were called **commuters**—and still are, for many people still ride trains to city jobs.

New Jersey really became a "city state" in 1880. That year, for the first time, the U.S. Census found that more New Jerseyans lived in city regions than in farm areas. That finding made the state officially *urban*.

Newark was New Jersey's leading city by the year 1900. It had the most people, the most industries, the biggest banks, the most insurance companies, many of the state's political leaders and the state's best educated men and women.

Close behind were Jersey City, Trenton, Paterson, Elizabeth and Camden. These, plus Newark, often were called the "Big Six," the centers of New Jersey strength.

Cities then were proud places. Fine homes lined the main streets, close to

Perhaps you believe cities always were big. The drawings of Trenton (above) and Newark were both made about 150 years ago. At that time, these cities were nothing more than little towns. Cities grow rapidly. People often find that their old-time village has become a city before they know what has happened!

the state's best stores. Parks were green and neat. Cities were the place to be!

People loved the cities at night. They shopped, studied in libraries, ate in restaurants and saw the latest movies. Every New Jersey city had at least 20 movie theaters.

Cities began to change in about 1950. Workers from outside began driving automobiles into cities rather than riding trains. That created traffic and parking problems.

As people found better jobs, they bought homes away from the cities—although most continued to work "downtown."

Industries began to leave the cities in about 1960, following workers to "the country." At first the movement of industry was slow. However, by 1985, former city industries were beside such highways as Routes 1, 10, 46, 130 and many others.

Cities were in a sad state by 1985. Because so many New Jersey leaders lived away from cities, it was difficult to interest state and national governments in city problems.

Cities always have had problems, even in days when they were strongest. Cities always have had crowded streets, slum sections, too many traffic jams and too little money.

As people have moved outward, problems have followed them. Many people realize that they have merely exchanged one crowded *old* city for a growing *new* city.

Now, let's look close up at the cities once called "the Big Six."

THE BIGGEST CITY

Newark's first settlers came from Connecticut in 1666—more than 300 years ago. They called their town beside the Passaic River, Newark, to remember a city in England.

Now Newark is New Jersey's leading city. About 325,000 people live there.

Broad Street, Newark's main avenue, was the widest street in colonial America when it was built in 1667. Tall buildings, some more than 30 stories tall, now line Broad Street, along with parks set aside by the founders.

Newark's many factories make chemicals, electrical machines, plastics, food, platinum, jewelry and other products.

One of the city's great businesses is insurance. The Prudential Insurance and Mutual Benefit Life Insurance companies both have their national headquarters in the city.

Newark has New Jersey's finest airport as well as Port Newark, an international seaport.

The city is a college center. Rutgers, The State University; New Jersey Institute of Technology and Essex County College educate about 30,000 students in Newark each year. The University of Medicine and Dentistry of New Jersey is also in the city.

Newark has a famed museum and a noteworthy library. Symphony Hall presents excellent concerts. The New Jersey Historical Society offers interesting exhibits and programs.

Newark is big and busy. It has both great problems and great possibilities. It is a city struggling to become great again.

Newark — or any city — can best be understood from the air. On the ground, tall buildings crowd in on the streets. That makes it difficult to know that modern streets have gradually changed from old wagon trails into today's busy, paved thoroughfares. Looking down on Newark, you can see that the streets do not form regular squares, as in modern towns. You can also see some marks of history — parks, church spires and even different kinds of buildings.

New Jersey's tallest buildings are in Newark. Many large corporations have their offices in those "skyscrapers," as such tall buildings are called. The area shown here is "downtown" Newark. Places where people live spread outward from this heart of the city.

THE FIRST CAPITAL

Elizabeth and Newark have been side-by-side neighbors for more than 300 years. In colonial days, a tree marked the boundary. An "E" was carved on one side, an "N" on the other.

The first people arrived in 1664, two years before Newark was settled. Elizabeth was the first New Jersey town founded by English-speaking people.

Elizabeth was New Jersey's first capital. The first legislature met there in 1668. Several of the first New Jersey Governors lived there.

Elizabeth gradually fell behind Newark. More people chose Newark as the place to live and work. People also left Elizabeth to found Westfield, Springfield and other towns.

Elizabeth's great hope now lies in its remarkable seaport, where there are docks for 25 ships. The Elizabeth port handles more container shipments than any other seaport in the world.

Container shipments reach Elizabeth port in locked trucks. The huge truck bodies are lifted off and placed aboard ships as if they only were small boxes.

Elizabeth workers make cookies, paper, chemicals, oil, clothing and other products.

This city is proud of its history. It has several old historic homes and some nice parks. Some say that although "Elizabeth is old, it thinks young."

Elizabeth's 300 years of history appear on Elizabeth's Broad Street, laid out in colonial days. Businesses have changed, of course. Often, as in all cities, stores are in buildings that once were homes. Broad Street's main historical building is the 1st Presbyterian Church, opened in 1786. The present church replaced an earlier building where Parson Caldwell preached. British troops burned it in 1780, perhaps because the parson was so active during the Revolution.

197

OLD DUTCH TOWN

This statue of Governor Peter Stuyvesant stands next to Jersey City's Martin Luther King School. Stuyvesant, who had a wooden leg, was called "Old Peg Leg" by Dutch settlers. In 1660, after several Indian attacks, Stuyvesant ordered settlers on the New Jersey side of the river to move into a town called Bergen. That town is now Bergen Square, a tiny part of Jersey City. Stuyvesant, a very tough governor, worked hard to insure that his struggling little colony would not perish.

Jersey City's first settlers came from New Amsterdam, as New York was called by the Dutch. They founded a village called Bergen in 1660. It was New Jersey's first town.

Bergen changed its name several times. It was called Paulus Hook in 1804, when a group led by Alexander Hamilton planned Jersey City.

Railroad tracks reached Jersey City in the 1830s. New piers were built along the city's five miles of waterfront. Industry settled near the docks.

Then, in about 1960, rail service began to decline. Jersey Central Railroad closed its station. The tremendous railroad yards were abandoned. The waterfront became an ugly, unused region.

Jersey City is changing. Today, much of the waterfront has become Liberty State Park.

Many old houses have been fixed up. People like them because New York City is so close. New office buildings are rising tall. Most of Jersey City's 220,000 residents feel that their city is on the move.

Jersey City's workers make pencils, spaghetti, steel, tin cans, luggage, chemicals, food and radios, among many specialties.

The city has two colleges—Jersey City State College and St. Peter's College—both on the city's high ridge.

The Statue of Liberty, the "Gateway to America," is in Jersey City waters. Jersey City reaches out for the world.

POWER

Paterson is the youngest of New Jersey's six best-known cities. It was founded in 1791, about two hundred years ago.

The city is built on rocky cliffs that surround the Great Falls of the Passaic River. The 70-foot-high falls thunder down into the gorge.

These days the falls are admired only for beauty. Once, however, the plunging water meant power to drive the wheels of dozens of mills.

Alexander Hamilton planned Paterson. He was an important leader with George Washington after Washington was elected President of the United States.

Hamilton knew that America must make its own machines, clothing and other products if it wanted to be strong. He urged using the power of the Great Falls. On that idea, Paterson became America's first planned industrial city.

Through the years Paterson's mills have made cotton, factory machines, railroad locomotives, silk and airplane engines.

No cotton, locomotives, silk or airplane engines are made in Paterson now. Instead, the old mills have industries that make such products as clocks, chemicals, clothing, machines, paper and textiles.

About 140,000 people live in Paterson. The city is a shopping and working center for many more men and women.

City officials have created a park at the falls. They are trying to preserve some of the old mills, remembering Paterson's industrial history.

City by the Falls: That's Paterson!

Twilight makes downtown Paterson stand out against the bright sky. The rounded dome is atop the Passaic County Courthouse, built in 1837. Nearby are the spires of several of the city's churches. The city spreads outward from the small part that we see here. Paterson is best known for its magnificent waterfalls, usually seen whenever New Jersey's beautiful places are shown. The city grew from industries founded to take advantage of the waterfall's power.

SEAT OF GOVERNMENT

New Jersey boys and girls know more about Trenton than any other city in the state.

Trenton is the State Capital. It is where the Governor works. It is where the State Assembly and State Senate make state laws.

Many new state government buildings have been constructed in recent years. Here, plans are made for schools, farms, industry, health and other state needs.

The city was founded by Quakers in about 1680. It was named Trent's Town in about 1720 to honor a leading resident named William Trent. His house still stands.

Trenton's most memorable day was December 26, 1776, when General Washington's ragged army smashed the enemy Hessians in the Battle of Trenton. Much of the city's history goes back to Revolutionary War times.

After the Revolution, it was hoped that Trenton would be the Capital of the United States. When the U.S. Capital was set at Washington, D.C., Trenton became New Jersey's capital in 1790.

Many thousands of school children visit Trenton every year. They see where Washington's army crossed the Delaware for the battle. They stop by the Old Barracks, where the Hessians lived. Some visit the Trent House.

Boys and girls enjoy the fine State Museum. They visit the capital building and see rooms where laws are made. Some even meet the Governor!

But how many realize that about 92,000 people live in Trenton? How many know that the Capital City is also a place of industry? Its workers make rubber, bridge cables, dishes, medicine, plastics, machines and other things. The city's motto is *Trenton Makes—The World Takes!*

New Jersey's State House is readily viewed from the Pennsylvania side of the Delaware River, as seen here. Our State House is the second oldest in continuous use in the U.S. The original State House was built in 1795. Traces of that old structure are found within the present structure. The governor, the State Senate and the State Assembly all use this building. The golden dome is visible for long distances.

COOPER'S FERRY

On one end of the state, Jersey City looks at New York. On the other end, Camden looks at Philadelphia.

Camden is older than Philadelphia by one year. It was founded in 1681 by William Cooper. Philadelphia started as a village in 1682.

At first, Camden was known as Cooper's Ferry. South Jersey farmers drove their wagons aboard the ferry owned by William Cooper. They headed for Philadelphia to sell their vegetables and fruit.

Cooper's Ferry became Camden in 1828. Six years later, the first railroad train chugged into town. The city sprouted.

Industry came. Joseph Campbell started canning tomatoes in 1869. About 30 years later, a Camden mechanic named Eldridge Johnson perfected his first phonograph. Mr. Campbell's tomato cannery became Campbell's Soup Co. Johnson's factory became RCA.

Camden's industry includes a big licorice maker. Other workers turn out leather, paper, chemicals and medicines.

Camden has many ties with Philadelphia. A high speed railroad line goes back and forth. Two bridges carry automobiles over the Delaware River between the cities. Those bridges are named for great men: Benjamin Franklin and Walt Whitman.

Walt Whitman was a noted poet. He lived in Camden from 1873-1893, the last 20 years of his life. Whitman liked cities and he loved America! His Camden home is now a historic site and he is buried in the city.

It is too bad Whitman is not still alive. Cities *need* poets to sing their praises!

Camden's waterfront park, along the Delaware River, is a part of a renewed hope that better times are here for the city. Camden suffered as much as any New Jersey city after many residents began moving eastward toward Cherry Hill and other areas. Much of Camden's history is close to this park, for the city's life always has depended on the river. At first, ferryboats linked Camden and Philadelphia. Then in 1926, the Benjamin Franklin Bridge was built across the river. That span, shown in the upper part of the picture, has been important in the changes that have come to Camden.

THE BIG TEN

	1987	1950
Newark	315,196	438,776
Jersey City	217,251	299,017
Paterson	138,200	139,336
Elizabeth	105,876	112,817
Woodbridge	94,007	35,758
Trenton	90,646	128,009
Hamilton	87,106	41,176
Edison	84,159	16,348
Camden	81,675	124,555
East Orange	77,140	79,340

THE CITIES

There are no skyscrapers in Woodbridge. Hamilton is a township; that might make you think it is a country place. There is no "downtown" in Edison.

Yet Woodbridge is now the fifth largest city in New Jersey, Hamilton seventh and Edison eighth!

During the past 25 years or so, many people have moved out of cities. They have created new cities in places that your parents might remember only as corn fields.

There are many examples in New Jersey of this kind of "new city." Most are not called cities. They might not look as you think cities should look. Yet they have crowds of people—and they are growing.

The "new cities" happened because of big new highways. People have moved out along such roads as the Garden State Parkway, the N.J. Turnpike, or Interstate Routes 78 and 80.

Before the Garden State Parkway was built, Ocean County had 56,622 people in the 1950 U.S. Census. Thirty years later, the 1980 Census showed 346,038 people in Ocean. That's six times as many people in 30 years!

Most of Ocean County's growth has been in Brick and Dover townships, both right off the Parkway. Brick had about 4,300 people in 1950. Today it's population is more than 62,000! Dover Township in 1950 had a popu-

"Heavy city traffic" is one reason given when people and businesses move to former New Jersey farm areas. This early evening winter photograph, taken outside a northern New Jersey office building, demonstrates how city problems follow people to "the country." Each morning and evening, workers headed for out-of-city offices create traffic jams. Such offices are usually near interstate highways, and such wide "super highways" often have big traffic problems. Worse, smaller highways and country roads are usually greatly overcrowded with cars.

iation of 7,700 compared to 72,000 today!

"New cities" rise at the expense of the old. As you can see on the chart to the left—Newark, Jersey City, Paterson, Elizabeth, Trenton and Camden all have had sharp declines in population since 1960.

When large crowds of people settle in one place, another city begins!

The "new cities" usually have several large shopping centers. These centers are not really "downtown," but they serve the same purpose. You can eat, shop, meet friends and go to the movies.

One danger of all cities is that they "just grow." Streets are laid out in winding or curving patterns that make it difficult for the traffic to move. More schools are needed. More and more automobiles are driven to shopping centers, schools and nearby industries.

Automobiles have become an absolute necessity in the new cities. There are no railroads to take people to jobs. Some places do not even have good bus service. Huge areas of former farmland have been paved to make parking spaces for industries, schools and shopping centers.

City problems catch up with people who thought they had moved to "the country." Soon there is pollution, noise, crowding and higher taxes.

New Jersey is first in *population density*, meaning the number of people living within an area.

People! New Jersey's new cities have them! Many think they do not want to live in cities. Yet they *do* want to live near other people. That's what makes cities out of corn fields!

MARKS OF HISTORY

We know that cities are people. Cities are places to work. Cities are where museums, colleges, stores and many other things are located. We know that nearly all cities have great problems.

Cities are also history. They are nearly all very old.

Look about any city. The street names often tell of the past. Some have the names of important people. Some tell of days that are nearly forgotten.

You can see city history in the parks. Statues of many prominent people are in Newark parks. A tall monument in Trenton is topped by a figure of George Washington. Bergen Square in Jersey City has a statue of Peter Stuyvesant, the Dutchman who started the city.

There are some unusual city "monuments." Paterson's West Side Park exhibits the first successful submarine in America, invented in 1878 by a Paterson school teacher named John Philip Holland.

Many old houses and buildings can be seen in every city.

Don't look only for places where Washington or some other great person stayed. History is also a matter of churches, factories, houses or old shipping docks. You might even find an

Morristown, often thought of as a small historical town, really is becoming a city. Here is Morristown's center. The old colonial village green is now a park. You can see some of the "marks of history" — an old church in the distance, a statue dedicated to Civil War soldiers. The "green" itself is historical. However, this picture also shows some of an area now filled with tall office buildings. These bring more workers to town. Nearly all arrive in automobiles. Traffic around the colonial green each day gets more difficult to control.

old city cemetery close to a factory or an apartment building.

History leaves its marks in other ways, some good, some not.

On the good side, Vineland's wide, shaded streets are due to history. Charles K. Landis, who founded Vineland in 1861, insisted that streets be wide and that all settlers plant trees.

Newark has two parks that were established more than 300 years ago—Washington Park and Military Park. In colonial days, soldiers used Military Park to practice their skills.

We have to remember that not all the marks of history are good.

For example, many city houses are 100 or more years old. Many were badly built in the first place and have never been improved. They are "historic houses"—but in this case, history is not pleasant.

Near the centers of Newark and Elizabeth, railroads run on high banks. These divide the cities as much as if they were wide rivers.

Finally, old cities were not planned. They "just grew."

Colonial streets were laid out along wandering Indian trails or paths that cattle took on the way from the fields to barns. Cows do not walk in straight lines.

It did not matter how crooked the streets were in days when not many people lived in town. It did not matter then how or where streets crossed. There were not many vehicles.

These days, however, trucks, buses and automobiles crowd the streets. Those one-time Indian trails and cowpaths cannot handle modern traffic.

Not everything, you see, is good just because it is old and "historic."

SILKEN STREETS

Much of a city's history can be seen in street names. Some are named for famous people, some for geographical features (Lakeside Drive, for example) and many bear names of trees (such as Maple).

One "tree street" found in most cities or larger towns is Mulberry Street, a reminder of an almost forgotten scheme that was supposed to make people rich.

About 150 years ago, people were told that silkworms could be raised to produce silk. Hundreds of people bought silkworms hoping to sell silk for high prices. Then they planted mulberry trees, since silkworms feed on mulberry leaves. Thousands of the trees were planted, along streets as well as in back yards.

The scheme did not work. The silkworms are gone, as well as most of the trees. At least a good street name remains!

CITY GROWTH

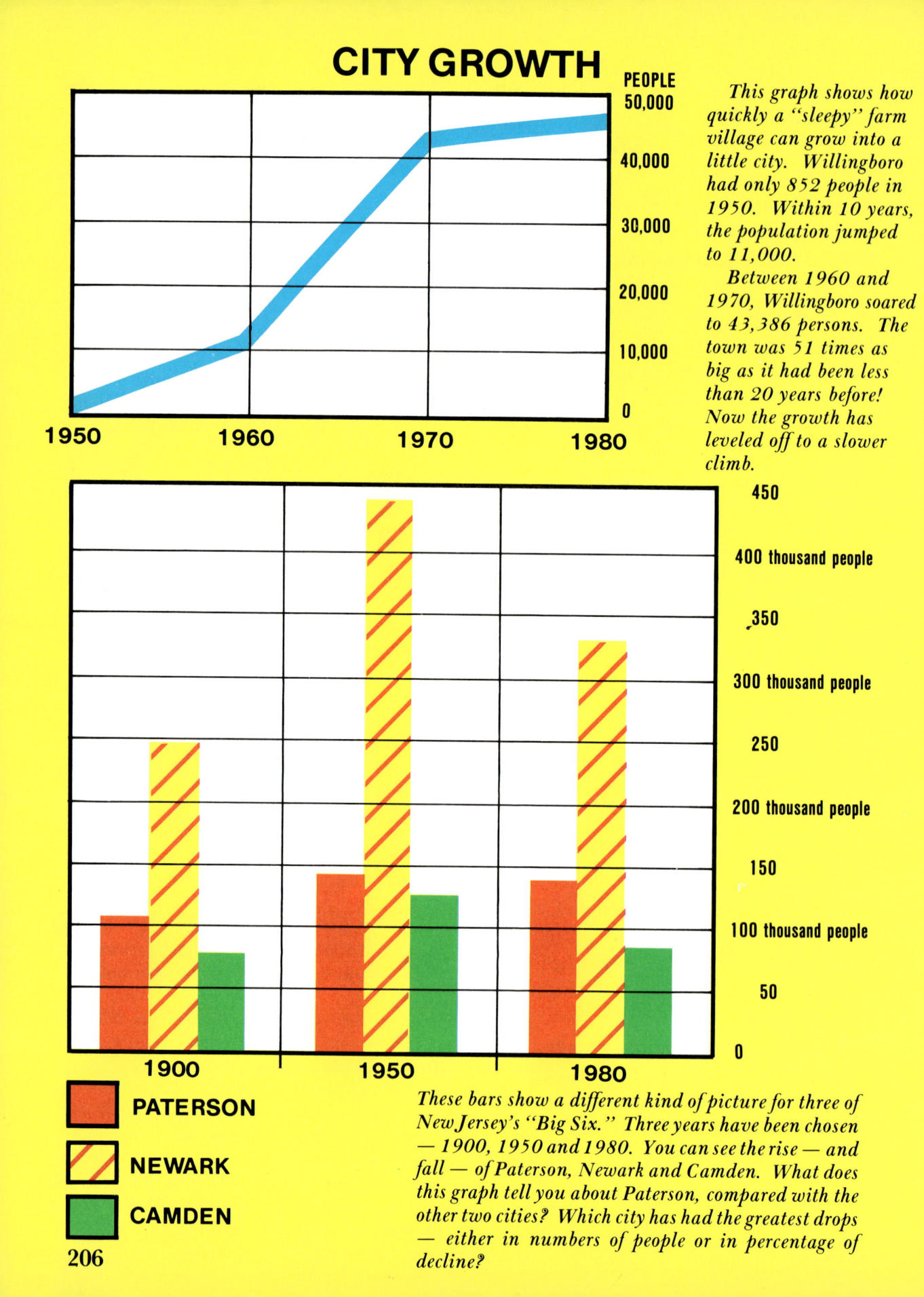

This graph shows how quickly a "sleepy" farm village can grow into a little city. Willingboro had only 852 people in 1950. Within 10 years, the population jumped to 11,000.

Between 1960 and 1970, Willingboro soared to 43,386 persons. The town was 51 times as big as it had been less than 20 years before! Now the growth has leveled off to a slower climb.

PATERSON

NEWARK

CAMDEN

These bars show a different kind of picture for three of New Jersey's "Big Six." Three years have been chosen — 1900, 1950 and 1980. You can see the rise — and fall — of Paterson, Newark and Camden. What does this graph tell you about Paterson, compared with the other two cities? Which city has had the greatest drops — either in numbers of people or in percentage of decline?

206

ENVIRONMENT

MAGIC CARPET NO. 12

♪ *Wide open spaces are New Jersey's claim,*
With wildlife, forests, parks for you.
Our state's natural beauty we'll enjoy,
But we'll protect, respect it, too.
   (Repeat Chorus, see page 9)

ENVIRONMENT. Think about that word. Remember it. That word will help to determine your life in the future.

Environment is everything in any area where we live — the air, the water, the sunshine; the trees, the flowers, the sidewalks. Environment surrounds us. We can't escape it.

If someone makes OUR air not worth breathing, we have a right to be angry. If someone dirties OUR water or litters OUR beaches, we should do something about it.

This state and this world are ours to enjoy. Let's give the environment our best!

207

NATURE'S SCHEME

There are places in the Pine Barrens where you and I could walk for 10 to 15 miles in a straight line without seeing a town, a house or even another person.

Along the busy Jersey Shore, parts of Sandy Hook and Island Beach are nearly as wild as they were 200 years ago.

The state still has deep forests, such as the great hardwood trees of the northern mountains and the dense pinelands of southern New Jersey.

Most people are amazed to learn that our state still is about 45 percent forest land. That is nearly half!

New Jersey is a state with more than 1,000 kinds of wildflowers, more than 200 kinds of trees, more than 400 kinds of birds, more than 50 kinds of wild mammals.

What difference do such things as forests, flowers, trees and mammals make?

Plants, trees and animals are special natural treasures. They are ours—to enjoy, respect and protect. They are as important to our **environment** as human beings.

Nearly everyone understands that we must try to keep our state, our nation and our Planet Earth as unpolluted as possible. The best way to begin understanding our environment is by knowing that nearby land is both beautiful and worth preserving.

New Jersey's open spaces and abundant wildlife surprise visitors. Most of them have only seen New Jersey only by way of the New Jersey Turnpike or along one of the state's other busy superhighways.

Often, people who fly into Newark International Airport or Atlantic

City's airport exclaim, "We didn't know that New Jersey is so *green*!" You could tell them more:

- By now, because you have learned about your state, *you* know that our forests and farms give us a "green look."
- You know about our famous Jersey Shore, 127 miles of fine white sand beaches.
- You know some of our state's long history. History and historic buildings are part of our total environment, too.
- You know that New Jersey has wide lakes, broad rivers and deep reservoirs.

When you read newspapers, watch TV or listen to the radio, you often will hear about such dangerous things as acid rain, air pollution, dirty water and horrible traffic tie-ups.

Those are all very much parts of New Jersey's environmental picture too—the unpleasant parts, caused by careless human beings.

Let's face it: in a state as densely populated as New Jersey, many suffer because of the careless acts of others.

Many groups and many individuals are fighting to protect New Jersey's environment. They know the value of clean, open space. Once a person sees how splendid our state could be, it seems only sensible to keep it unpolluted.

Environmental knowledge helps us understand the role of human beings on earth.

Nature has created roles for all living things—birds, animals, flowers, trees PLUS people. We are merely one part of nature's scheme for a good planet.

Come along. Let's look closely at New Jersey's environment. We'll learn about the "good things"—our parks, our seashore, our lakes and ponds, our wild and open land.

We will look carefully. Along the way we see deer grazing, see a rattlesnake sunning itself on a mountain rock or hear an Eastern Goldfinch singing our "state song!"

We will also learn about pollution. Let's get angry about it! You and I can—and should—help to determine the quality of where we live.

WILD ORCHIDS

Tell this to everyone you know. Orchids grow wild in New Jersey!

You may recognize this as a lady slipper. It is also a delicate wild orchid, although not commonly known as such. White and pink lady's slippers are found in many parts of New Jersey — but you have to know where to look!

Orchids begin to bloom in the Pine Barrens in May, when the beautiful arethusa is found. Our orchids come in many colors — white, purple, yellow, pink and even some in green.

If you find a wild orchid, "take it home" only in a photograph. Orchids almost always die if transplanted into home gardens.

HERE ARE YOUR PARKS

Would you like to hike, play ball, explore a "ghost town" or go camping?

Would you like to paddle a canoe, find bog iron or hook a big trout?

Would you like to swim in the ocean, water-ski on a lake or see a plant that eats insects?

You can—in one of New Jersey's 43 State Parks or 40 State Forests spread from High Point to Cape May. These include woodlands and seashore, mystery towns and lakeside swimming docks, playgrounds and snowmobile trails.

There is very little difference between State Parks and Forests, as far as using them is concerned. State Forests were established mainly to protect woodlands. However, all of the Forests have varied kinds of park uses. Some of the State Forests are heavily enjoyed.

Whether parks or forests, the state-owned lands offer many exciting possibilities.

Most have picnic groves, fishing spots, campgrounds, hiking trails and playgrounds. Several have areas for swimming. Some have programs to help you and your classmates learn about nature or history. A few contain "ghost towns."

Two familiar state-owned "ghost towns" are Allaire (in Monmouth County) and Batsto (in Burlington County). Long ago, both villages rang with the sights and sounds of iron making. The two areas have been reconstructed to show you how people once lived and how they worked.

New Jersey's most unusual State Parks are the Round Valley and Spruce Run reservoirs. Their primary purpose is to store water, but land surrounding each of these **reservoirs** is

Preserving areas of natural beauty has long been important to the people of New Jersey. Essex County proudly boasts the first county park commission in America, established in 1895. Local and county parks are not always large and filled with activity. Sometimes, all we want is a quiet spot to enjoy the warmth and beauty of spring. Such "pockets" of green are especially popular with picnickers.

open for sailing, fishing, swimming and picnicking. People *can* use reservoirs for fun!

The State Parks and Forests belong to all of us. Find out about them. Write for your own map and information to: *Division of Parks and Forestry, Department of Environmental Protection, CN404, Trenton, NJ 08625.*

There are many other kinds of New Jersey areas open to the public. Your school undoubtedly is close to some kind of park or recreational area—city, town, county, state or even large region owned by the federal government.

A few counties do not have county park systems including Salem, Sussex and Warren. Find out about your own county park systems.

The largest federal (or national) parkland in New Jersey is The Delaware Water Gap National Recreation Area. It covers 28,000 acres of land, just north of Delaware Water Gap. These acres are located in Warren and Sussex counties.

Federally-owned lands in our state also include four National Wildlife Areas—most notably Great Swamp in Morris County and Brigantine in Atlantic. These are not *parks*, but the very large areas can be enjoyed by hikers, bird-watchers, nature lovers and all people who just enjoy being outdoors.

More than 800,000 acres of open space—parks, forests and wildlife **refuges**—are now owned by various government agencies in New Jersey. That is very close to *one-fifth* of all the land in our state!

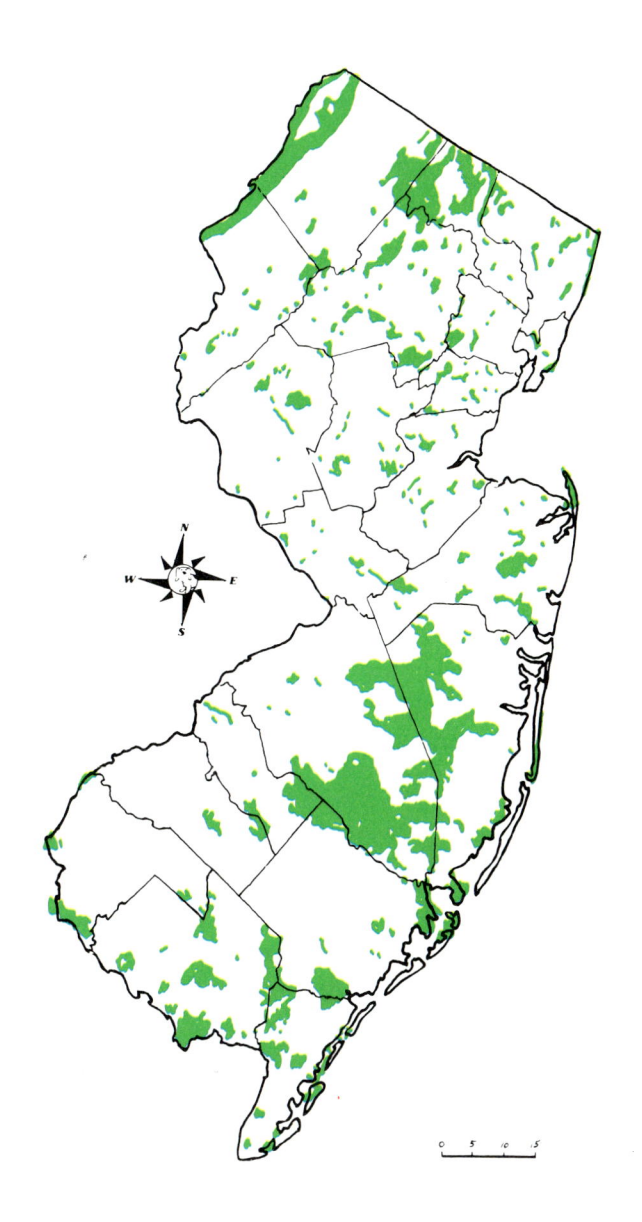

From high above, New Jersey is a lovely shade of green! Over the years, the state's voters have worked for the "greening" of New Jersey by voting YES for new parks and reserves.

These parks and forests are a precious heritage right now, for you and me. They will remain a heritage for all people in all the years ahead.

211

PATCHES OF BLUE

Let your eyes wander over a map of New Jersey. Look at the many "patches" of blue. These are map symbols, to show where our lakes and ponds are located.

There are about 50 quite large lakes and ponds in the state. About 750 more smaller lakes or ponds are found on county maps. Adding farm ponds or very small ponds used mainly for landscaping, it is believed that New Jersey may boast of as many as 3,000 "patches of blue."

The biggest lake is *Hopatcong*, set in thick hardwood forests shared by Sussex and Morris counties. Lake Hopatcong is about seven miles long. Its shoreline, dented by many coves, is about 40 miles around.

We share our second biggest lake, *Greenwood*, with New York State. The six-mile-long lake is about half in New Jersey.

Lake Marcia, in High Point State Park, is our "highest" lake. Easily seen from the High Point Monument, Marcia is 1,570 feet above sea level.

Most of the "patches" are in the northern part of the state. This is because the **glacier** (see page 60) dug out hollows where lakes or ponds formed. You can spot the larger lakes easily on a map—*Hopatcong, Greenwood, Culvers, Owassa, Mohawk, Swartswood, Wawayanda, Highland Lakes* and so on.

You will see that many of the lakes have Indian names. Every body of water was important to the Lenape.

Southern New Jersey lakes are quite small, although a few, such as *Union Lake* near Millville, *Mirror Lake* near Browns Mills or *Lake Lenape* near Mays Landing, are large.

Most of the state's lakes and ponds once were necessary for industry. Dams were placed across streams to store water. When the water was released, it poured out to drive gears and grinders in grain mills or sawmills.

Steam, followed by electricity, made waterpower less vital about 90 years ago. Gradually, lakes and ponds became used for recreation. These days, all-year homes surround most bodies of water.

Several northern New Jersey lakes were dammed up to provide water for the Morris Canal. "Canal lakes" included *Hopatcong, Cranberry, Greenwood, Pompton* and *Musconetcong*. The canal is gone. The dams and the lakes remain.

Lake Mohawk is one of the state's largest man-made lakes. Once the area near Sparta was an unpopulated woodland valley, drained by the slow-moving Wallkill River. A dam was built across the valley in 1926. Lake Mohawk rose behind the dam. If you did not know that, you would think the lake had always been there.

Some of New Jersey's largest "blue patches" are reservoirs. As you have

A lake: water enclosed by land; big or small, natural or man made, it matters not. Our lakes from the smallest to the largest sparkle like jewels! Many were created by building dams, much like the one above. Lake Hopatcong (upper left) was once two large ponds. A dam built in the 1830's to provide water for the Morris Canal, connected the ponds. Hopatcong, our largest lake, is 6½ miles long and measures 1½ miles across its widest part. At its deepest spot, the lake reaches down 50 feet. Islands dot its surface. Imagine living on an island and traveling home by ferry! More than 50 families do just that! They live on Raccoon, the lake's biggest island.

learned, Spruce Run and Round Valley reservoirs both permit use of the water and shoreline for recreational purposes.

One theme runs through the story of New Jersey's "patches": Nearly all once were "working" lakes or ponds.

That means that they were necessary or useful—to run mills, to provide canal water, to provide recreation, to store up drinking water and to provide pleasant settings for homes.

Even the little ponds that rise when beavers dam up a stream are useful. They give the beavers the kind of home that they need and want.

Big or small, man-made or natural, our lakes and ponds make any map colorful. Much more important, they are very necessary to help provide a good New Jersey environment.

THE JERSEY SHORE

The Jersey Shore is certainly our state's most important natural treasure. It is also the most threatened region in all of New Jersey.

Here are a few reasons why the Jersey Shore is treasured:

- It is 127 miles of seaside, with dozens of beaches. Millions of vacationers each year enjoy our state's white sands and rolling tides.
- It is the remarkable natural beauty of such places as Sandy Hook, Island Beach and thousands of acres of marshes where shore birds dwell.
- It is the high dunes at Avalon and Island Beach, covered with rare plants and often the places where shore birds lay their eggs.
- It is **bays** and **sounds**, where people water-ski, sail boats, try to hook flounders or cast fishing lines from piers and docks.
- It is the vast and mysterious Atlantic Ocean, sometimes rough, but usually peaceful enough in summertime for swimming and surfing.

Any of us easily can visit our shore. If we are lucky, we live close to it. Either way, we can take home such personal treasures as seashells, nice tans and memories.

The Jersey Shore "treasure" is not only natural beauty or water sports, however. Each year, visitors to our seaside spend billions of dollars—for rents, food, clothing, gasoline, beach toys and suntan oil.

It is probable that the Jersey Shore is the state's largest and most productive industry.

Despite the "treasure," few of us even think of the threats to our Jersey Shore—unless something such as the "green slime" of August 1985, keeps us out of the surf.

That green slime was no mystery. It

was quickly traced to overworked sewage plants, especially along the southern part of the seashore.

Doesn't it make you wonder how communities that depend so much on visitors could so uncaringly dump sewage into the ocean?

Some cities tow garbage scows out on the Atlantic Ocean and dump their garbage into our ocean. Sometimes it washes ashore and closes beaches as it did in 1987 and 1988.

Liners and freighters passing along the coast also throw garbage into the sea. Occasionally, a tanker or ship may release oil into the ocean. If even a small amount is carried in by the tides, the black, sticky mess can ruin the beaches for a few days.

Too many visitors leave their personal garbage on the sand—aluminum cans, bottles, old beach chairs or other junk. It's almost as bad as garbage washed in from the sea.

Nature also throws mighty punches at the Jersey Shore.

Sometimes a powerful hurricane rips up boardwalks, blows down homes, smashes windows and whips sand into seaside streets. Some storms can even cut temporary inlets through seaside towns.

Each day, each hour, even every minute, the ocean waves move the beach sands. Currents take sand from one seaside place and put it on another beach. That is why some Jersey Shore beaches are so narrow, some so wide.

We can't stop nature. However, we can respect the **dunes**, nature's own protection against roaring winds. We can hope that builders won't put up houses in places where nature's power can sweep them away.

Most important, day to day, we can get angry at people who pollute our beaches. If they are big city garbage dumpers, we can—*and should*—write letters to our governor or our legislators.

The Jersey Shore is *our* treasure—to enjoy and to protect.

Beachcombing, shell collecting, fishing and birdwatching are favorite ways to pass a day at the shore. Surf fishermen try their luck by "casting" from the coast. Others prefer to venture out aboard boats. Either way, a day's catch might include bluefish, cod, flounder, sea bass, weakfish, porgies and more! The heaviest saltwater fish caught in our waters was a bluefin tuna. It weighed 1,022 pounds!

The heron, left, is just one of many New Jersey shore birds. At least 10 varieties of heron alone can be seen along our coast.

215

PEOPLE WHO CARE

People CAN do something about threats to their environment!

More than 25 years ago, in 1960, powerful leaders in New York City decided to build a giant jetport in Morris County's Great Swamp.

The city leaders believed that no one would care what happened to a swamp.

People DID care. They protested in public meetings. More important, they raised more than a million dollars to buy most of the Great Swamp. They gave the land to the U.S. Government as a National Wildlife Refuge.

The Great Swamp refuge now includes more than 6,000 acres in Morris and Somerset counties. Amazingly, the huge sanctuary is less than 15 miles from Newark, our state's largest city.

One of the earliest battles to save an especially precious piece of New Jersey land began more than 90 years ago when quarry owners blasted away at the Palisades overlooking the Hudson River.

The Palisades has been a natural wonder since explorers first saw it more than 350 years ago. The cliff towers more than 500 feet above the river.

When road builders wanted rock and stone in the 1880s, companies began blasting down parts of the Palisades. Members of the New Jersey State Federation of Women's Clubs demanded that the state legislature stop the blasting.

The bold and mysterious Palisades remind us of New Jersey's geologic past and the people who battled to save this natural wonder.

The women won! Blasting was stopped forever. The towering cliff became Palisades Interstate Park, controlled jointly by New Jersey and New York. It was the first park in the United States where ownership was shared by neighboring states.

Much more recently, determined people have preserved much of the Pine Barrens.

The N.J. Audubon Society first pressed for a Pine Barrens National Monument in 1965. In 1977, the U.S. Congress made the Pine Barrens our nation's first National Reserve. Now a N.J. Pinelands Commission seeks the best uses for the woodland.

Trees are important in the Pine Barrens. So are rare plants and animals. The best reason for saving the region, however, is that clean drinking water is in natural underground reservoirs.

It has been estimated that there are 17 trillion gallons of water beneath the Pine Barrens. That's 17—*followed by 12 zeroes*! That's a lot of water!

Saving land and water is important in a state as crowded as New Jersey.

The good news is that there are thousands of adults working for land preservation. These are the kinds of people who saved the Palisades, the Great Swamp, the Pine Barrens and dozens of other vital areas.

New Jersey's first state park was set aside in 1906. Now we have more than 800,000 acres in parks, forests, refuges and other public lands—owned by local, county, state or federal governments.

Our state has three other national Wildlife Refuges in addition to the Great Swamp. The Forsythe National Wildlife Refuge at Brigantine covers about 20,000 acres. Two, Killcohook and Supawana, near Pennsville, are small.

Remarkably, the Forsythe Refuge is close to Atlantic City. The city's casino hotels are easily seen, just across Reeds Bay.

Birdwatchers and wildlife scientists visit the refuge at Brigantine, coming from many parts of the world. In the fall, flocks of as many as 150,000 birds gather there.

That refuge is mostly **marshland**. Jersey Shore marshes may look like swamps, but those wetlands are very necessary. They provide places where salt water fish can lay eggs. Birds nest in the grass. Wetlands are where life begins.

People do fight to save our land.

Still, there are also too many people who know little of the value of swamps, forests, beaches and other natural areas.

You can help. Get information. Get interested!

KEEP IT CLEAN!

Nature lovers have a rule they follow whenever they visit any place:

Leave it cleaner than when you came!

We hear so much about dirt and litter on our streets, in our parks and beside our picnic tables. We see beer cans and broken bottles in our streets.

PROTECTING OUR ENVIRONMENT

Pollution is a BIG problem, especially in a state as densely populated as New Jersey. Every bit of land, water and even air is precious! Every person must learn to care and behave responsibly.

State government must also play a role to improve and protect the environment. The New Jersey Department of Environmental Protection serves as our state's official "watch dog." D.E.P., as it is called, cares for the state's natural resources, monitors air and water quality, as well as manages all state parks and recreation areas. It also works to reduce or eliminate pollution from sewage, industrial chemicals, noise, pesticides and other sources. Fish and game programs are under its control.

D.E.P. even regulates boating on our lakes. By reviewing plans and issuing permits, the agency protects our open spaces from becoming over-developed. Headquartered in Trenton, the Department of Environmental Protection employs over 2,000 people. These government workers are dedicated to making New Jersey a better place to live for us as well as future generations.

Who is to blame? The answer is plain: People like you and me.

Many New Jersey boys and girls, by themselves or in school groups, are working to make their world better. They do not merely write letters or blame somebody else. They get to work.

One school class in Morris County "adopted" a brook. It flowed through their town, near their school. They traveled along both sides of the stream, and carried away old soda and beer cans, papers, automobile tires and boots.

When the boys and girls found a thick film of oil on their stream's water, they took the story to their town newspaper. That action forced the person responsible to stop dumping oil into the stream.

School children in Mercer and Warren counties have "adopted" old cemeteries. They received permission to clean away rubbish and put stone walls back in place. They helped to set up toppled-over gravestones and made grass grow again!

Groups of boys and girls in schools near the Pine Barrens have received permission to "take over" small pieces of woodland. They clean away fallen branches. They help remove anything that might burn in a forest fire. They pick up junk that people have thrown from cars!

There are many other examples of boys and girls who work to clean up their state and their world. They

Time spent out-of-doors exploring streams, fields and forests teaches us about things we cannot learn in books. As our knowledge grows, so does our appreciation for nature's wonders. The boys and girls below are at the New Jersey School of Conservation at Stokes State Forest, in Sussex County. Each year more than 10,000 New Jersey students spend from two to five days at Stokes. During their stay, students come face to face with animals in the wild. These include beavers, snakes and deer. Outdoor instruction includes classes in geology and ecology. Stokes State Forest and other environmental education centers around the state are "classrooms without walls!"

don't waste time talking about why someone else should clean up a river or the Atlantic Ocean! They set to work to improve what is *close at hand!*

Is there a very old abandoned cemetery, a littered park or a dirty playground near your school? Can you find a neglected woodland near by?

Talk the matter over with your teacher, with other classes and with your principal. Perhaps your school can DO something to improve the environment.

Maybe your school playground could use some cleaning up. Perhaps the sidewalk in front of your own house is littered with papers or cans or bottles that someone else has thrown away. Pick up, clean up! Make your world better!

If you do "adopt" a brook, a cemetery, a playground or a park, call up the newspaper. The editor might like to tell your story.

The reason for newspaper stories is not just to get credit, although there is nothing wrong with credit if you do something worthwhile! The reason is to let other people know that someone cares!

Many people never follow the rule of leaving a place cleaner than they find it.

So it comes down to each of us. The best thing is not to throw junk away carelessly. However, if we pick up someone else's litter, remember: we won't let *their* junk spoil *our* world!

219

Over 1,000 wildflowers carpet New Jersey in colors bright and beautiful. It's tempting to pick a bunch, but better to leave wildflowers for all to enjoy. Instead, collect their names: marshmallow, lizard's tail, turkey-beard, milkwort and sneeze-weed are just a few to get you started!

Creepers, chirpers, hoppers, crawlers: all call New Jersey home! Among our 15 kinds of frogs is the spring peeper (upper left). Though quite a noisemaker, he measures just an inch in length! Another, the Pine Barrens' carpenter frog, is not found anywhere else in America. Underfoot are 19 varieties of snakes. Most are harmless, such as the pine snake (left) and the green snake (above). If an award were given to our strangest reptile, the hognosed snake would win. When frightened, he mimics a rattler. If that fails, he plays a cobra. As a last resort, he plays dead! Amongst birds, the skimmer (middle left) might win for appearance!

221

Little New Jersey boasts 110 kinds of mammals. That's hard to believe, but true! Many live in our parks and forests. Our list includes the red fox, otter, beaver, cottontail rabbit, whitetail deer, porcupine, bobcat and black bear. Some, like the bottlenose dolphin, the harbor porpoise and the 80-foot long fin whale live along our shore, in the deep Atlantic.

Wherever you live, animal neighbors are near. Be on the lookout. Though shy, all are waiting for your eyes!

GOVERNMENT

MAGIC CARPET NO. 13

All government does things we cannot do,
Tasks too big for you 'n' me.
Nation'l, state, and county; local, too.
Offer help we're glad to see.
    (Repeat Chorus, see page 9)

The United States is noted throughout the world because we people have so many rights and freedoms. If we don't like our government's leaders, we can vote them out of office.

Most of us are citizens because we were born here. Foreigners must earn their citizenship.

If we want to make sure that the United States continues to belong to the people, we must learn about governments — town, county, state and national. If we know about government — and if we act as proud citizens — we can make all the difference.

223

GOVERNMENT? WHO'S THAT?

Most of you have seen your town or city mayor, in person or in newspaper pictures. Some of you may know the name of your State Senator. A few of you have even met the Governor of New Jersey. Practically everyone has seen the President of the United States on TV.

These are the kinds of people that come to mind when we or our parents and teachers talk about government.

Some praise "the government." Others say only bad things about it. Some people argue that "government" ought to do more. Others argue it ought to do less.

Who is really responsible for government in your town, in your state or in the United States?

Think about that.

Is government just one big powerful man? Is it just a few big powerful people who take control and tell the rest of us how to live, what to wear, what to say and what to read?

Some countries do have that kind of government. People in those nations have very little to say about their lives. When one person runs a country by himself, he is called a "dictator." That means he "dictates" what all people can do, what they can think and where they can work.

In the United States, government is exactly the opposite. Our country is in the hands of the people. Our Declaration of Independence said in 1776 that our government gets its power from "the governed." That means power from the people.

Why do we need government at all? Why does your town or city, your county or your state *need* government? Wouldn't it be better if we could all do anything we wanted, whenever we wanted to do it?

Good government does not try to hold us down. After all, this country belongs to us. Good government tries to help all people and tries to make it possible for all of us to enjoy the best things in the country.

Government does the many kinds of things that we could not afford to do by ourselves as individuals. It builds streets, bridges and sewers. Government provides police and firemen. Government builds most schools and colleges. It builds airports. It sometimes builds houses and apartments that people can live in at fair rents. Government can help people who do not earn enough to live properly.

Many people take very little interest in government—except to blame it when things go wrong. Most forget that WE are the government in this country.

WE are the government because we can vote in secret. If we do not like the people in office, we can vote against them. Often, however, not even half the people who can vote in our state bother to use the right.

People in our country can help to get the kind of government they want by voting. A person must be 18 years old to vote in New Jersey. YOU will be 18 by the time you get out of high school. You must register to vote, and you must be a U.S. **citizen**.

How does a person get to be a citizen? That is a good question! Turn the page to find out who are citizens, entitled to vote and to enjoy the many rights of people in the United States.

TO BE A CITIZEN

See if you can answer these questions. *This is not a test!* In fact, it would be very surprising if you could answer all the questions. Try these, and see how lucky you are if you were *born* a citizen of the United States.

Try these questions:
- *How long do Congressmen from New Jersey serve?*
- *How are United States laws made?*
- *Name the 13 Original Colonies.*

Those are just a few of the kinds of tough questions that people born in foreign countries must answer if they want to become United States citizens. They must study very hard. They must be prepared to answer questions on history and government.

Millions of people born in other nations have passed such tests to become U.S. citizens. Some went to night school to learn how to pass the tests.

They have wanted very much to be citizens of our country. They are very proud to pass the examination.

Perhaps some of your parents or grandparents or neighbors took such tests and became citizens. Ask them what citizenship means to *them*.

These are new citizens of the United States. They are being "sworn in," meaning that they are promising to be loyal to the nation and to obey all laws. These citizens were part of a large swearing-in ceremony that was conducted at Liberty State Park. Many nations were represented.

Those born in any of the 50 states and in Puerto Rico or other United States possessions are all citizens, too. We are *given* something that millions have struggled hard to earn.

You are also a citizen if you were born in another country and your parents were United States citizens. Some children in Army or Navy families are born in other countries. If their parents are U.S. citizens, they are automatically citizens, too.

What difference does it make to be a citizen of the United States?

Most important, you can vote. You can be a candidate for public office if you wish. You can be appointed to a government job. You can travel anywhere in this country without getting special permission.

Being a real U.S. citizen is more than just being born in the right place. It is more than passing a test.

Real citizens are persons who learn about our government, who take part in our country's activities and who work to make their town, state and nation better.

Let's look in the next eight pages at some kinds of government—in towns, in counties, in the State of New Jersey and in the United States.

You will see how you and your families, are a part—a *very important part*—of government.

227

GOVERNMENT CLOSE BY

Suppose your school had no playground. Suppose your city had no streets or sidewalks. Suppose your house was on fire.

What could you do about any of those *all by yourself*? Almost nothing!

That is why we have *local government*. People work together in our towns, as citizens, to provide what their place needs. We cannot build schools, playgrounds, streets or sidewalks as individuals. We cannot be our own firemen or policemen.

Local governments vary in size, because towns and cities are different. The word used for any local government is **municipality**. Cities, towns, boroughs, townships and villages are different kinds of municipalities in New Jersey.

You can't tell how *large* a place is by its name.

Newark is a city. Everybody knows that. Corbin City in Atlantic County is also a city. About 250 people live there! Port Republic calls itself a city. Its population is about 850!

Perhaps you think a village is a very small place. Ridgewood is a "village." It has about 25,000 residents! South Orange, another "village," has a population of about 16,000.

New Jersey has 567 municipalities. The largest in population is Newark, with about 325,000 people. The smallest is Tavistock in Camden County. The Tavistock population is 9! The next smallest is Teterboro (Bergen County). Only 21 residents live there!

Another way of rating towns is by *area*. Vineland (a city) is easily the largest city in area—69.5 square miles. It is not the largest *municipality*, however. That honor goes to Hamilton Township in Atlantic County. It is 115 square miles in area—larger than Hudson County!

New Jersey's smallest town in area is East Newark (Hudson County). It is one-tenth of a square mile. Most town parks are that large!

Find out about your own place. How many square miles does it cover? How many people live there? What kind of municipality is it—borough, city, village, township or town?

Think of things that citizens of your municipality do together that they could never do as individuals. Start with your street. Who built it? Who maintains it? Who plows the snow?

Perhaps you might attend a meeting of your town government with your parents or your teacher. You might visit "city hall," or whatever your local government building is called.

Ask questions. Local government belongs to everyone, including *you*!

Local government is not easy to understand. Let's start by thinking of your classroom as a "town." You are a "citizen" of that "town." What do you do together with other children? How do you cooperate to make your "town" a better place?

Could you elect your own "mayor" and other "officials" for your "town?" What problems in your "town" might be like those in your municipality? Can you offer ways to solve these problems? Remember, when YOU are the government, you must try to understand the problems of others!

TOWN TO TOWN

Your town is on one side of a wide New Jersey river. My town is on the other side.

Your town has a grocery store and a hardware store. My town has neither of those, but it does have a shopping mall and a movie theater. Your town does not have those. We need *your* town. You need *our* town.

Which of our municipalities should spend the money to build the bridge that we both want and need? Your town—or mine?

Most of us often want to travel from our municipality to another. Who should build the road between towns? Should each town build a section? Suppose that your municipality paves the road with concrete? Should my place be permitted to pave our section with logs? Suppose that we can only afford logs?

You can see that a bigger government is necessary to provide services that involve several places. In New Jersey, as you know, we have 21 counties. These are the "bigger government."

County government builds bridges between towns. It constructs highways that link municipalities. It provides county hospitals for people who are old or mentally ill. It may provide county parks, playgrounds, campgrounds and picnic areas.

Those who run county government

So far, we have been talking about your classroom as the "local government" in your school. Now let's see how your "town" (classroom) fits into "county government." We can think of your "county" as all of the classrooms (or "towns") in the same grade — such as 4A, 4B and 4C.

Classrooms at the same grade level have some things you would like to do together. Perhaps you might want to plan an assembly program. Maybe you could schedule a trip. Your "towns" could elect your own "Freeholders" to plan the activities! The "Freeholders" would be "building bridges" between rooms in your school.

are called **freeholders**. The name comes from colonial days, when only those who owned property could vote. Since property was called a "freehold," owners were freeholders. They elected a "Board of Chosen Freeholders" to represent them in county business.

Each county has a town that was chosen to be the **county seat**, where county government is carried on. County seats are easily found on road maps (or this book, pages 250 and 251).

The main building in the county seat is the county courthouse. Important trials are held there. Most New Jersey courthouses are old, historic buildings.

Each county has a "Hall of Records," where important documents are kept. These documents are more than just county or municipal records. Personal documents are also filed, such as property deeds or wills. Some business records are also on file.

Visit your county seat. Look at the courthouse and other county buildings. When was the courthouse built? Is it in a central place in your county? Is it big enough to take care of all county business in these busy days? Have other buildings been erected to share county business?

Perhaps you can get a freeholder to tell you about the courthouse and about county government. Maybe a lawyer in your town would come to your class to talk about deeds, wills and other documents.

JOINING THE 21

Some things are just too big and too expensive for even two or three counties to do together.

Bridges across either the wide Passaic River or the broad Raritan River would be good examples. So would roads that connect heavily-populated areas. Some major roads might be too expensive even for 10 to 12 counties to build together.

Our next higher level of government to do such "big" jobs is the *State Government*. It unites our 21 counties to provide important things needed by all people in the state.

A bridge over the widest part of the Raritan River would all be in only one county—Middlesex. People from everywhere in the state and the nation would use it.

Should only the people living in Middlesex County bear the cost of taking *everyone* over the river? Of course not! State government must help.

State government also pays most of the cost for education at Rutgers, The State University of New Jersey. State money also supports our nine state colleges and our 17 county colleges.

College education benefits nearly all people in the state. Not all people can afford to attend private colleges. That is why some public higher education should be available at the lowest cost possible. This support can best be given by the state government.

Our state government is centered in

Nearly all of the buildings in this picture are used by some form of state government. You recognize the State House dome, to the right. All of the white, state-owned structures have been built since 1963, when a huge program of constructing state buildings was begun. If you have been to Trenton on a field trip, you recognize the rounded building, top left. It is the planetarium. Nearby are the State Library and the State Museum. The large building in the lower edge is the War Memorial Building. It is not owned by the state.

Trenton. Many of you have seen the State Capitol and other state buildings.

The head of our state government is the Governor of New Jersey. New Jersey voters can vote for a governor every four years.

New Jersey also has **legislators**. They are men and women elected to represent varied districts of the state. The legislators make state laws. They approve the money spent to pay for state services.

New Jersey has two kinds of legislators. One group is called the *State Senate*. The other is named the *State Assembly*. Members of the Senate are called Senators. Assembly members are called Assemblymen or Assemblywomen.

There are 40 Senators and 80 members of the Assembly.

Legislators are very important to New Jersey. Can you find the names of your Senator and Assembly member? Ask any five adults if *they* know their legislators. You may be surprised! Many people do not realize the part that state government plays in all of our lives.

Thousands of people who are not elected also are employed in state government. These men and women work in various departments, such as Labor and Industry, Education, Agriculture, Transportation and Health.

One department that closely affects each of us is the Department of Environmental Protection. It seeks to keep our water and air clean. It also maintains our state parks, forests and historic sites.

This is the bottom line: state government is still *we, the people!*

So, your classroom is "local government" and your grade level is "county government." What would "state government" be in your school?

All the grades together would be "state government!" Anything that happens in your school affects everyone.

Perhaps your school has a Student Council. It should include "legislators" from every part of your school. It is important that legislators try to protect the rights of even the smallest and weakest of all of us.

233

UNITED WE STAND

Our country is the *United* States of America. That means the states have joined to form a strong *nation*. Our national government unites the 50 states. It helps us to do things together that we could not accomplish as individual states.

Suppose New Jersey was always at war with our nearest neighbors, Pennsylvania or New York? Or suppose all the states in the North fought all the states in the South?

That happened once. The North and the South fought in what was called the Civil War. It was fought more than 100 years ago, in the years between 1861 and 1865. That terrible war nearly split the nation into two pieces!

Our states must cooperate, or fall. That is why we have the U.S. Government in Washington. By cooperating, stronger states can help weaker ones. We can build interstate highways that reach from the Atlantic Ocean to the Pacific. We can protect ourselves against outside enemies.

If there were not a United States Government, we probably would always be arguing with our neighboring states. We would say, "YOU build the bridges over the Delaware!" They would say, "No, YOU build them, New Jersey!"

You know that the head of our U.S. Government is the President. We vote for a President every four years.

We, the people of New Jersey, also take part in the U.S. Government even more directly. We elect two U.S. Senators and 14 Congressmen to speak for us in Washington.

Our two Senators represent all of New Jersey. Our Congressmen, in the House of Representatives, speak for various *sections* of our state. New Jersey is divided into 14 *districts*, which are supposed to be nearly equal in population. Each district has a Congressman. Do you know the name of *yours*?

Our national government does not merely work between states. It does many things within state borders.

The U.S. Government pays for and runs big natural areas, such as The Great Swamp and Brigantine National Wildlife Refuge. It operates the U.S. Coast Guard along the Jersey Shore. It operates lighthouses along our coast. It keeps the deep channels open in our main rivers.

U.S. money helps run our railroads. Fort Dix and Fort Monmouth are both national military installations. Picatinny Arsenal near Dover is owned by the United States.

Remember reading about the aviation research being done at NAFEC near Atlantic City? That is accomplished with U.S. money.

New Jersey's most unusual historic site is the Morristown National Historical Park. It includes Washington's Headquarters in Morristown and nearby Jockey Hollow. United States money has been used there to preserve history since 1933. That year the Morristown Park was established as the first national historical park.

Government in Washington might seem far away. Yet remember that we the people have the power to control our U.S. Government. As long as people vote, *we* have power!

Sometimes we states have to give up some things for the sake of a better nation. If we did not, the United States would be so divided that we surely would fall.

235

EVERYTHING IS FREE?

You probably would like more playgrounds, more baseball fields and more parks. Your parents want good schools, better roads and good water to run from the faucets in your home. All families would like to enjoy good swimming beaches.

Perhaps your class has taken a trip to Washington Crossing State Park or Barnegat Light. Someday you may want to attend Rutgers, the State University, or one of the state colleges. You might want to go to one of the county colleges.

Playground, baseball fields, parks, roads, colleges: Everything is free, right?

Wrong! Everything costs money, even when the government builds it. Remember, WE are the government!

Often we, the government, decide to build things that will cost a lot of money. Our schools, roads and public parks are good examples. There is only one way to get the money. We pay taxes.

Everybody pays taxes, one way or another.

Most people pay "income taxes" to both the U.S. Government and the State of New Jersey. Gasoline prices include heavy taxes. We pay a state "sales tax" on nearly everything we buy except for food and clothing.

Most New Jersey tax money comes from what are called "property taxes." That means any person who owns land and buildings, must pay taxes on them. Most property taxes go to the local government where the property is located.

Property owners also pay "county taxes" to provide money for what we want county government to do for us. Money from the New Jersey sales tax goes to our State Government.

Industry pays taxes, too. We might think, "That is fine. *They* can afford it!" However, industry usually just adds the cost of that tax to the price we pay for what we buy. So *We*, the people, really pay industry's taxes as well as our own!

We pay other kinds of "taxes" without thinking about it. Every toll that we pay on the Garden State Parkway or the New Jersey Turnpike is really a "tax." The toll money pays for the roads without regular tax money from "the government."

Some people think that "the government" should pay for nearly everything that we use together. They say that if "the government" pays, then we all would have more money for ourselves.

There is one thing wrong with that. You know what it is. The *only* money that government has comes from taxes. *We* pay the taxes!

Taxes are the price we pay to have whatever we, the people, agree is necessary or worthwhile.

TAXES
U.S. CONGRESS
N.J. LEGISLATURE
TOWN GOVERNMENT
COUNTY GOVERNMENT
EVERYTHING IS FREE... ...RIGHT?
SCHOOL
PARKS
BALL FIELD
F.D.
RUTGERS
STATE COLLEGES
FARM AID
POLICE
PUBLIC LIBRARY
PARKWAY AND TURNPIKE

GLOSSARY

archaeologist. A scientist who learns about past people's lives by finding and studying the things a group has left behind.

barracks. A building where soldiers live.

barter. To exchange things without the use of money.

bay. A part of ocean or sea that reaches into the coastline.

canal. A man-made waterway for boats.

cargo. Goods transported on a ship, truck, plane or train.

cartographer. A mapmaker.

citizen. A person who by birth or choice becomes a member of a nation.

climate. The kind of weather a place has throughout the year.

colony (colonies). A settlement belonging to a distant country.

commuter. A person who each day travels a long distance between home and work.

continent. A very large body of land. The globe has seven continents.

corridor. A long passageway.

county. A division of a state for the purpose of government. New Jersey is divided into 21 counties.

county seat. A town or city that is the home of a county's government.

degree. A part of a circle that measures one-360th of the total.

dune. A hill of sand formed by nature.

Equator. An imaginary line around the globe, located halfway between the North and South Poles.

environment. Our natural surroundings: air, water, living things, etc.

fossil. The remains of a plant or animal that, over a long period of time, have turned to stone.

freeholder. A person elected to share the responsibilities of county government.

geology. A science that deals with the earth's history, especially as recorded in rocks.

geologist. A scientist who studies the earth's natural history.

glacier. A large body of slowly moving ice.

harbor. A sheltered body of water where ships may anchor or tie up at docks.

hemisphere. Half of sphere (or ball shape); half of the earth.

Hessian. Soldier from Germany paid to fight against the Americans during the Revolution.

immigrant. A person who leaves a homeland to live in another country.

import. To bring goods from another country or any other distant place.

industry. A business that provides a product or service.

irrigate. To bring water to farm fields by pipes, ditches or canals.

latitude. Distance north or south of the Equator. Lines that measure latitude run east-west around the globe.

legislator. A person elected to make laws for the state or nation.

longitude. The distance east or west of the prime meridian. Lines that measure latitude run north-south around the globe.

Loyalist. A colonist "loyal" to England and therefore unwilling to join the American fight for independence.

manufacturing. The making of products by hand or machine.

marshland. An area of soft, wet land; often covered with grass-like plants.

massacre. The violent and cruel killing of large numbers of people.

mastodon. An extinct animal resembling an elephant.

militia. An army made up of citizens with some military training, but called into service only during emergencies.

Minutemen. Citizens during the Revolution who were ready to leave their homes and fight at a moment's notice.

municipality. A community with its own government.

nursery. A farm where plants and trees are raised for sale.

ocean. A large body of salt water. The world has four oceans.

ornamental. A plant used to decorate the property of a home or business.

Patriot. Any colonist who believed that America should fight for independence from England.

peninsula. Land that extends out into water and is almost surrounded by it. Because of the Delaware River on one side, New Jersey can be called a peninsula.

port. A place where ships load or unload freight cargoes.

prehistoric time. Refers to the time before the start of a written history.

privateer. A captain of a private armed ship (not part of the regular navy) who is permitted by the government to make war against enemy ships.

Redcoats. Name given by American colonists to the British troops because they wore red uniform coats.

refuge. A place where wildlife is protected from harm.

refugee. A person who flees from danger, usually to a foreign country.

reservoir. A place where water is stored for future use.

sapling. A young, thin, green-trunked tree.

scale. The part of a map that compares the map's size to the actual place being mapped.

skirmish. A minor battle in a war.

specialize. To limit oneself to one business or subject. In agriculture, when a farmer limits his kinds of crops.

sound. A long stretch of water that often connects two larger bodies of water or forms a channel between the mainland and an island.

state. One of the divisions of a country with a national government. Our country, the U.S.A., has 50 states.

steerage. A dark, cramped area below the main decks of a ship and very close to the ship's steering apparatus. Here, immigrants paying the lowest fares were housed for the journey across the Atlantic Ocean.

symbol. Something that stands for another thing: the N.J. State Seal is a symbol of our state government.

succotash. An Indian stew of corn and lima beans.

tanker. A ship that has huge tanks for carrying oil.

textile. A cloth that is woven, by hand or on machines.

thoroughfare. A main road or means of travel (colonists often called rivers thoroughfares).

tinker. A person who likes to putter and can fix all sorts of things.

tourism. Travel for pleasure.

tunnel. A passage under the ground or through a mountain for cars, trucks, buses or trains.

turnpike. A road on which a person must pay a toll in order to travel.

urban. City-like; opposite to "country."

village green. A grassy, open area (usually square) at the center of a colonial town where people met to exchange ideas, news and goods.

wampum. Beads made from shells and used by Indians as money.

NEW JERSEY "FIRSTS"

Everything on these two pages is a New Jersey first — invented, manufactured, discovered, played or organized in our state. This is just a sampling. You probably can find some "firsts" in your own town or county. If you do, please let us know!

First AIR VOYAGE in America, made in balloon from Philadelphia to Deptford, 1793.

First BASEBALL game played under organized rules, Hoboken, 1846.

First BLUEBERRIES grown for markets, Whitesbog, 1916.

First BOARDWALK laid on sand, Atlantic City, 1870.

First CANNED TOMATOES packed at Jamesburg, 1847.

First CHINA made in America for use in White House, Trenton, 1918.

First FIRST AID KITS made in New Brunswick, 1890.

First FM STATION went on air at Alpine, 1937.

First FOOTBALL game played by college teams; Princeton-Rutgers, 1869.

First GLASS factory successfully operated in America. Salem County, 1739.

First IRON BEAMS for use in construction, Trenton, 1854.

First PATENT LEATHER in America, Newark, 1819.

First LOCOMOTIVE in America, steam-powered, made at Hoboken, 1825.

First ELECTRIC LIGHT, made practical by Thomas Edison, Menlo Park, 1879.

First PERMANENT MAGNET, previously considered impossible, Newark, 1887.

First MISS AMERICA chosen, Atlantic City, 1921.

First MOVIES made and shown in West Orange, 1889.

First MOVIE WITH A PLOT made near Edison's West Orange studio, 1903.

First MOVIE STUDIO in the world, West Orange, 1893.

First PLASTIC in America, "Celluloid," made in Newark, 1873.

First PHONOGRAPH invented by Edison at Menlo Park, 1877.

First REVOLVER, or repeating pistol, Paterson, 1836.

First ROCKET ENGINES made at Pompton Plains, early 1940s.

First ROLLER BEARINGS, Newark, 1885.

First SILK FACTORY in the United States, Paterson, 1838.

First SMOKE DETECTOR, perfected in Jersey City, 1900.

First CONDENSED SOUP (add water, heat and serve), Camden, 1897.

First STEAMBOAT in America ran from Burlington to Philadelphia, 1786.

First STEAM ENGINE brought to New Jersey from England in 1753; operated at Arlington, 1755.

First SUBMARINE in America, Paterson, 1878.

First TEFLON, the well-known "non-stick" plastic, developed at Arlington, 1943.

First THERMOS BOTTLE made in Vineland in the 1880s.

First TRANSISTOR made by three-man science team, Murray Hill, 1948.

First TV for home use made in Upper Montclair, 1933.

First TV SHOW successfully broadcast from Whippany to New York, 1927.

First TV TAPE perfected at RCA's Princeton lab, 1951.

First VITAMIN B1 produced chemically at Roselle, 1934.

First VOLTMETER measuring electric current, Newark, 1888.

First WAX PAPER made in Garfield, 1887.

NEW JERSEY DATES

1524 Italian captain, Giovanni da Verrazano, explored parts of northern N.J.

1609 Henry Hudson, English captain sailing for Holland, explored Jersey coast, Raritan Bay, Hudson River.

1630 Dutch settlers in what is now Hudson County.

1638 New Sweden started beside lower Delaware River.

1660 Dutch Governor Peter Stuyvesant founded Bergen (now part of Jersey City); 1st N.J. town.

1664 England took over land between Delaware and Hudson rivers, named it New Jersey.

1665 Elizabethtown, Woodbridge, Piscataway, Middletown and Shrewsbury settled by Long Island and New England families.

1666 Newark established by settlers from Connecticut.

1668 1st N.J. Assembly met at Elizabethtown.

1675 John Fenwick and English colonists founded Salem, 1st Quaker colony in America.

1681 Burlington named capital of West New Jersey.

1686 East New Jersey capital located in Perth Amboy.

1702 East and West New Jersey united into one colony.

1739 America's 1st successful glass works established in Salem County.

1746 College of New Jersey (now Princeton University) started. Moved, Newark to Princeton, in 1756.

1758 Lenape reservation opened at Indian Mills; one of 1st reservations in U.S.

1764 Sandy Hook lighthouse erected; now America's oldest continuously-lit lighthouse.

1766 Queens College founded. Renamed Rutgers College in 1825 because of small gift of money from Colonel Henry Rutgers.

1773 New Jersey began to turn against England, opposing taxes and British laws.

1774 Greenwich patriots burned tea in their village, December 22.

1776 Washington's troops smashed Hessians in a crucial battle at Trenton, December 26.

1777 After defeating British at Princeton (January 3), Washington's army went to winter camp at Morristown.

1777 Colonial troops repulsed British and Hessians: Battle of Red Bank in Gloucester County.

1778 Washington's army fought British to standstill in Battle of Monmouth, June 28.

1778 American army spent winter of 1778-79 in and near Somerville.

1779 American army returned to Morristown; winter of 1779-80 worst of the entire war.

1780 British and Hessians twice defeated in moves toward Morristown: at Connecticut Farms (now Union), June 6, and at Springfield, June 23.

1783 Princeton was temporary capital of U.S. when Continental Congress met at Nassau Hall, June to November.

1787 New Jersey 3rd state to approve U.S. Constitution.

1790 Trenton chosen as permanent state capital.

1791 Paterson founded at the Great Falls as America's 1st planned industrial city.

1811 Steam ferry started, Hoboken to New York.

1819 Seth Boyden of Newark made America's 1st patent leather.

1826 Boyden produced America's 1st malleable iron.

1831 Part of Camden & Amboy, 1st N.J. railroad, finished near Bordentown.

1832 State's 1st daily newspaper, "Newark Daily Advertiser," started.

1834 Delaware & Raritan Canal completed, New Brunswick to Trenton. Extended to Bordentown, 1838.

1836 Morris Canal, completed from Phillipsburg to Jersey City. Started in 1825, took 11 years to build.

1838 Alfred Vail perfected Samuel Morse's telegraph at Morristown.

1844 New State Constitution adopted, replacing Constitution of 1776.

1848 U.S. Lifesaving Service begun as idea of New Jerseyan William Newell.

1848 James Marshall of Lambertville discovered gold in California, setting off the great "gold rush."

1849 Dr. Solomon Andrews, Perth Amboy, began making world's 1st successful dirigibles.

1853 Teachers from eight counties founded New Jersey Education Association (N.J.E.A.).

1854 Atlantic City begun as oceanside terminal for new Camden & Atlantic Railroad, starting big-scale tourism.

1855 New Jersey's 1st teacher training schools opened in Trenton, Paterson and Newark.

1862 Fort Delaware on Pea Patch Island near Salem became prison for Southern soldiers captured in Civil War. More than 12,500 prisoners on the tiny island; about 2,500 died.

1865 Paterson companies topped Philadelphia as nation's leading locomotive builders.

1869 Rutgers defeated Princeton 6-4, in 1st intercollegiate football game.

1869 Joseph Campbell opened tomato cannery in Camden.

1873 Immigrant families from Italy settled on Vineland farmlands.

1875 Voters eliminated word "white" from state voting laws.

1876 Thomas Edison opened world's 1st research laboratory at Menlo Park.

1877 Edison invented phonograph. He called it his "favorite invention."

1878 John Holland, Paterson school teacher, submerged 1st U.S. submarine in Passaic River.

1879 World's 1st practical incandescent lamp made by Edison.

1880 U.S. Census showed 1,131,116 people in New Jersey; 1st time population topped one million mark.

1884 Grover Cleveland, who was born in Caldwell, elected President of U.S.

1887 Edison moved laboratory from Menlo Park to West Orange.

1888 "Blizzard of '88," March 11, closed railroads, factories and schools.

1889 Edison's 1st movie machine made at West Orange.

1891 New Jersey became 1st U.S. state to pay state money for road building.

1893 World's 1st movie picture studio, "The Black Maria," completed at Edison's West Orange laboratory.

1893 World's 1st "certified" milk guaranteed pure, produced at Caldwell.

1908 1st radio broadcast from experimental station in Newark.

1912 Woodrow Wilson, Governor of N.J., elected U.S. President.

1914 World War I began. New Jersey factories supplied arms.

1917 Fort Dix opened to train U.S. soldiers for World War I.

1921 WJZ, world's second radio station, established in Newark. 1st program: 1921 World Series.

1922 WOR began broadcasting from Newark. 1st eastern station to schedule 15-minute news broadcasts.

1926 Benjamin Franklin Bridge opened, Camden to Philadelphia.

1927 1st wireless TV broadcast, Whippany to New York.

1927 Holland Tunnel opened under Hudson River, connecting Jersey City and New York.

1928 Newark Airport started. In 1931, completed airport was called "busiest in the world."

1931 George Washington Bridge opens: Fort Lee to New York. Bayonne Bridge completed: Bayonne to Staten Island.

1933 National Historical Park, 1st in U.S., created in Morristown.

1937 1st tube of Lincoln Tunnel opened, connecting Weehawken to New York.

1941 New Jersey workers began making huge supplies of arms for World War II.

1945 Rutgers University officially named the State University.

1947 New State Constitution approved by voters; replaced 1844 Constitution.

1948 Transistor, one of world's great inventions, perfected at Murray Hill.

1951 Delaware Memorial Bridge, Salem County to Wilmington, Del., dedicated.

1953 N.J. Turnpike, 118-mile-long toll road, completed across state.

1954 Garden State Parkway, 143 miles long, completed from Cape May to New York State line.

1957 Walt Whitman Bridge connected Camden and Philadelphia.

1959 Savannah, world's 1st nuclear-powered commercial vessel, launched at Camden.

1961 Voters approved 1st of several "Green Acres" proposals to protect N.J. environment.

1962 Astronaut Walter M. Schirra, Jr., a New Jerseyan, completed six orbits of the earth.

1964 State celebrated 300th anniversary of being named New Jersey.

1968 Garden State Arts Center opened in Monmouth County.

1969 Edwin Aldrin of Montclair was one of the two men who were first to walk on the moon.

1971 Sandy Hook included in U.S. Gateway National Recreational Area.

1976 Meadowlands sports complex opened in East Rutherford.

1978 1st casino opens its doors for gambling in Atlantic City.

1978 U.S. Congress established Pinelands National Reserve. 1st such reserve in the nation.

1985 Population of New Jersey rose above 7½ million people for 1st time.

245

FAMOUS NEW JERSEYANS

ABBOT, Bud (1895-1974). Asbury Park man; noted comedian with Lou Costello.

ALLAIRE, James (1785-1858). Bought Howell Iron Works in Monmouth County in 1822. His iron making town is now Allaire State Park.

ALLEN, Elizabeth (Died 1919). Taught first in Atlantic City, then Hoboken. In 1871, became a leader in struggle to win better pay and privileges for teachers.

ANNIN, Benjamin (1817-1895). Founded flag making company. His sons opened world's largest flag making company at Verona, 1916.

ANDREWS, Solomon (1806-1872). Perth Amboy doctor, inventor; made and flew world's 1st successful dirigibles, 1849 to 1865.

ARONSON, Louis (1869-1940). Newark inventor and manufacturer. Invented: time fuse for airplane bombs, windproof matches and "voice" for "Mama dolls."

BARRY, John (1745-1803). Born in Ireland, came to America, 1760. Appointed 1st U.S. Navy officer, 1775. Led ships into battle from Bordentown. His birthday, Sept. 13, celebrated in N.J. schools.

BARTON, Clara (1821-1912). Established 1st successful N.J. free school at Bordentown in 1853. Civil War nurse and founder, American Red Cross.

BOARDMAN, Alex (1830-1900). Railroad conductor. Planned and built first boardwalk in Atlantic City, 1870.

BOURKE-WHITE, Margaret (1906-1971). One of the greatest American photographers; graduate of Plainfield H.S.

BOYDEN, Seth (1798-1870). Inventor. Perfected in Newark: 1st patent leather, 1st malleable iron, many other things, including huge strawberries.

BURR, Aaron (1746-1836). Princeton University graduate. 3rd Vice President of the U.S.

CALDWELL, Rev. James (1734-1780). Elizabeth minister active in Revolution.

CLARK, Abram (1725-1794). Rahway surveyor and lawyer. Called "Poor Man's Lawyer." Signed Declaration of Independence.

CLEVELAND, Grover (1837-1908). Born in Caldwell. Twice elected as U.S. President. Died in Princeton.

COLLINS, Isaac (1746-1817). Burlington printer. Started 1st N.J. newspaper, "New Jersey Gazette," in 1777.

COLT, Samuel (1814-1862). Paterson inventor. Made world's 1st six-shot revolver at his Paterson gun mill in 1836.

COOK, George H. (1818-1889). Geologist, mapmaker, farm scientist. First head of N.J. Agricultural Experiment Station (part of Rutgers University).

COSTELLO, Lou (1908-1959). Paterson comedian; Abbott and Costello movies often seen on television.

CRANE, Stephen (1871-1900). Newark-born man who wrote great Civil War book, *The Red Badge of Courage*.

CROMWELL, Oliver (1747-1853). Burlington County black soldier; served six years during the Revolution in 2nd N.J. Regiment. Died at 106.

CROSBY, Harrison (1815-1875). First to pack tomatoes in tin cans. Did research and canning at Jamesburg.

DANA, John Cotton (1856-1929). World famed Newark Library director. Also founded Newark Museum.

DIX, Dorothea (1802-1887). Her report on horrible N.J. jails and places for insane forced state in 1844 to build new State Hospital for mentally-ill.

DODGE, Mary Mapes (1838-1905). Wrote book, *Hans Brinker, or the Silver Skates* at her Newark home. People of Holland called it a fine story of their land.

DORRANCE, John T. (1873-1930). Developed first canned condensed soups at Campbell Company in Camden.

DOUGLASS, Mabel Smith (1877-1933). Jersey City woman who led drive for a N.J. woman's college (now called Douglass College). Became 1st dean when college founded, 1918.

DURAND, Asher (1796-1880). Maplewood artist; won fame for his engravings, portraits and landscape paintings.

EDISON, Thomas A. (1847-1931). Probably the world's greatest inventor. Spent last 60 years of life in N.J.

FENWICK, John (1618-1683). Established Salem in 1675 as 1st Quaker colony in America.

EINSTEIN, Albert (1879-1955). German-born scientist; lived and worked in Princeton from 1933 until his death.

FITCH, John (1743-1798). Trenton arms maker. Made 1st American steamboat, ran it on Delaware River in 1787.

FORESTER, Frank (1807-1858). English-born writer; settled in Newark, wrote famous books on outdoor life, nature, hunting and fishing.

FRANCIS, Joseph (1801-1893). Toms River inventor. Perfected unsinkable lifeboat to save people aboard wrecked ships.

FRANK, Morris (1908-1980). Trained and used 1st Seeing Eye dog in U.S.; made headquarters in Morristown, 1930.

FRENEAU, Philip (1752-1832). Monmouth County writer and Revolutionary War leader. Called "Poet of the Revolution."

GARIS, Howard (1873-1962). Newark newspaperman who wrote well-known "Uncle Wiggily" stories and books about a "rabbit gentleman" and his friends.

GILBRETH, Lillian (1878-1972). Montclair psychologist/engineer. Internationally known for insistence that human beings, not machines, were most important in successful industry. Mother of 12 children. Her story told in *Cheaper by the Dozen*.

GOODWIN, Hannibal (1822-1900). Newark minister who invented flexible photographic film, used in cameras and for making motion pictures.

HADDON, Elizabeth (1681-1762). Born England, came to America in 1701, founded Camden County town named for her.

HANCOCK, Cornelia (1840-1884). Salem Quaker who volunteered as nurse in Civil War. Worked after war to aid newly-free blacks in the South.

HART, John (1711-1779). Hopewell farmer; signed Declaration of Independence.

HOBART, Garrett (1844-1899). Born in Long Branch, became successful Paterson businessman. Elected U.S. Vice President, 1896.

HOLLAND, John P. (1840-1914). Irish-born schoolteacher. Came to Paterson in 1873, launched 1st American submarine in Passaic River in 1878.

HOPKINSON, Francis (1737-1791). Bordentown writer, poet and musician. Signed Declaration of Independence.

HUDDY, Joshua (1740-1782). Defended important Toms River saltworks. Captured in 1782; executed by British.

HYATT, John W. (1837-1920). Invented Celluloid, 1st American plastic, in 1872. Opened huge Newark factory in 1873 to make it.

INNESS, George (1825-1894). First great American landscape painter. Lived and painted in Montclair.

JOHNSON, Eldridge R. (1860-1910). Made Edison's "talking machine" practical by inventing flat records and perfecting regular speeds of operation.

247

JOHNSON, Robert W. (1845-1910). Started making medical plasters in Orange in 1874. Later, with his brothers, opened Johnson & Johnson, world's largest maker of surgical dressings.

KILMER, Joyce (1886-1918). New Brunswick poet; wrote poem "Trees." Taught in Morristown, later lived in Mahwah. Killed in France in World War I.

LAKEY, Alice (1857-1935). Cranford woman who talked throughout the nation on impure foods; leading force in nation's 1st Pure Food and Drug Act, 1906.

LAWRENCE, James (1781-1813). Navy captain, born in Burlington. Won fame in War of 1812. Wounded, he pleaded with crew: "Don't give up the ship!" He died of wounds, but crew saved ship.

LENOX, Walter (1859-1920). Trenton pottery maker who made 1st American china used in White House, 1918.

LIVINGSTON, William (1723-1790). 1st governor of State of New Jersey after independence from England was declared, in 1776.

LANDIS, Charles K. (1833-1900). Founder of Vineland, one of America's first planned cities.

MAASS, Clara Louise (1876-1901). East Orange and Newark nurse. Sacrificed her life in Cuba in 1901 during tests to prove mosquitoes carried yellow fever.

MACCULLOCH, George (1775-1858). Morristown schoolteacher; dreamed up plans for Morris Canal while fishing at Lake Hopatcong in 1822.

MARSHALL, James (1812-1855). Lambertville man who went to California in 1844 and discovered gold in 1848. This set off the celebrated "gold rush."

MASON, John (1832-1890). Vineland glass maker. In 1858 perfected 1st glass container for fruits and vegetables, the "Mason Jar."

MAXIM, Hudson (1853-1927). Invented Maximite, shock-proof highly explosive, and smokeless gunpowder.

NAST, Thomas (1840-1902). One of greatest cartoonists of all times. Lived in Morristown last 30 years of life. There he drew a "fat, jolly" Santa Claus as well as symbols for political parties.

NEWELL, William (1817-1901). While working as a doctor at Manahawkin, organized what is now the Coast Guard to save lives of shipwrecked passengers.

PAUL, Alice (1885-1977). Moorestown woman known worldwide as fighter for equal rights for women. Was a leader in getting women the right to vote.

PETERSON, Thomas (1840-1890). 1st black voter cast his ballot at Perth Amboy. Right to vote guaranteed to all citizens by 15th Amendment to U.S. Constitution.

PHILBROOK, Mary (1872-1958). First woman lawyer to be accepted as member by N.J. Bar Assn. Worked to improve rights of women and children.

ROBESON, Paul (1898-1976). Scholar, athlete, actor, concert singer. Lived in Princeton and Somerville. Won All-American honors in football; top student in his class at Rutgers.

ROEBLING, John A. (1806-1869). Trenton bridgebuilder who 1st used wire cables on suspension bridges. Died while constructing the Brooklyn Bridge.

SHAHN, Ben (1898-1969). Painter from town of Roosevelt; won national fame for his murals and other artworks.

SOMERS, Richard (1778-1804). Atlantic County captain in U.S. Navy. Killed in Tripoli while fighting Mediterranean pirates.

STEVENS, John (1749-1838). Hoboken inventor. Made 1st ocean-going steamboat in 1804 and constructed 1st American steam locomotive in 1825.

STILL, James (1812-1885). Called "Black Doctor of the Pines" because of skill in curing pineland people with local herbs and medicines.

STOCKTON, Annis (1736-1801). Poet who gave name "Morven" to the notable Princeton house. Wife of Richard Stockton.

STOCKTON, Richard (1730-1781). Princeton lawyer who signed Declaration of Independence. Became ill, died after British constantly sought his capture.

STOUT, Penelope (1622-1712). Dutch woman, seriously wounded at age 20 during shipwreck off Sandy Hook. Survived to marry Richard Stout of Monmouth County. They had 10 children.

TERHUNE, Albert Payson (1872-1942). Wrote much-loved and widely-read stories of collie dogs that he raised on his Pompton Lakes estate.

TREAT, Mary (1830-1923). Distinguished Vineland botanist and naturalist. Noted for her studies of Pine Barrens plants.

TUBMAN, Harriet, (1820-1913). Leader in the plan that helped escaping black slaves to gain freedom. Worked at times at Cape May hotels to finance her work.

VAIL, Alfred (1802-1859). Morristown inventor; made Samuel Morse's telegraph instruments work. Perfected message system known as the "Morse Code."

WARD, Samuel A. (1847-1903). Newark composer; wrote music for "America The Beautiful."

WESTON, Edward (1850-1936). Invented and built dynamos for electric lights; invented the photoelectric cell, much used in alarm systems, door openers, etc.

WHITE, Elizabeth (1872-1954). Developed and marketed world's 1st cultivated blueberries, 1916. Most popular modern blueberry varieties developed by her.

WHITMAN, Walt (1819-1892). Great American poet. Lived last 19 years of his life in Camden, where his home still stands.

WILLIAMS, William Carlos (1883-1963). Medical doctor, Bergen and Passaic counties. Delivered thousands of babies but his fame is for writing poems about Paterson area.

WILSON, Woodrow (1856-1924). Virginia born, attended Princeton University, became its president in 1902. Elected governor of N.J. in 1910. Twice elected President of the U.S., 1912 and 1916.

WITHERSPOON, John (1722-1794). Came from Scotland in 1768 to be president of College of New Jersey (now Princeton). Fifth and last New Jersey signer of Declaration of Independence.

WRIGHT, Patience (1725-1786). Bordentown Quaker; modeled figures from bread to amuse her four children. Before her death, became known as America's first sculptor.

COUNTIES OF NEW JERSEY

COUNTY	COUNTY SEAT	AREA SQ. MI.	RANK IN AREA	POPULATION 1987	RANK IN POPULATION	DATE FOUNDED	NOTED FOR
Atlantic	Mays Landing	567	4	208,500	15	1837	Miles and miles of beach. Famed seaside resorts, including Atlantic City.
Bergen	Hackensack	235	15	830,400	2	1683	One of East Jersey's 4 original colonies. Offers scenic pleasure of the Palisades. Home of Meadowlands Sports Complex.
Burlington	Mount Holly	827	1	388,000	11	1681	Only county to stretch from Atlantic Ocean to Delaware River. Home of much of Pinelands, America's 1st National Reserve.
Camden	Camden	227	16	496,300	7	1844	Most heavily populated southern county. Industrial and transportation hub. Some farming left.
Cape May	Cape May Court House	265	14	94,200	19	1692	Town of Cape May, America's oldest seaside resort. Vacation spot of Presidents including: Lincoln, Grant and Harrison.
Cumberland	Bridgeton	500	6	137,600	16	1748	Home of N.J.'s 1st oyster fleet. Industries include: agriculture, food processing, glass making. "Tea party" at Greenwich, 1774.
Essex	Newark	127	19	844,500	1	1683	One of East Jersey's 4 original colonies. Home of Newark, our largest city. The "University County" — 10 colleges here.
Gloucester	Woodbury	329	11	213,000	14	1686	A "garden spot," leading producer of fruits and vegetables. First settled by Swedes.
Hudson	Jersey City	46	21	547,200	5	1840	State's most densely populated county. New Jersey's 1st village, Bergen (Part of Jersey City). Home to Miss Liberty.
Hunterdon	Flemington	437	3	98,900	18	1714	Scenic county with rolling hills and picturesque farms. Host to annual Flemington Fair!

250

County	Seat			Population		Year	Description
Mercer	Trenton	226	17	327,100	12	1838	The "Capital County," home of our state government. World famous Princeton University here.
Middlesex	New Brunswick	319	12	645,700	3	1683	One of East Jersey's 4 original colonies. Home of Rutgers, the State University. Menlo Park, site of Edison's lab.
Monmouth	Freehold	477	8	553,600	4	1683	State's first iron furnace at Tinton Falls, 1675. Birthplace and home of superstar Bruce Springsteen!
Morris	Morristown	490	7	419,400	9	1739	Home of Great Swamp Wildlife Refuge. Twice the winter home of General Washington and his troops.
Ocean	Toms River	638	2	403,000	10	1850	Explored in 1614 by Dutch captain Cornelius Mey. Today, our fastest growing county. Many seaside resorts here.
Passaic	Paterson	194	18	463,700	8	1837	America's 1st planned industrial city: Paterson. Home of Passaic River's Great Falls. A major manufacturing center.
Salem	Salem	347	10	65,400	21	1694	America's 1st glass factory here, 1739. One of state's most rural counties; almost half of land in farming.
Somerset	Somerville	304	13	221,600	13	1688	Winter headquarters of General Washington at Somerville, 1778-79. At Gladstone, U.S. Equestrian Team makes its home.
Sussex	Newton	527	5	124,300	17	1753	Here NJ highest spot: High Point, 1803 feet above sea level. A sports lovers delight: hiking, skiing, camping, more!
Union	Elizabeth	103	20	502,500	6	1857	State's "youngest" county. Home of scenic Watchung Mountains. Lots of flat land for industry and homes.
Warren	Belvidere	362	9	87,200	20	1824	At Belvidere, the "Shoe Tree," over 300 years old. Splendors include Delaware Water Gap and the fertile Great Meadows.

251

INDEX

A
Absecon Lighthouse, 47
Agriculture 37, 44, 45, 50, 51, 80, 81, 90, 91, 93, 109, 118, 124, 125, 140, 149, 155, 164, 171-188, 193, 209
Airports (Airplanes), 11, 146, 147
Algonquians, 67 (see also: Indians)
Allamuchy, 68
Allentown, 187
Alliance, 125
American Revolution (see Revolution, American)
Amphibians, 221
Animals, 37, 63, 70, 84, 85, 176, 177, 182, 183, 185, 208, 217, 221, 222 (see also: animal names)
Appalachian Trail, 36, 37
Apple Pie Hill, 42
Apples, 45, 156, 178, 179
Arthur Kill, 149
Asparagus, 172, 180
Atlantic City, 13, 46, 47, 143, 145, 147, 154, 159
Atlantic County, 23, 179, 181, 182, 211, 229, 250
Atlantic Highlands, 47
Atlantic Ocean, 22, 23, 34, 46, 49, 50, 67, 79, 94, 110, 120, 121, 148, 214, 215
Automobiles, 39, 133, 144, 145, 149, 152
Avalon, 214

B
Bader Field, 147
Balloon travel, 147
Barnegat Bay, 110
Barnegat Light, 47
Barnsboro, 59
Batsto, 43, 93, 159
Bay Head, 47
Bayonne, 48, 49, 124, 149, 159, 191
Bayonne Bridge, 151
Bays, 47, 214
Beach Haven, 47
Beans, 172, 181
Bedminster, 105
Bees, 18, 184, 185
Belleville, 191
Bell Laboratories, 168
Benjamin Franklin Bridge, 150, 151, 201
Bergen, 80, 198
Bergen County, 23, 55, 81, 110, 117, 140, 141, 154, 228, 250
Bergen County Historical Society, 73
Birds, 19, 158, 161, 208, 215, 221
Blacksmiths, 158, 161, 208, 215, 221, 222
Bloomfield, 52
Blueberries, 45, 172, 178, 179
Bog Iron, 93, 157
Bogota, 60
Boonton, 57
Bordentown, 92, 101, 140
Boston Tea Party, 100
Boundaries, 17, 34, 35, 38, 49
Bound Brook, 104, 105, 141
Boyden, Seth, 160
Brick, 40, 202
Bridges, 52, 135, 136, 150, 151, 161, 201, 232
Bridgeton, 52, 113
Brigantine, 211, 217, 235
Brotherton, 75
Brotmanville, 125
Burlington, 83, 86, 92, 134, 142, 158
Burlington County, 22, 23, 44, 112, 126, 179, 181, 250
Burnet, Daniel, 129
Burr, Aaron, 129

C
Caboto, Giovanni & Sebastian, 78
Caldwell, 129
Caldwell, Rev. James, 107
Camden, 40, 41, 48, 91, 124, 132, 135, 139, 143, 145, 147, 148, 149, 150, 151, 159, 161, 164, 165, 191, 192, 194, 201, 203, 206, 250
Camden County, 23, 126, 179, 182, 228, 250
Campbell, Joseph, 164, 201
Campbell Soup Company, 164, 180, 201
Canals, 140, 141, 152, 158, 212
Canneries, 180
Cape May, 10, 13, 30, 34, 35, 44, 46, 47, 52, 62, 92, 110, 134, 145
Cape May County, 23, 47, 83, 126, 250
Cape May "diamonds," 10
Cape May Lighthouse, 47
Carmel, 125
Casinos, 154
Chatham, 92, 124
Chemical Industry, 165, 167
Cherry Hill, 191
Chestnut Neck, 110, 111
Chickens, 44, 172, 175, 176, 177
China (pottery), 167
Cities, 40, 41, 124, 160, 172, 189-206, (see also: names of cities)
Citizenship, 225, 226, 227
Clark, Abraham, 101
Cleveland, Grover, 129
Clifton, 40, 202
Climate, 12, 13, 14, 17, 50
Coast (see Jersey Shore)
Cohansey, 68
Cohansey Creek, 52, 100
Colleges and Universities, 59, 81, 92, 93, 100, 101, 161, 169, 193, 196, 198, 232 (see also: names of colleges and universities)
Colonial New Jersey, 38, 46, 49, 73, 74, 77-96, 116, 134, 135, 136, 137, 140, 156, 157, 158, 174, 175
Colonies (13 Original), 94, 95
Colt, Samuel, 129
Columbus, Christopher, 78
Commuters, 143
Constitution (of New Jersey), 101
Continents, 15, 26, 27, 28, 31
Cooper, William, 201
Cooper's Ferry (see Camden)
Copper, 164
Corbin City, 228
Corn, 70, 180, 181
Counties, 22, 23, 49, 230, 231, 250, 251 (see also: county names)
County Seats, 22, 23, 231
Courthouses, 22
Covered Bridges, 150
Cows (see Dairies)
Cranberries, 45, 125, 172, 178, 179
Cranberry Lake, 212
Cromwell, Oliver, 112
Crosswicks, 83
Cuba, 126
Culvers Gap, 128
Culvers Lake, 212
Cumberland County, 23, 44, 100, 101, 140, 177, 179, 180, 181, 250
Czechoslovakia, 118, 119

252

D

Dairies, 37, 44, 176, 177
Declaration of Independence, 94, 100, 101, 224
Deepwater, 151
Defiance, 111
Delaware (State of), 34
Delaware and Raritan Canal, 140, 141
Delaware Bay, 34, 50, 63, 100, 110, 148, 159
Delaware Memorial Bridge, 144, 151
Delaware River, 34, 44, 48, 56, 80, 81, 82, 102, 103, 104, 114, 132, 138, 140, 149, 150, 151, 152, 201
Delaware Water Gap, 56, 86, 211
Deptford, 147
Dey Mansion, 113
Dinosaurs, 58, 59, 62
Dover, 40, 92, 157, 161
Dover Township, 202
Drovers, 138
Dutch, 23, 79, 80, 81, 82, 83, 91, (see also: Holland)

E

Earth (world), 16, 26, 56, 58, 78
Earthquakes, 54, 57
Eastern Hemisphere, 28
East New Jersey, 83, 86, 135
East Orange, 40, 129, 191
East Rutherford, 182
Edison, Thomas A., 161, 162, 163
Education, 73, 96 (see also: colleges and universities)
Egg Harbor City, 117
Electricity, 162, 163
Elizabeth (Elizabethtown), 40, 48, 49, 82, 86, 92, 93, 94, 101, 102, 124, 132, 138, 148, 149, 151, 156, 158, 164, 191, 192, 194, 197, 203
Ellis Island, 17, 120, 121, 122, 123, 124, 125, 126, 127
England, 23, 78, 79, 82, 83, 84, 92, 94, 95, 98 (see also: Revolution)
Environment (and Ecology), 207-222
Equator, 27, 28, 29
Essex County, 23, 62, 250
Europe, 27, 28, 75, 79, 84, 116, 117, 118, 119, 120, 121, 122, 123, 126
Ewing, 191
Explorers, 67, 78, 79

F

Factories (see Industry)
Fair Haven, 63
Far Hills, 57, 124
Farms (see Agriculture)
Farrand, Rhoda, 109
Ferryboats, 135, 137, 150, 152
Finley, Samuel, 90
Fishing, 47, 70, 89, 215
Fitch, John, 142
Fithian, Rev. Phillip, 112
Flowers (grown on farms), 175, 176
Flowers (wild), 42, 208, 209, 220
Ford Family (Morristown), 106, 107
Ford Mansion, 106, 107, 113
Forsythe National Wildlife Refuge, 217
Fort Dix, 42, 126
Fort Lee, 102, 151, 191
Fort Mercer, 105, 112
Fort Monmouth, 126, 169
Fossils, 54, 55, 59, 62, 63
Fourth of July, 100, 101
France (French), 78, 79, 83
Franklin (town of), 38
Franklin, Benjamin, 201
Franklin, Governor William, 134
Freehold, 92, 105, 113
Freneau, Philip, 112
Frogs, 221
Fruits, 45, 50, 172, 178, 179, 185 (see also: names of fruits)

G

Garden Spot, 44, 45
Garden State, 44
Garden State Parkway, 144, 202
Geography, 33-52
Geology, 53-64
George Washington Bridge, 144, 151, 161, 191
Germany (Germans), 117, 119, 126, 128, 165 (see also: Hessians)
Glaciers, 55, 60, 212
Gladstone, 183
Glassboro, 157
Glassmaking, 43, 93, 116, 117, 157, 159, 166
Glen Rock, 55
Gloucester City, 160
Gloucester County, 23, 44, 55, 105, 113, 149, 179, 181, 185, 250
Goethel's Bridge, 151
Goldfinch, 19
Government, 126, 200, 223-237
Governor, 95, 101
Great Britain (see England)
Great Meadows, 173
Great Pathway, 40
Great Swamp, 61, 103, 211, 216, 235
Greenwich, 101, 112
Greenwood Lake, 38, 212
Growing Season, 44, 50

H

Hackensack, 80, 92
Hackensack River, 80, 92, 136, 151, 158
Haddonfield, 58, 137, 138
Hadrosaurus, 58, 59
Half Moon, 79
Hamilton, 40, 191, 202, 229
Hamilton, Alexander, 198, 199
Hancock, Cornelia, 129
Hancock House, 81, 113
Hancock's Bridge, 110, 113, 129
Hanover, 92
Harbors (see Ports)
Hart, John, 101
Harvey Cedars, 46
Hays, Mary Ludwig (Molly Pitcher), 105
Hemispheres, 28, 29, 31
Hessian Soldiers, 102, 103, 105, 107, 110, 113, 200
Hibernia, 92
High Bridge, 161
Highland Lake, 212
Highlands, 13, 33, 38, 39, 157
High Point, 10, 36, 37, 212
Highways (see Roads)
Hobart, Garrett, 129
Hoboken, 80, 117, 124, 142, 143, 150, 159, 191
Holland, 78, 80, 81, 119
Holland, John Phillip, 204
Holland Tunnel, 151
Holly, 184
Holmdel, 168
Hopewell, 101
Hopkinson, Frances, 101
Horses, 11, 44, 175, 182, 183
Horseshoe Crab, 63
Howell, Richard, 99, 101
Hudson County, 23, 48, 80, 117, 143, 148, 166, 229, 250
Hudson, Henry, 79
Hudson River, 34, 48, 57, 79, 82, 106, 107, 132, 135, 150, 151, 217
Hunterdon County, 23, 140, 177, 185
Hurricanes, 51, 215
Hyler, Capt. Adam, 111

253

I

Immigrants, 115-130, 164, 194
Indian King Tavern, 137
Indians, 23, 49, 65-76, 134, 179
Industry, 40, 92, 93, 126, 153-170, 172-188, 193, 194, 196, 197, 198, 199, 200, 201, 212, 214
Inns (or Taverns), 136, 137
Inventors (Inventions), 160, 161, 162, 163, 168, 169
Ireland (Irish), 83, 117, 119, 128
Iron, 38, 39, 43, 92, 93, 108, 109, 117, 156, 157, 158, 159, 160, 161
Irrigation, 50, 181, 186
Island Beach, 208, 214
Isle of Jersey, 82
Italy (Italians), 78, 117, 118, 119, 128

J

Jersey City, 40, 41, 48, 80, 117, 124, 136, 137, 140, 143, 151, 158, 159, 166, 191, 192, 194, 198, 203
Jersey Meadows, 61
Jersey Shore, 13, 33, 34, 46, 47, 51, 79, 92, 108, 109, 134, 143, 154, 159, 208, 209, 214, 215
Jockey Hollow, 106, 107, 109, 112, 113, 235
Johnson, Eldridge, 201
Johnson, Robert Gibbons, 45

K

Kearny, 191
Killcohook National Wildlife Refuge, 217
Kill Van Kull, 48
Kittatinny Mountains, 36, 37, 68

L

Laelaps, 59
Lake Hackensack, 60, 61
Lake Hopatcong, 38, 140, 212, 213
Lakehurst Naval Station, 42
Lake Passaic, 60, 61
Lakes, 38, 39, 60, 61, 212, 213
Lambertville, 129
Landis, Charles K., 205
Latitude, 24, 25, 26, 27, 28, 29, 31
Lenape (see Indians)
Lettuce, 180
Liberty Bell, 101, 113
Liberty State Park, 41, 198
Lighthouses, 47, (see also: names of lighthouses)
Lincoln Park, 62
Lincoln Tunnel, 151
Little Egg Harbor, 86
Livingston, 129
Livingston, William, 101
Log cabins, 81, 86
Long Beach Island, 46
Long House, 69
Longitude, 24, 25, 26, 27, 28, 29, 31
Loyalists, 95, 110
Lucy (see Margate Elephant)

M

Maass, Clara, 129
Macculloch, George, 140
Madison, 124, 139
Mammals (see Animals)
Manasquan, 110
Manito, 75
Mannington Township, 59
Manufacturing (see Industry)
Manville, 124
Maps, 15-32
Margate Elephant (Lucy), 14
Marshall, James, 129
Marshland, 64, 214, 217
Mastodons, 59, 62, 68
Matilda (mastodon), 59
May's Landing, 52
McConkey's Ferry, 103, 113
Meadowlands Sports Complex, 12, 61, 154, 182
Medicine, (see Pharmaceuticals)
Meeting Houses, 83
Mendham, 49
Menlo Park, 162
Mercer County, 23, 126, 129, 250
Metuchen, 104
Michigan, 179
Middlesex County, 23, 162, 164, 251
Middletown, 83, 86, 92
Military Ocean Terminal, 149
Militia, 94
Mills (see Industry)
Millville, 160, 184
Minerals, 38
Minutemen, 98, 99, 107, 110, 111
Monmouth (Battle of), 98, 105, 113
Monmouth County, 23, 63, 112, 126, 134, 157, 177, 179, 181, 184, 187, 251
Moorestown, 129
Morris Canal, 52, 140, 141, 159, 212
Morris County, 12, 23, 61, 105, 109, 157, 182, 211, 212, 216
Morristown, 92, 98, 103, 104, 106, 107, 109, 124, 134, 138, 147, 204
Morristown National Historic Park, 235
Mountains, 35, 36, 37, 38, 50, (see also: mountain names)
Mt. Holly, 138
Munsee (see Indians)
Murray Hill, 168

N

National Aeronautics Facility Experiment Center (NAFEC), 169
National Wildlife Refuges, 211, 216, 217
New Amsterdam, 80, 81, 198
Newark, 39, 40, 48, 49, 61, 82, 86, 92, 94, 117, 124, 129, 132, 134, 136, 140, 148, 158, 160, 191, 192, 194, 196, 197, 203, 205, 206, 228
Newark Bay, 49, 148
Newark International Airport, 11, 40, 146, 147, 196
Newark Museum, 41
New Brunswick, 80, 81, 92, 93, 94, 104, 110, 111, 124, 138, 140, 141, 160
New England, 82, 83, 84
New Jersey Day, 83
New Jersey Department of Environmental Protection (D.E.P.), 211, 218
New Jersey Division of Travel and Tourism, 154
New Jersey School of Conservation, 219
New Jersey Turnpike, 133, 144, 191, 202
New Sweden, 80, 81
Newton, 52, 138
New Village, 144
New York (Battle of), 102
New York (State), 34, 35, 36, 38, 49, 60, 75, 212, 217
New York Bay, 48, 79
New York City, 40, 61, 80, 93, 98, 105, 110, 124, 132, 135, 136, 140, 143, 150, 151, 159, 191, 216
Norma (town), 125
North America, 28, 29, 31

O

Ocean City, 47
Ocean County, 23, 179, 202
Oceans, 15, 26, (see also: Atlantic Ocean)
Oil Refineries, 149, 166, 167
Old Barracks, 94, 95, 113, 200
Old Tappan, 110
Old Tennent Church, 113
Orange, 92, 129, 158
Orchids, 42, 209
Oswego River, 219
Outerbridge, 151

254

P

Paine, Thomas, 112
Palisade Mountains, 57, 102, 216, 217
Palisades Interstate Park, 217
Passaic, 124
Passaic County, 22, 23, 251
Passaic River, 49, 80, 136, 151, 196, 199
Paterson, 40, 41, 56, 124, 129, 143, 158, 159, 160, 161, 191, 192, 194, 199, 203, 204, 206
Paterson Falls, 41, 138, 158, 199
Paterson Museum, 73
Patriots, 95
Paul, Alice, 129
Paulus Hook, 136, 198
Peaches, 45, 172, 178, 179
Peninsula, 34, 47, 62
Pennsylvania, 30, 34, 36, 102, 103
People (see Immigrants, Colonists, Indians)
People, Famous, 129, 246-249 (see also: names of people)
Peppers, 180, 181
Perth Amboy, 49, 60, 83, 90, 93, 124, 134, 151, 164
Pharmaceuticals, 167, 169
Philadelphia, 40, 48, 83, 93, 98, 100, 101, 104, 105, 110, 130, 132, 135, 136, 140, 142, 143, 147, 148, 150, 175, 191, 201
Phillipsburg, 52, 140, 161
Pike, Zebulon, 129
Pine Barrens, 10, 33, 42, 43, 91, 93, 108, 118, 134, 157, 159, 179, 208, 219
Pinelands Commission, 217
Piscataway, 82, 86
Pitcher, Molly, 105
Plainfield, 92, 158
Pluckemin, 105
Poets, 41, 112
Pollution, 209, 214, 215, 218
Pompton Lakes, 212
Ports, 41, 47, 48, 120, 132, 133, 148, 149, 196, 197
Preakness, 113
Precipitation (see Rainfall)
Prehistoric Times, 54-64
Princeton, 101, 129, 140
Princeton (Battle of), 98, 103
Princeton University, 93, 100, 101, 169
Printz, Johan, 81
Privateers, 110, 111
Products (see Industry, Agriculture)
Pumpkins, 174

Q

Quakers, 83, 86, 90, 96, 200

R

Rahway, 104, 158
Railroads, 133, 142, 143, 150, 152, 158, 161, 194, 198, 201
Rainfall, 50
Raritan River, 49, 80, 92, 151, 158
Recreation, 154, 159, 214, 215
Red Bank (Battle of), 98, 105, 112, 113
Red Coats, 102, 103, 105
Refuges, National Wildlife, 211
Regions (see Geography)
Religions, 83, 86, 90, 91, 96, 117, 118, 119, 125, 126, 127
Reptiles, 221
Research, 11, 40, 126, 162, 163, 168, 169
Reservoirs, 38, 39, 50, 217
Revolution, American, 21, 23, 95, 97-114
Ridgewood, 228
Ringwood, 92
River Edge, 73
Rivers, 48, 49, 68, 73, 80, 132, 134, 135, 136, 150, 151, (see also: river names)
Roads (and Highways), 132, 134, 135, 136, 138, 139, 144, 145, 202
Robeson, Paul, 129
Rockaway, 52, 92
Roebling, John, 161
Rogers, Thomas, 158
Roseland, 62
Rosenhayn, 125
Round Valley Reservoir, 39, 213
Rutgers University, 59, 81, 92, 169, 196, 232
Rutherford, 61

S

Salem, 83, 86, 92, 133, 134, 148, 149, 177, 211
Salem County, 23, 44, 45, 59, 113, 129, 140, 144, 151, 157, 179, 181, 251
Salem Oak, 14
Salt, 108, 109
Sandy Hook, 13, 34, 47, 62, 79, 111, 208, 214
Saxton Falls State Park, 141
Sayreville, 124
Scale (on map), 21
Scheyechbi, 67
Scotland (Scots), 83, 119, 158
Seasons, 29, 50, 51
Seaville, 83
Sections of New Jersey (see Geography)
Sergeantsville, 151
Settlers (see Colonists)
Sewell, 55
Ship Bottom, 47
Ships and Shipping, 78, 79, 84, 90, 120, 121, 123, 132, 133, 148, 149, 159, 164, 165, 215
Shrewsbury, 83, 92
Shunpike, 139
Singer, Isaac, 164
Size (of New Jersey), 16, 17, 50
Slavery, 90, 91
Snakes, 221
Soil, 42, 44
Somerset County, 22, 23, 105, 183, 216, 251
Somerville, 98, 105, 113, 129
Song ("New Jersey's the Place for Me"), 9, 15, 33, 53, 65, 77, 97, 115, 131, 153, 171, 189, 207, 223
Sounds (bodies of water), 47, 214
South Orange, 228
Soybeans, 187
Spinach, 172, 180
Sports, 12, 13, 39, 154
Springfield, 92, 138, 197
Springfield (Battle of), 98, 107
Spruce Run, 39, 213
Stagecoaches, 136, 137, 152
Stanger Family, 157
State Animal, Bird, Flag, Flower, Insect, Tree, 18
State Capital, 200, 232, 233 (see also: Trenton)
State Capitol, 14
State Motto, 19
State Museum, 41, 59
State Parks and Forests, 22, 211, 217
State Seal, 19
State Symbols, 18, 19, 44
Staten Island, 151
Statue of Liberty, 14, 17, 41, 121, 130, 198
Steerage, 120, 121
Stevens, John, 142, 152
Still, James, 91
Stockton, Richard, 101
Stockton, Robert, 129
Stokes State Forest, 36, 219
Strawberries, 45, 160, 178, 179
Submarine, 204
Succasunna, 92, 138, 157
Summit, 124, 138
Sunrise Mountain, 36, 37
Supawana National Wildlife Refuge, 217
Sussex County, 12, 23, 44, 52, 59, 176, 211, 212, 251
Sweden (Swedish), 80, 81, 119
Swedesboro, 81, 175

255

T

Tavistock, 228
Taxes, 94, 95, 100, 134, 236, 237
Tea Party (see Greenwich)
Teterboro, 146, 228
Textiles, 160, 161
Tinton Falls, 157
Tolls, 138, 139, 236
Tomatoes, 45, 164, 172, 180, 181
Toms River, 52, 92, 108, 109, 110
Tories (see Loyalists)
Tourism, 46, 143, 154, 149
Trains (see Railroads)
Transistor, 168
Transportation, 11, 131-152, 158, 159, (see also: Ships, Roads, Canals, Bridges, Ports)
Trees, famous, 14
Trees (forests), 42, 43, 156, 159, 208, 217
Trent House, 200
Trent, William, 200
Trenton, 40, 48, 86, 92, 94, 113, 124, 138, 142, 147, 160, 161, 165, 191, 192, 194, 200, 203, 232
Trenton (Battle of), 98, 102, 103, 114, 200
Tuckerton, 92, 110
Tunnels, 150, 151, 152
Turnpikes, 138, 139
Twin Lights, 47

U

Unami (see Indians)
Union County, 23, 149, 251
United States, 16, 30, 31, 99, 100, 101, 116, 117, 118, 119, 120, 121, 122, 123, 124, 125, 126, 234, 235
United States Equestrian Team, 183

V

Vegetables, 44, 45, 50, 170, 172, 180, 181, 185, 187, (see also: vegetable names)
Vernon, 59, 62
Verrazano Bridge, 161
Verrazano, Giovanni da, 67, 69
Volcanoes, 56, 57
Vineland, 118, 205, 229

W

Waksman, Dr. Selman, 169
Wallace House, 105, 110
Wallkill River, 212
Walt Whitman Bridge, 151, 191, 201
Wampum, 72
Warren County, 12, 23, 44, 144, 173, 177, 211, 251
Washington Crossing State Park, 113
Washington, George, 98, 102, 103, 104, 105, 106, 107, 113, 114, 132, 199, 200
Washington's Headquarters (at Morristown), 103, 104, 106, 107
Watchung Mountains, 57, 61, 103, 104, 107
Water, 34, 217 (see also: Rivers, Lakes)
Waterloo, 141
Weather, 50, 51
Weehawken, 151
Westfield, 92, 197
West New Jersey, 83, 86, 96, 135
West Orange, 163
Whippany, 168
Whitall, Anne Cooper, 112, 113
Whitman, Walt, 41, 201
Wicke, Tempe, 112
Wigwams, 68
Wildwood, 47
Willingboro, 206
Wistar, Caspar, 157
Witherspoon, John, 101
Wizard of Menlo Park (see: Edison, Thomas)
Woodbine, 125
Woodbridge, 40, 60, 83, 86, 191, 202

Z

Zinc, 38
Zucchini, 180

PHOTO SOURCES

ACAD. OF NATURAL SCIENCES OF PHILA. 19
ANNIN & CO.: 167 (right)
AT&T BELL LAB.: 155 (bottom), 167 (top left), 169 (right)
THE BETTMANN ARCHIVE: 126
BUITONI FOODS: 166 (lower right)
CAMPBELL SOUP CO.: 188 (upper left)
CHOROSZEWSKI, WALTER J.: Cover, 13 (top), 14 (left), 127, 150 (right), 151, 167 (lower right), 198, 199, 200, 201, 204, 208, 216, 227
FRAUNCES TAVERN MUSEUM: 105, 107
GENERAL DRAFTING CO.: 21
GENERAL MOTORS CORP.: 166 (right)
GREAT ADVENTURE AMUSEMENT PARK: 154
H. ARMSTRONG ROBERTS, INC.: 203
LEONARD LEE RUE III: 222
LIBRARY OF CONGRESS: 90, 116, 120, 121 (right), 123 (upper right, middle right, lower left)
MARSHALL-CLARK MANUFACTURING CORP.: 166 (upper left)
MUSEUM OF THE CITY OF N.Y.: 124
NATIONAL ARCHIVES: 121 (left), 123 (lower right)
N.J. DEPART. OF TRANSPORTATION: 41 (top)
N.J. DIV. OF TRAVEL & TOURISM: 13 (lower left, lower right), 14 (lower right), 137, 150 (left), 182
N.J. TURNPIKE AUTHORITY: 133 (middle)
N.J. SCHOOL OF CONSERVATION: 219 (bottom)
NEWARK PUBLIC LIBRARY, N.J. ROOM: 43 (lower left), 164, 193, 195
PUBLIC SERVICE ELECTRIC & GAS CO. OF N.J.: 11 (upper left), 41 (bottom), 146 (bottom), 147 (upper right and lower right), 155, 169 (left), 184, 193 (left), 196
U.S. DEPARTMENT OF LABOR: 125
WASHINGTON CROSSING STATE PARK, PA: 114
WHARTON STATE FOREST: 220, 221
ALL OTHER PHOTOS FROM THE COLLECTION OF JOHN T. CUNNINGHAM